Queer Brown Voices

Queer Brown Voices

PERSONAL NARRATIVES OF LATINA/O LGBT ACTIVISM

Edited by Uriel Quesada, Letitia Gomez, and Salvador Vidal-Ortiz

University of Texas Press   *Austin*

Requests for permission to reproduce material from this work should be
sent to:
    Permissions
    University of Texas Press
    P.O. Box 7819
    Austin, TX 78713–7819
    http://utpress.utexas.edu/index.php/rp-form

♾ The paper used in this book meets the minimum requirements of
ANSI/NISO Z39.48–1992 (R1997) (Permanence of Paper).

LIBRARY OF CONGRESS CATALOGING-IN-PUBLICATION DATA
Queer brown voices : personal narratives of Latina/o LGBT activism /
edited by Uriel Quesada, Letitia Gomez, and Salvador Vidal-Ortiz. —
First edition.
     pages   cm
    Includes bibliographical references and index.
     ISBN 978-1-4773-0232-3 (cloth : alk. paper) — ISBN 978-1-4773-0730-4
(pbk. : alk. paper) — ISBN 978-1-4773-0233-0 (library e-book) —
ISBN 978-1-4773-0234-7 (non-library e-book)
    1. Hispanic American sexual minorities—Political activity—United
States.   2. Gay activists—United States.   3. Sexual minorities—
Identity.   I. Quesada, Uriel, editor.   II. Gomez, Letitia, editor.
III. Vidal-Ortiz, Salvador, editor.
    HQ76.8.U5Q44 2015
    306.76089′68073—dc23   2014046939

doi:10.7560/302323

To the memory of all Latina/o lesbian, gay, bisexual, and transgender activists, living and dead, who made their voices heard, whether in spaces of visibility or invisibility, and who devoted their loving energy to improving the lives of their communities

Contents

Preface

LETITIA GOMEZ

*I*N 2009 I WAS INSPIRED TO COLLABORATE WITH SAL-
vador Vidal-Ortiz and Uriel Quesada on this book, primarily as a way to satisfy my personal need to document the period of
LGBT Latina/o activism that I experienced in the 1980s and 1990s, *la
época de oro* (a phrase coined by José Gutiérrez to describe this period
of our history when Latina/o LGBT groups and organizations flour-
ished in the United States and Puerto Rico). In my view, this period
has been significantly underdocumented—and when it has been documented, the accounts have included errors about the people involved
and the sequence of events. This book aims to offer new perspectives
on the history of Latina/o activists and their organizations. The result of a collaborative effort between sixteen people, *Queer Brown Voices*
covers more than three decades of activism and several geographical locations across the United States and Puerto Rico, from Los Angeles to
San Juan. The personal narratives within give the reader a glimpse into
the lives of the activists and reveal why it was important to them to participate in the LGBT Latina/o movement of the late 1970s, 1980s, and
1990s. My hope is that this collection will serve as an introduction—
a primer, if you will—to what I anticipate will be a wealth of stories to
be told in the future. Sadly, there are some stories that will never be
told from the first person, because we lost so many gay Latinos to HIV/
AIDS in the 1980s and 1990s and have lost several lesbian Latina activists in the years since. Fortunately, due to activists' efforts to collect and
archive their own history, we have access to documents and other materials that show firsthand proof of organizing efforts, even when the
original voices are lost. José Gutiérrez's chapter, in particular, shows the
extent of activists' efforts both to make history and to preserve it.

In 2007 Salvador, Uriel, and I were involved with the GLBT Latino History Project (LHP) in Washington, D.C. In 2009, out of our experiences of working on the LHP archives, planning to conduct oral histories, and facing the challenges of making such histories public, we began to collaborate on this project. In the process of identifying and finding potential contributors for this book, we first reached out to activists whom Salvador and I knew from our own previous activist work. We also received referrals from colleagues linking us to activists whom we did not know but felt would be important contributors, and we did research to identify activists in regions we wanted to include. We then contacted activists from across the United States and Puerto Rico with an invitation to join us in the process of writing and editing this work as well as to participate in interviews for oral history chapters. Initially, we asked all the contributors to address a few basic questions on an abstract, while as editors we discussed topic areas that we strongly felt needed to be included. Although we received many abstracts for the book, personal challenges, time conflicts, busy work schedules, and even editorial differences limited the completed chapters to a total of fourteen contributions. While it was a self-selected sample of activists, we intended to have as much gender parity, regional representation, and balance between lesbians, gay men, and transgender people as possible (none of the activists self-identified as bisexual). We also sought to have a balanced number of activists from the 1970s, 1980s, and 1990s.

Queer Brown Voices blends two types of first-person narratives. Six chapters are based on first-person essays written by our contributors, and eight chapters are based on oral history interviews (a number of them recorded in Spanish) that were all conducted and edited between June 2011 and June 2012. We used an interview guide to conduct the oral history interviews; it included questions very similar to those asked of the essayists so that the content between both formats would be consistent. The process of collecting the narratives was time-consuming because we were working with the contributors' schedules and developing the format of the chapters as we received submissions. Our work included supporting the drafting of chapters (in the case of the first-person essays) and sharing and exchanging them back and forth, sometimes six to eight times. It was also challenging, at times, to set up an oral history interview date and time with potential contributors, especially because we wanted to have two editors present at each of the interviews. I particularly enjoyed the experience of conducting the oral interviews, because of their collaborative nature and the opportunity to reflect on the interviews with my coeditors afterward.

Regardless of whether activists wrote or we interviewed them, the editing process was extremely rigorous. We shared multiple drafts with each other before sending a draft back to a contributor. We also held numerous conference calls to debate some of the potential challenges in each and every one of the chapters you will read. As editors, we never questioned who was going to be the author, regardless of the modality; we decided that the activist was author. Our editorial role was to be actively engaged with the material and, in most cases, to provide a close line-by-line editing. In addition, because we were assisting, in a way, in the creation of a narrative and in identifying key points in the narrators' lives, we asked for further information or suggested cutting down on some information that seemed less central to the narrative we were collectively producing. Similarly, we edited out information from the oral histories that was less relevant to the goals of the project.

As editors, we were committed to keeping the activists' own voices and stories intact as much as we could. We also tried to see the drafts from our own present and past points of view: as scholar, activist, or scholar-activist; as U.S. Latina/o, third-generation Chicana, or immigrant; as gay, lesbian, or queer identified; as mestizo or light-skinned Latinas/os. We also asked the contributors for more detail and clarification, for fact verification, and for more analysis of the facts. Each discussion and the ensuing suggestions for rewriting gave us a clearer understanding of the history at each of the sites discussed by the activists. Uriel and I wrote the chapters based on oral history interviews, and Salvador and I translated the transcriptions of interviews conducted in Spanish, all the while keeping faithful to the voices of the activists, which was especially true in the translation of the oral histories from Spanish to English.

As we read the contributors' drafts over and over, we sought to maintain a commitment to the storytelling format, even when details contained in a personal narrative contradicted the greater story of the movement. These inconsistencies in the narratives, acronyms, names of organizations, names of people, and specific dates of events are a factor of differences in how activists recall events many years after they took place. For some activists, the names and places and dates are less important than the events; others have a photographic memory when it comes to those details. In most cases we corroborated the information by contacting the activists. When this was not possible we sought alternative sources, such as archived materials. Herein is one learned benefit and value of archiving materials. As we were developing this book, we learned of several LGBT Latina/o activist collections housed at universities, in addition to history projects like the GLBT Latino History Project we had already worked on together. Given the overlapping histories and shared participation of some of the activists included in this book, some organizations are mentioned repeatedly. This is a reflection of the interconnectedness of Latina/o activists during that period of time. For example, most of the book's contributors were somehow connected to the National Latino/a Lesbian and Gay Organization, LLEGÓ.

Another one of our challenges was to determine how to handle translation of the Spanish-language contributions, which included four oral history interviews and one essay. We shared the original transcription or chapter with each other along with a draft of the translated document. In the process, we sometimes identified words in Spanish that had no clear equivalent in English. For instance, in Adela Vázquez's chapter she uses the term *bugarrón*, which is Cuban slang for a heterosexual man who does not identify as gay but who "tops" other men. We decided that such a term was better left in Spanish, as it conveys a meaning not easily translatable. In the end, we believe the intent of the narrative will be understood by readers of English. We also decided to keep colloquial expressions in their original sense when stated in Spanish (even when problematic to us as editors) to maintain the spirit of what the activists said. One example is when Adela Vázquez talks about women born female, and she refers to them as "normal" women. While we do not see trans as abnormal, because it was said both in the Spanish context and in the voice of a trans woman, we knew what she meant to convey.

In the spirit of LGBT organizing we met several times, retreat style, to read and make final edits to all of the chapters; to draft our preface, introduction, and conclusion; and to finalize other editorial details. We also engaged in numerous conversations where we discussed the implications of the contributors' statements—aspects of gender, class, and ethnicity, as well as the influence of the narrators' sexual identities on some of the ideological positions they took—in order to better understand the meaning of what they were telling us. What you see in this book is the result of four years of such thought and discussion.

Our goal is to provide the reader—and especially the young LGBT Latina/o—with knowledge about the history of Latina/o LGBT activism in the last three decades of the twentieth century. Our expectation of students, scholars, and historians is that they see an opportunity to build upon our work and to contribute further to the body of evidence of LGBT Latina/o activism and its positive impact on the larger LGBT Latina/o community. I have never found this goal to be more important than today. In 2008 I participated in a workshop on creating a national agenda of LGBT Latina/o issues where the majority of participants had no idea that there had once been a national Latina/o LGBT organization (LLEGÓ). Up until the 1980s, the gay and lesbian movement in the United States was largely known as white. People of color were not highly visible in news coverage by either the gay press or the mainstream press. Nor were people of color visible in key leadership positions in the nascent gay and lesbian organizations that were formed after Stonewall. Worse, sexism, racism, and classism served to exclude lesbian and gay people of color from influencing decision making—and even excluded them from entrance to some gay bars. Hence, in the 1980s some of us were compelled to act and to get involved in our communities. Organizations, support groups, and clubs for lesbian and gay people of color seemed to sprout up overnight in major urban areas of the United States and Puerto Rico. This vibrant local and national community of activists focused both on organizing in their communities to create space for Latinas/os in a predominantly white gay and lesbian culture and on creating national visibility so as to be included in discussions on the issues of the day. I was then, and will forever be, proud of being part of that history.

For Latinas/os, whose issues are not solely gay issues, being viewed as "other" was one element to factor in when becoming an activist. In 1988 at a national gay and lesbian conference I heard a white gay peer announce to the room that he wanted us (people of color) to "check our color at the door" because it would get in the way of working together on what was deemed more important (to him)—gay liberation. The messages I received from that experience were "being free to be gay and lesbian is most important" and "I don't care about your Latino issues." I later witnessed this again during national march platform discussions on whether to include immigration issues. I am sure I am not the only Latina/o or person of color to recount such experiences.

As Salvador, Uriel, and I collected the stories of our peers during 2010 to 2012, we encountered many similarities. I found aspects of my own coming-out experience mirrored in some of the other contributors' essays and oral histories. Having come out in a predominantly white gay and lesbian environment, I was immediately faced with racism, sexism, and classism. I remember feeling isolated and asking myself, "Where do I fit in?" The gay and lesbian bars of 1980s Houston were mostly white. The organizations that existed were also mostly white, and they reflected the values and experiences of the dominant gay and lesbian society—values that were not necessarily my own.

The stories collected for this book recount personal experiences during a period of time in which activists came together to support each other and to work toward common causes that had meaning to them as gay, lesbian, bisexual, and transgender Latinas/os. You will find that relationships with lovers, family, friends, and community are important features of many of the narratives. Indeed, reflecting on my personal experience as a Latina lesbian activist brought back so many fond memories of people whom I met along the way. Many remain good friends today, like Dennis Medina, Gloria Ramirez, Laura Esquivel, and Brad Veloz. But the experience also brought forth painful memories of watching dear activist friends, like Arcadio Torres and Joe Perez, die in their youth of AIDS. Many talented, bright, and loving individuals were lost in the 1980s and 1990s to what was then an unmanageable disease.

For practical reasons we decided to make the turn of the century the book's end point. First, for the purpose of the oral histories, we needed a specific period of time around which to center the narratives. Second, we were most interested in the period of the 1970s, 1980s, and 1990s as the height of Latina/o LGBT activism. Yet after collecting the narratives, we realized that one cannot set arbitrary limitations of time to convey a historical set of processes, and for that reason you will see that some of the chapters do not simply end in 2000. Many of these activists continued their involvement with groups and organizations beyond that time. Ultimately, the recounting of these later experiences offered a richer sense of the life narratives of the activists involved.

I will be eternally grateful to Salvador Vidal-Ortiz, who prompted me to think about this book with the question, "Well, what do you want to do about it?" He asked this in response to my anger and disappointment that a scholar had published as fact an untruth regarding the identity of the founder of LLEGÓ. Salvador's question and his offer to help publish this book opened my eyes to the possibility of documenting Latina/o LGBT history for future generations. I also wanted to set the record straight on some events in the history of Latina/o LGBT activism that had not been committed to paper by the activists themselves or had been portrayed inaccurately. Uriel Quesada has my highest admiration for his gentle prodding and for helping us stay on task during the last four years. Both Uriel and Salvador brought their academic experience in writing and publishing to bear, which was a tremendous learning experience for me, a nonacademic. These two gentle, smart, passionate men were a pleasure to work with. We exchanged hundreds of emails and spent hours on conference calls discussing our progress via Skype and encouraging each other in spite of our individual busy lives and schedules. They were also extremely generous in sharing their access to some financial resources that, combined with our personal contributions, helped bring this book to you. It was an intense, but ultimately easy, collaboration, and we enjoyed many moments filled with laughter.

Finally, I am extremely grateful to the contributors, who freely gave their time to be interviewed for the oral histories or to write their personal stories. That they shared their stories with you is as much a labor of love as the valuable time they have devoted to activism, so deeply felt, on behalf of their Latina/o LGBT communities.

MAY 2014

Acknowledgments

*F*IRST AND FOREMOST, THIS BOOK WOULD NOT BE in front of you were it not for the fourteen contributors, the main actors in the story we tell. Their invaluable time and energy and countless hours of communicating with us—addressing edits, expanding their ideas for clarity, and even looking for relevant articles, documents, and pictures from the end of the twentieth century—have all made the book a reality. Our gratitude to you is immense.

We wish to thank the University of Texas Press—in particular, Theresa J. May, whose investment in this project in her last years before retirement invigorated our belief in the collection of essays. Theresa wanted this book for the UT Press and convinced us that Texas, above all other presses, was a perfect home for the manuscript. Kerry E. Webb, a senior editor at Texas, has been extremely supportive of our project. We wish to thank the manuscript reviewers; they offered caring and constructive feedback, which, along with suggestions from friends and colleagues, gave us direction to produce a book that makes sense to a wider audience.

This project became, literally, a labor of love and passion with little resources. We spent our personal funds, used extra frequent-flier miles, and depended on the love of friends, who generously allowed us to stay with them while we conducted interviews for the oral history chapters. Salvador wants to thank, in particular, Bill Blum in San Francisco and Elda Albino Rivera and Juan Carlos Delgado Román in San Juan for their unending support whenever he traveled to conduct oral histories there. We also received support from students, faculty, and community members who offered assistance with locating sources, identifying archives, and suggesting linkages across the stories in these chapters; they too helped enhance the collection of essays. In particular, Leti wishes to thank Noriega James, who volunteered to take pictures of some of the archives.

The sources of funding we did have access to were of great support for the completion of this project. Salvador received an award from American University's College of Arts and Sciences Mellon Grant, which helped cover copyright and images from the University of Texas at Austin archives, as well as indexing, editing, and other costs. Uriel received a Faculty Research Grant from Loyola University New Orleans that helped with data management, particularly the arduous work of transcribing the interviews. We also want to thank the librarians of the Rare Books and Manuscripts Division at the Nettie Lee Benson Latin American Collection at UT Austin, particularly Michael Hironymous. We came up with all kinds of requests, and they always helped us find a solution. Those archives are a world of knowledge waiting to be tapped into. We also want to thank Stanford University Libraries' Adan Griego, the National Minority AIDS Council, and the New York Public Library for their help regarding some images for the archival component of this book.

We would like to thank Nadia Reiman, Christina Schott, and Lisbeth Philip, our amazing and patient transcribers, for doing a great job. They really cared to preserve every single detail of each interview, be it in Spanish or English. J. A. Cunningham helped create the first version of the index. His work gave us a sense of how to approach this important task. Luz Guerra provided us with a comprehensive and thorough final index.

Finally, we would like to thank our friends and partners for their encouragement and support throughout this project. Our sense of community—with each other and with that extended "family"—has given us much energy to complete the book.

Queer Brown Voices

Brown Writing Queer:
A Composite of Latina/o LGBT Activism

SALVADOR VIDAL-ORTIZ

ONE OF MANY BEGINNINGS AND MANY VOICES

A pink map of the Americas upside down—that was the first
visible sign for me that a Latina/o LGBT/queer presence in the United
States was strengthening.[1] The year was 1993, and many of us attended
the March on Washington for Lesbian, Gay, and Bi Equal Rights and
Liberation.[2] That map was a T-shirt from the Latino Caucus of the
AIDS Coalition to Unleash Power (ACT UP). In 1993 as we arrived
in Washington, D.C., for a third national march, there was already a
strong Latina/o queer presence throughout the United States, represented by organizations such as the D.C. Metropolitan Area Coalition of Latino Lesbians and Gays in Washington, D.C.; Ellas en Acción, Asociación Gay Unida Impactando Latinos/Latinas A Superarse,
and Proyecto Contra SIDA Por Vida in San Francisco; Las Buenas Amigas (itself derived from Salsa Soul Sisters, a women of color group)[3]
in New York, as well as other groups being formalized there, like Latino Gay Men of New York and Latinas and Latinos de Ambiente New
York; and the Austin Latina/o Lesbian and Gay Organization, Gay and
Lesbian Coalition de Dallas, and the Gay Chicano Caucus (eventually
becoming Gay and Lesbian Hispanics Unidos of Houston) in Texas.
Other organizations existed in Puerto Rico,[4] groups such as Colectivo de Concientización Gay (later Colectivo de Lesbianas Feministas),
Coalición Orgullo Arcoiris, and Coalición Puertorriqueña de Lesbianas y Homosexuales. By 1993 the first nationwide organization, the National Latino/a Lesbian and Gay Organization (LLEGÓ), founded in
1988, had begun to offer services, in large part due to health funding

provided by the Centers for Disease Control and Prevention (CDC).[5] A large presence of Brown queers who had been visible since the 1970s in their own cities, regions, and states were now, between the second and third "gay and lesbian" marches, becoming more established and visible at the national level.[6] Brown was being written into queer in a slow but steady manner. Yet both Brown and queer still functioned as shameless markers that signaled outsiderness to heteronormativity and whiteness, as I will discuss later on.

As a member of ACT UP Puerto Rico, I was also at the march to address issues of access to treatment for those infected with HIV and, equally important for me and my fellow ACT UP members, to address HIV-related discrimination and to advocate for more prevention and education funds. Walking on the National Mall, where the AIDS Memorial Quilt was displayed, we could see the countless names—and recognize friends and lovers and family members—of those lost to AIDS because of homophobia, inadequate treatment, and ignorance. While queer Latinas/os, as a movement, weren't in decline, we were nevertheless affected by HIV/AIDS—and little to nothing was being done then. Just as Brown was becoming visible and organized, the impact of AIDS in our lives was both prompting the establishment of organizations and movements while also taking many of our Latina/o brothers and sisters from us.

This first moment marked my beginning of Latina/o activism at the U.S. national level,[7] but many elements of change existed before and after. In the 1970s and 1980s, in addition to the discrimination and hatred faced by Latina/o queers in housing, employment, education, and access to health care, gays and lesbians also faced homophobic violence. In the 1990s fighting homophobia in the health-care system became increasingly important, as breast cancer and other health concerns impacted many of our sisters and brothers. And all the while, as these internal processes of reconfiguration and change, of loss and rebirth, were taking place, Brown queer people were visible organizing and fighting for equal rights. Brown queer activists confronted these issues in their neighborhoods, in community-based organizations, in political movements, on college campuses, and in the government. As referenced in the title, *Queer Brown Voices*, Brown is not a mere color but a way of seeing (and of being seen by) the world; it is a form of identification that supersedes both "Hispanic" and "Latino" ethnoracial categories.[8] Indeed, as I note later on in this introduction, Brown (capitalized) often *becomes* queer.[9]

The histories of Latina/o LGBT activism have not been told as graciously as those of the "mainstream" LGBT movement (with mainstream being a term to use with apprehension, of course, but one that points to a primary, often hegemonic, way of producing a "common" agenda). The former have been rewritten in the service of simpler projects of visibility (for the sake of portraying a mainstream Latina/o community devoid of sexual minorities or of portraying national LGBT organizing—and leadership—as white). Organizations bolster a racial politics that generally stays within a black-and-white binary, effectively erasing Latinas/os (and Asians and Pacific Islanders, Native Americans, and multiracial LGBT people) from the process, while a heteronormative Latina/o mainstream agenda also ignores LGBT populations. While the U.S. homophile movement of the past forty to fifty years is well documented, Latina/o LGBT people have received little attention in these historical accounts, even though people like José Sarria, Sylvia Rivera, and Jeanne Córdova were activists and leaders before Harvey Milk and others of their era (on José Sarria and Sylvia Rivera, see Retzloff 2007; on Jeanne Córdova, see Faderman and Timmons 2006 and Gallo 2007; on all three, see Stein 2012).[10] History books (see Katz 1992 and D'Emilio 1983) do not reflect the fact that numerous LGBT Latina/o organizations were extremely active in their local communities from the late 1970s through the 1980s and 1990s, working on issues of immigration, health care, HIV/AIDS, and inclusion in the gay and lesbian movement for equal rights. Other foundational readers on lesbian and gay history used in universities (Chauncey 1995; Duberman, Vicinus, and Chauncey 1989) rarely document the presence of queer people of color active in the movement. In visual media, sometimes the portrayal of a racially marked LGBT person is distinctive from the (majoritarian) "rest"—a good example is the portrayal of Harvey Milk's Mexican lover (Jack Lira) in the movie *Milk*. Or worse, when a history does mention LGBT Latinas/os who were active in the movement, the reference is factually incorrect, leaving the unknowing reader to believe it historically accurate.

As a case in point, recent books such as Amin Ghaziani's *The Dividends of Dissent* (on the four gay and lesbian national marches in Washington, D.C.) incorrectly credit a single individual with the founding of LLEGÓ.[11] Like *Dividends*, other books addressing the historical LGBT movements misrepresent histories of activism. Sometimes such works portray ethnoracial minorities as contesting mobilization among other gay and lesbian activists; as a result of this view (from outside), queer activists of color are deemed disruptive of a "national" agenda (one selected by a few leaders). And in the process, the contributions of and challenges faced by those who are "multiply minoritized" seldom get to be read as part of history.[12]

Queer Brown Voices utilizes personal narratives and oral histories to document community-organizing efforts among Latina/o queer activists during the 1970s, 1980s, and 1990s and to counter that movement's invisibility. The first-person stories serve as historical, counter-hegemonic accounts of activism outside of mainstream "gay and lesbian" organizing, and as such they shift the dialogue away from pervasive national mainstream issues (such as same-sex marriage). In weaving this web of stories we, the editors, seek to develop a new type of history that counters the invisibility of Latina/o queers in U.S. mainstream history and LGBT studies. Moreover, we intend this book to offer more than a response to that invisibility, aiming for it to be read as a newer kind of cultural history making, one that offers the reader insights into the social movements of that era and the interconnectedness of many of these stories. More than giving visibility to Latina/o LGBT subjects, we seek to trouble assumptions about homogeneity within social movements. Even these fourteen narratives show heterogeneity within a "Latina/o LGBT" movement; those differences range from national/cultural identifications, to gender, gender identity and expression, to socio-economic status, racial background, age, and the relationship between politics and sociocultural activism.

One could indeed just focus on the basic question of visibility: were lesbian and gay, and later on LGBT, Latinas/os involved in the LGBT movement? The chapters in this book unequivocally show we were. If we take the second half of the twentieth century, from the Mattachine Society and the Daughters of Bilitis, where there is little documented presence of queer Brown members; to the next four lesbian and gay marches; to the shortage of leadership positions for Latina/o queers at organizations like the Human Rights Campaign (HRC) and the National Gay and Lesbian Task Force (NGLTF), we can indeed see a general pattern of marginal participation, although that pattern is beginning to shift.[13] *Queer Brown Voices* builds on the initial issue of invisibility (the yes or no type of question), and moves beyond it to explore the factors, political atmosphere, and social elements that fostered the emergence of queer Latina/o organizing in the last three decades of the twentieth century (the how and where—in other words, which forces influenced such emergence). We seek to show that the contemporary gay movement, emergent since the 1960s–1970s, as well as the fight for civil rights, the quest for social justice in Central America, the relationship some queer Latinas/os had to solidarity in Cuba and pro-independence in Puerto Rico, and the challenges they faced in their work with the struggles of "third-world women," were elements that influenced some of these activists' paths, a conclusion not only manifest in this volume but also in others (see Ramirez-Valles 2011). In these, and in other personal narratives,[14] it becomes evident that work within other progressive movements influenced the decision of Latina/o queers to organize around sexuality, gender, and race.

Queer Brown Voices fills a gap in the activist literature on multi-identity politics while it links to academic areas such as ethnicity, race, immigration, sexuality, and gender. This book engages sociology, anthropology, history, American studies, women's and feminist studies, LGBT/sexualities studies, and AIDS cultural studies by weaving these local stories into a minoritarian reading of activism seldom encountered in academic circles. Oftentimes, in academic work that engages the voices of queers of color, LGBT identities are foregrounded, and ethnoracial experiences are ignored; in addition, gender discussions might be suppressed for the sake of unifying the narratives (to produce a singular voice of "unity"). This book aims to incorporate all the "selves" of those telling the first-person accounts; it shows the complex experiences of several activists because those experiences need to be told. It also, and perhaps most importantly, begins to compose a missing history of late twentieth-century Latina/o LGBT movements and community organizing in the United States and Puerto Rico. There are too many first moments, too many organizations, and way too many activists' his/herstories. We are only beginning to draft such a history here, and we encourage others to continue this work by expanding the timeframe we set out to include in these chapters.[15]

In what follows you will see the chapters ordered chronologically; the activists' first involvement in Latina/o LGBT activism served as our criteria. These stories address challenges such as lacking family support, growing up facing discrimination (as Latinas/os in predominantly white spaces, as women in predominantly male spaces, and as gay people in predominantly Latina/o spaces), embracing sexuality or gender identity, challenging heteronormative or racist assumptions, and dealing with the impact of AIDS. As you will see, these stories are, and are not, singular voices: while they do not seek to represent the communities from which they come, the stories do bridge groups of activists from many U.S. cities and Puerto Rico, effectively creating a web of social movements through the personal telling of each individual narrative. This telling, however, is multilayered—and intersectionality and queer studies are critical tools for understanding the impact of these complex narratives.

INTERSECTIONALITY AND LATINA/O, QUEER, AND FEMINIST THEORY

As editors, we initially approached this project through a lens of intersectionality, which we take to mean the connecting and coproducing ways in which a difference-turned-inequality is enacted, either conceptually (in terms of prejudice and stereotyping) or behaviorally (in terms of discrimination) (for a similar interpretation, see Grzanka 2014). Intersectionality as a concept operates in terms of both multiple identities (and more importantly, the crossing and connecting of these identities to make for a complex social location faced with layers of privilege and oppression) as well as the structural elements that impact someone's life.

Although intersectionality was initially a feminist of color project developed by Crenshaw (1991) and Collins (2000), it is oftentimes presented as a strictly feminist project devoid of any racial markings.[16] A complex proposal indeed, intersectionality aims to show the praxis, the method, and the theory of these multiply-lived locations, power-based structures, and related social arrangements. Its value perhaps resides in the instability of its aim in seeking to locate a multiply-layered subject, its sources of oppression, the possibilities for liberation, and the systems through which that power is set up and sustained.

While debate exists about the possible reach of the field and whether or not sexuality is an appropriate dimension of intersectionality, the theory, as a framework, has influenced the work of queer scholars. Of particular note are examinations of queer diasporas (Patton and Sánchez-Eppler 2000; Gopinath 2005), queer migrations (Luibheid and Cantú 2005; Cantú 2009), and the queer of color critique (Ferguson 2004; Muñoz 1999; see also Muñoz 2009). The latter becomes central to our understanding not of identity crossings and structural issues but of oppressive systems of heteronormativity, whiteness, and misogyny, as noted in Muñoz (1999). This book thus grounds its work not only on intersectionality for the sake of speaking to multiple identities, as intersectionality might be read by some, but on the queer of color critique for simultaneously thinking of racial and sexual formations in the United States (Ferguson 2004) and on the promise of a possible better future, always unattainable and yet conceptually feasible—a set of actions, hopes, and thoughts that reach for the "then and there" of Muñoz's *Cruising Utopia* (2009). This book enacts the quest for a more equal world, one where Latina/o LGBT people are not effaced by such pervasive whiteness in social movements (Bérubé 2001) or for the sake of more recent attempts to multiculturalize difference and thus render racism, sexism, and other elements out of a register with gayness.

Queer Brown Voices, like an array of other recent work, puts Latina/o studies and queer studies in conversation with one another (Lima and Picano 2011; Cantú 2009; Hames-García and Martínez 2011). Partly because of differences in genre, partly because of our focus on a balance that incorporates cisgender male, cisgender female, and trans Latinas/os, and partly because our book views social movements through a personal lens, our method of using first-person accounts loops back into Moraga and Anzaldúa's work (1981; see also Alexander 2005; Guzmán 2006; and Perez 2005). The next section elaborates on the use of personal accounts to theorize the social.

FROM PERSONAL STORIES TO SOCIAL MOVEMENTS

By telling the his/herstory of Latina/o LGBT activism through first-person accounts in the form of *testimonios*, autobiographies, memoirs, and oral histories, we aim to show a composite of stories that link to each other in different ways: through shared political issues, other activists and organizations, or discriminatory practices experienced by more than one activist. Thus this volume follows in a tradition of Latina/o writings (Latina Feminist Group 2001), Latina lesbian writings (Moraga and Anzaldúa 1981), and first-person narratives (Berger and Quinney 2005), including LGBT narratives, in which the personal evokes the social; a story may begin with an individual, but it is more than just the sole narrative of the individual. (Leti Gomez addresses the issues of testimonial writing and authorship more fully in the preface.)

Personal narratives are, by necessity, a central element of the book. It was our belief that a collection of stories, along with archival-based visual documentation (of the contributors or the organizations they were involved with) would provide the book with a significantly new and perhaps more complex version of events while remaining, as other oral history scholars have suggested, simple in its implementation (Janesick 2007; 2011). We sought stories that, if powerfully told, would provide enough detail and description to illustrate broader social issues through first-person accounts. We caution the reader that even though these stories use the concept of "I" in their making, they are not *just* singular stories; instead they represent a complex set of elements, including experiences of social marginalization (based on gender, sexuality, or ethnoracial identification); of living in the flesh and of desire; of growing pains and successful turnarounds; and of organizing people from different backgrounds to work for a cause (or set of causes).

We sought to avoid the social/cultural history division as framed by, on the one hand, memory studies (where wars, the Holocaust, and the ending of communism in Eastern Europe serve as significant markers—what is, for some, the official history) and, on the other, the tradition of oral history (itself rooted in democratization processes, decolonization, and the feminist movement from the 1960s) and the ways both of these approaches have been used (Hamilton and Shopes 2008, ix–xi). We view these first-person accounts as bridging from the phenomenological sense of experience and the stories told by individuals (important in oral histories) to the broader purpose of accounting for social, economic, cultural, geopolitical, and other structural elements (key to memory studies). This bridge between the individual and the social is a central reason for our use of personal narratives to tell the story.

First-person accounts have been common for gays and lesbians as a "self-writing" of one's biography (Cohler 2008) that documents experiences of being a member of a minority group, living with HIV, or having someone near to oneself die of AIDS; sexual stories, in particular, have a longstanding value for sexual minorities as telling both the everyday and the so-called intimate (Plummer 1995). We conceived of oral history in particular, a qualitative research method, as a great way to articulate the struggles, successes, and historical elements of any given organization or movement; and we thought the first-person narratives would provide an exercise resembling autoethnography (see Ruiz-Junco and Vidal-Ortiz 2011), an increasingly recognized method in the humanities and the social sciences. Writing first-person accounts resulted in an exercise of verifying facts, as did the oral histories.

In particular, we wanted to bridge previous work on the use of personal stories in order to discuss social issues that were relevant to Latina/o LGBT activists from the 1970s to the 1990s, thus considering social movements beyond "mainstream" portrayals. First-person accounts that illustrate a narrative development, a series of struggles, a link (as indirect as it may be) between a person's formation and his or her participation in a movement or organization, or a significant outcome on the notion of the "self" based on that participation are the type of accounts that help social science and humanities scholars, as well as activists (and the scholar-activists "caught" in between), to understand the impact of a given movement. In sum, we view oral history, like Janesick (2007; 2011), as a social-justice project and value the use of first-person narratives as sources to better understand inequality, and pride, today.

We wished to connect the workings of small-scale social movements (of social, cultural, and political groups composed of Latina/o LGBT people) with that historical moment of the last decades of the twentieth century: the proliferation of movements and 501(c)(3) community-based organizations on a quest for LGBT Latina/o rights. And so these stories undoubtedly have to address what we call the "corporatization" of movements and activism, which, along with an understanding of the workings of social-movement groups, is the topic to which we turn next.

MOVEMENTS FOR SOCIAL CHANGE IN THE LATE TWENTIETH CENTURY

As you will see in some of these chapters, the work in the 1970s and 1980s was done by word of mouth, with little resources. Meetings and conferences at that time depended on personal funds and the dovetailing of objectives (e.g., activists attending a "gay and lesbian" March on Washington would also convene for the purposes of international or U.S. Latina/o organizing). Cell phones were of course not yet developed, and the lack of networking technology impacted the level of organizing done locally.

Undoubtedly, too, the impact of AIDS was felt among all communities of color beginning in the 1980s. The sources of AIDS-related funds (for prevention, technical assistance, care, etc.) that emerged in the late 1980s were instrumental in funding (and sometimes organizing) LGBT Latina/o groups. In addition, the world of philanthropy and foundations supported a lot of sustainable development of these groups. While major donors funded (sometimes after dying) "mainstream" organizations such as the Human Rights Campaign, Latina/o LGBT groups faced limited funding due to lack of available resources in an economically disadvantaged community. Our communities responded in innovative ways to support the already visible work of organizations throughout the United States and Puerto Rico. LLEGÓ, for instance, utilized some of the funding they received in the mid-1990s to offer seed funds as technical assistance to community-based Latina/o LGBT groups.

In the late 1980s and early 1990s there seemed to be a boom in the number of local Latina/o LGBT groups emerging. At that time a lot of people, myself included, were paid to be "professional Latina/o queers."[17] (While the term "queer" was still potentially radical in the mid-1990s, it was, to some extent, used as shorthand for LGBT.) The government and corporations began to pitch in—although not everyone benefited, since not a lot of lesbian- and trans-specific funding was available, and there were politics around funding for HIV/AIDS that only or mostly affected (nontrans) gay men. For instance, Adela Vázquez notes how she was the first trans woman hired at Proyecto Contra SIDA Por Vida—with funding allocated for "men who have sex with men" (MSM), which brought significant challenges to activists who believed that such funding needed to only go to gay men's services.[18] Laura Esquivel, too, talks about the challenges of the professionalization of the Latina/o LGBT movement in Los Angeles, precisely at a historical moment when local groups were facing a transition from grassroots to professional networking. That change is discussed next.

HOW ORGANIZATIONS CHANGE AND SHAPE A MOVEMENT

The 1980s and 1990s saw the emergence and professionalization of a movement that was originally focused on action and activist mobilization. While the mid- and late 1970s witnessed small grassroots efforts to organize locally, because of a number of factors addressed below, the last two decades of the twentieth century became a battleground for the establishment and institutionalization of larger units that sought to give the broadest possible visibility to Latina/o LGBT people, as well as to other people of color groups, through the nonprofit system. This process began before the 1980s, in the 1950s and 1960s, but was rooted in previous historical moments.

As Luz Guerra, one of our contributors and a consultant for many progressive organizations, notes in her evaluation of progressive funders and the designation of technical-assistance services for communities of color,[19] this move to become "official" is the inherent process of "internalization of structures of domination" (Guerra 1999, 34) to which many movements fall prey (domination here might be read as a certain domesticity that suppresses different cultural or operational values). Even groups that are not trying to operate as nonprofits are often coached (through technical assistance, training, and strategic-planning processes, for instance) to imitate corporate models of the agencies that do register and apply for 501(c)(3) status. According to Guerra's report, this process is part and parcel of the "NGOization" of the movements that started much earlier in the century with the 1934 Indian Reorganization Act, which eliminated traditional forms of indigenous governance by imposing, for instance, corporate-board-style leadership and majority voting (35). Guerra points to a link between government reorganization of indigenous groups and the reorganization of the social movements fighting for radical change; the founding, and later funding, of nonprofit organizations was one way of engaging with a forced restructuring to adhere to the "mainstream" (in this case, legal, capitalist-driven goals) expectations of governance and leadership that Guerra deems colonizing (including, as noted before, styles of leadership and forms of decision making). Moreover, because the 501(c)(3) status of nonprofits prohibits direct involvement in political activity (Smith 2007), the NGOs (nongovernmental organizations) that achieve 501(c)(3) status are made to act in docile ways toward the capitalist agents that, oftentimes, such communities organized against in the first place.

This "NGOization" requires shifting goals and developing agendas with aims, deliverables, and outcomes. It also requires donors, external funding (often in the form of external grants, a time-consuming enterprise in and of itself), and a board or advisory body that may oversee the implementation of the vision and mission of the organization. The people involved in the everyday operations of NGOs have what Guerra calls "the pressure to manage two different spheres of work":

> One sphere has to do with developing organizational capacity, and building and maintaining institutions. These are skills that are typically considered under the rubric of "organizational development," and include how to run an activist nonprofit organization, how to structure and work with that organization's leadership, how to ensure that staff and volunteers have the skills needed for their day-to-day work—both internal to the organization and in their program work—and how to finance our activist work and sustain our organizations. The second sphere of work extends outside of our organizations to the broader move-

ments for social change; rather than institutional capacity, it is concerned with "movement building for the long haul." This sphere includes how we gain the skills we need to maintain ourselves and our communities beyond our organization, how to collectively plan and work for social change, and how to build mass-based movements to sustain our vision. (Guerra 1999, 27)

From the interviews she conducted, Guerra noted how activists, funders, and technical-assistance providers all spoke about the challenges of developing a radical "world changing" agenda (political education) while working toward the next payroll commitment (running an agency). Moreover, there is a challenge to consciously fight racism, sexism, classism, and homophobia among the staff of an organization, the executive office, the board of directors (or any other body serving in an advisory or "oversight" capacity), and the organization's constituents. It is this dual project of serving broader social-change goals while paying staff's salary and the office rent that is (to some) a necessary evil (for a debate, see Smith 2007), one that absolutely changes the conditions of sustaining a social-change agenda. In the following chapters you will see how this applies to LLEGÓ as a federally funded agency, but you will also read about it in terms of the toll taken on the lives, relationships, and social worlds of these Latina/o LGBT activists. This "NGOization" is only one of the elements linked to the corporatization of LGBT Latina/o movements, the topic discussed below.

CORPORATIZATION OF MOVEMENTS AND ACTIVISM

Jane Ward's *Respectably Queer: Diversity Culture in LGBT Activist Organizations* (2008) is relevant to this discussion as well. Her research, based on ethnographic participation and interviews, links three Greater Los Angeles nonprofits: the L.A. Gay and Lesbian Center (the country's oldest LGBT community-service center), Christopher Street West (the organization in charge of organizing the city's Pride events), and Bienestar (a Latina/o health initiative focused primarily on Latino gay men). Ward's goal is to push the envelope in terms of the (already discussed) concept of intersectionality by looking at the challenges that diversity poses in these organizations. She also exposes neoliberal ideology in an identity-politics framework based on sexuality (the three organizations focus on LGBT or sexuality issues), where diversity becomes consumption (of otherness), different class status becomes a deficit (for the working class), and gender inequality is not an element addressed in such spaces (rendering women's health issues, and women, invisible). Diversity is commodified in these LGBT spaces through an effort to professionalize and legitimize the organizations within a businesslike model so as to enhance their public image. Ward asks, "What is (still) queer about queer approaches to difference?" In posing that question she bridges the limits of intersectionality (the classic study of race, class, and gender as the central axes of social life and analysis) with the three empirical sites, which focus primarily on sexuality and thus with a queer theoretical formulation of identity slippages and elusiveness. And she notes the challenges of intersectionality at every turn of the research, in that multi-issue politics are quite difficult to manage in these sites. Her concept of "queer intersectionality" inspires our thoughts about the organizing challenges, and community successes, of the communities represented in this volume's narratives.

Laura Esquivel recounts here her experiences of racism at the L.A. Gay and Lesbian Center; fast forward two decades and we see the establishment of a "diversity day" at the center, which most people of color interviewed by Ward viewed as an imposition of corporate cultural values (to respect diversity), while the organization's structural elements (who held the decision-making power) remained untouched. (Work on organizations shows that there is no change, and that institutions remain as racist as they were before, when they only include people of color in front-desk and low-managerial positions.) The businesslike model of treating diversity issues like a written quarterly report is instrumental in understanding how the corporatization of these LGBT organizations impacts queer people of color.

Taken together, Guerra's report and Ward's research articulate some of the same challenges faced by the contributors to this book: Olga Orraca Paredes shows the tension created by having to prioritize between organizational sustainment and social change in her work as a LLEGÓ board member; we also see this in Adela Vázquez's narrative about working for a project that struggled to provide services while having a social-change agenda; and Letitia Gomez articulates the challenges of activists becoming professionalized while lacking the necessary tools to run an agency.

LLEGÓ and other, more local, organizations faced these challenges—and endured them—for decades; some organizations morphed into new projects (Proyecto Contra SIDA Por Vida, for example, has been revived through El/La, a trans-Latina group in San Francisco's Mission District), while others closed their doors—with LLEGÓ doing so in 2004. Many of these groups were social, sociocultural, and political (non-AIDS-service organizations or nongovernmental organizations). While many of these movements owe much funding, technical assistance, and even their very existence to HIV/AIDS funding, a lot of other (nonpaid) organizing has also taken place—and remains. Perhaps because there were multiple types of mobilizations during the 1980s and 1990s (from AIDS activism, community organizing, NGOs, and politics, to someone's home cooking as a basis for mobilization), some have survived. Mona Noriega's chapter, for instance, discusses social gatherings and food preparation for Latina lesbian peers, a model that continues to be used to this day.

Ward's and Guerra's work invites us, as editors, to think about a queerness that is not implicitly white, but intentionally Brown—and a Brownness that shows the intersectional limitations of the people and organizing efforts we illustrate here. Because of the uses and applicability of "queer" in these chapters, what follows is a discussion of complicating queer and Brown as elements that articulate each other, sometimes in and through each other.

WAYS OF DOING QUEER AND BROWN

Queer Brown Voices takes inspiration from the possibilities of queer as a destabilizer of identities, or as an indicator of what is slippery, excessive, and thus uncontainable by identity frameworks (such as LGBT). Queer has two meanings in this volume: first, the common usage, as shorthand for LGBT (a nontheoretical use), and second, as a verb, to mean the act of queering something. The instances when an action *does queer something* are most productive to us in this book. Queer is also a concept that responds to, although almost in opposition, homonormative forms of being gay (and of living gayness), forms that reproduce normative binary forms of gender (male/masculine, female/feminine), sexuality (monogamous, within marriage/the couple, etc.), and even race and class (well-to-do-white as a norm of what is read socially and culturally as being gay).

Along the same lines, we see Brown as queer because it serves to destabilize categories too: in the case of the United States, Brown serves as a rupture between the white/black binary of its racial system. Brown bodies are those bodies that break away from the expectation of whiteness as the norm. Yet Brown bodies are also queered in that they are seen as suspicious, as already delinquent, especially in relation to immigration but also to not fully participating in U.S. citizenry. As Gomez illustrates in her chapter when talking about the Washington, D.C., of the 1980s, to be either queer or Brown was a source of potential harassment; either one was enough of an outsider marker to place people at risk of facing violence. Brown also helps us debunk the simple gay-equals-white perception of gay movements; by refuting the invisibility of Latina/o queers, Brown emerges as a new form of thinking beyond gayness (even when Latina/o bodies may inhabit the sign of gayness).

Among our contributors, most squarely assume a gay or lesbian identity. (A minority used queer to denote their identity, or moved from gay or lesbian to queer.) Yet there are several ways in which that gay or lesbian identity is destabilized: the contributors' Latina/o backgrounds impact the ways they experience gayness and how they assume their identities; their sense of being gay or lesbian is impacted by the ways in which whiteness erases their own sense of self; finally, they expressed that they have to exclude a part of their selves in order to participate in the normative ways gayness is portrayed in contemporary U.S. society. But the contributors often queer Brown by way of their acts—from simple forms of socializing and organizing (with queer acts such as sponsoring *bailes* with *rancheras* and other Latina/o music, and doing so in Latina/o neighborhoods despite being cautioned of supposed homophobia in Latina/o communities) to their broader vision of the movement.

As activists, many of the contributors whose identities might have been noted as gay or lesbian were thinking of queerness within a political milieu that assumed sexuality as the beginning, not the end point of their activism (see chapters by Dennis Medina and Gloria Ramirez). They queer Brown as they make sense of a political agenda that may be about, at the time, Central American or Cuban solidarity, gender parity, transnational linkages, or even pornography and the erotic (we see these most saliently in the contributions of Gloria Ramirez and Luz Guerra, although we see the sense of political urgency to connect U.S. sexuality struggles with other struggles in chapters by David Acosta, Jesús Cháirez, and other contributors).

Queer Brown organizing almost always responds to the (seemingly innocent) question posed by white gays and lesbians: "Why would you organize by yourselves? You are being separatists!" Many of us have experienced the anger that erupts after that demand for "unity," even more so when an answer has been offered to try and explain why it is necessary. Brown thus serves as a reminder to "mainstream" LGBT movements that there are other issues besides sexuality—and as we see in Ward's work, those who challenge that (white) norm by bringing up race, ethnicity, gender, or class may feel the response from entitled white LGBT "leaders" whose job becomes to mark queer Brown organizing as delinquent.

Take multi-issue women-led organizing as a prime example. The Esperanza Peace and Justice Center has always been a queer Brown space, not an LGBT space—and has been made to pay for it by some in the San Antonio white gay establishment who attempted to censor and defund the center's work. Queer there, as in other chapters, is a political formation that connects sexuality to many other issues and does not privilege sexuality, or sexual orientation, as the prime reason for organizing. In a way, what fuels the anger of many white gay leaders in these instances is that sexuality is not voiced centrally, in what Manolo Guzmán (2006) has noted as "the love that cannot stand not being not named."

QUEERING BROWN ISSUES

Anger fueled many of this book's contributors (see the chapter by José Gutiérrez particularly, but also David Acosta, Dennis Medina, and Moisés Agosto-Rosario), as did frustration and first-hand experiences with discrimination (see chapters by Olga Orraca Paredes, Gloria Ramirez, Luz Guerra, and Leti Gomez). Refusing to serve as a translator (as Moisés Agosto-Rosario did with ACT UP) and instead forming one's own political platform are queer acts based on anger at being reduced to a peripheral role rather than being given an equal chance to hold a position of leadership. Queer in this case is about establishing an area of expertise and interest by and for oneself and not coordinated or decided by others—and doing so without apology.

Some of the chapters illustrate processes of racialization (the act of being marked, some say raced, by virtue of one's phenotypic characteristics, accent, way of dressing, etc.) that clearly go beyond national identity. Moisés Agosto-Rosario, a very light-skinned, blue-eyed Puerto Rican, illustrates the challenges of moving to the United States and beginning to identify not only as Latina/o but as a person of color;[20] Adela Vázquez, too, describes the processes of being marked as a person of color in U.S. society, while noting that for many Latinas/os there is a common erasure of the blackness inherited by many of us. And in various narratives from activists in Texas (Cháirez, Medina, and Gomez), we see the necessary move from one's social location as Chicana/o or Tejana/o to *becoming* Latina/o in order to build a movement based on

Latina/o experience. These stories queer what it means to be racialized in U.S. society when you are not a white or a black USAmerican. More broadly, the politics of race and people of color, not as a skin color–based identity, but as a coalitional one, are seen in the contributions of David Acosta, Gloria Ramirez, Luz Guerra, Mona Noriega, and Laura Esquivel.

The topic of gender equality and the need for gender spaces is something we see implicitly in Gloria Ramirez's chapter, but it is most explicit in Laura Esquivel's contribution. We also see this in the context of Latina/o spaces—how leadership and retreat events were often organized for Latinas/os only and the negotiations that were required with participants' non-Latina/o partners. These processes of enunciation of one's own space offered opportunities to talk, to truly discuss the meaning of diversity and of organizing along gender or ethnic lines, and thus enhanced organizing for LGBT Latina/o communities.

Queer and Brown are here ways of twisting and troubling the normal assumptions about both sexuality and race, for LGBT Latinas/os initially, but in the long run for all. We saw these processes take place as we edited and compiled this work. And as such, we see the challenges and richness that result when organizing is embedded with processes of queering Brown and when organizers challenge, by merely being nonnormative, the status quo in Latina/o spaces and in "mainstream" LGBT spaces. We conclude by turning to our process of reconstructing this history through these narratives.

CONTINUING TO DOCUMENT OUR HISTORIES

Whether oral history interview or first-person written narrative, the storytelling in these chapters is but a fraction of the history being told. Reconstructing history through checking facts is not the same strategy as remembering events and naming names. We have sought to do both in order to stay true to the recollection of events and, to the extent possible, have verified through other sources the veracity of many of these events. We have contacted additional activists, sought archives (in Austin and San Francisco), and repeatedly asked the contributors to do the same in order to guarantee a triangulation of information. But memory is never complete; it never is the now, the present, nor can it be fully recaptured. These are, in the end, incomplete pieces of a puzzle that merits the effort of pulling them together in order to achieve a queer futurity of then and there (Muñoz 2009).

Queer Brown Voices' contributors are Latina/o lesbian, gay, and transgender activists from cities such as Houston, San Francisco, New York, San Antonio, Philadelphia, Austin, and Chicago. Some talk about their experiences of living in Puerto Rico, a country with a highly complex relationship with the United States and linked in many ways to its Latina/o queer politics.[21] The contributors are Mexican American, Chicana/o, Tejana/o, Mexican, Puerto Rican, Dominican, Colombian, and Cuban. They have been involved with LGBT-advocacy groups, human-rights groups, and other movements since the late 1970s through to the 1990s (and many continue such work in the present). Most of our contributors have completed at least a bachelor's degree, with many being exposed to an exchange of ideas common in educational (and related progressive) settings. We sought gender parity, trans inclusion, and various levels of socioeconomic experiences. Yet as editors, we must insist that this book is a primer for the work ahead and that we need many more volumes, archives, and published works that show the value of these earlier generations of LGBT Latina/o activists.

In the stories that follow, the discrimination experienced by the contributors is divided almost in half in terms of discrimination based on Latina/o identity versus discrimination based on gender expression, gender identity, or sexual orientation. But there is also a strong sense of pride, of participation in a shared Latina/o culture that in many instances cuts through the discrimination faced. It is that richness that we envision will offer a more grounded sense of what organizing meant for Latina/o LGBT people during the decades covered in this book. Some chapters center on the story of a person, and how that individual's sense of life and commitment to justice came about and influenced his or her work in an organization or as part of a movement; others showcase the history of an organization and weave the individual's life and personal story as a secondary telling that emerges through the organization's story. In either scenario you can see issues such as micropolitics, discrimination (on account of being a woman, LGBT, or Latina/o in male, mainstream Latina/o, or gay white spaces), and strategic mobilization across the work of the organization or movement. Some of the chapters show coalition building among feminists, women of color, and people of color, a type of organizing that was less common than other types in gay and lesbian circles at the time, and still is.

Like the incredible work produced by Horacio Roque Ramírez, both alone ([2015], 2011, 2008, 2007, 2005) and in collaboration (Roque Ramírez and Boyd 2012), as well as newer oral history and archives scholarship (for a recent case, see Torres 2014), we aim to promote greater recognition of the socially relevant issues found in these personal, yet never individual, accounts. Again, our focus on these activists should only be considered a primer for more scholarship and activist work to intersect. At the same time, we consider these contributors to be an incredible source of resilience; simply, a combined force of greater magnitude—larger than each of their individual narratives. Herein lies the power of the research and writing we share with you, the perseverance of an insightful and resourceful multilayered activism.

We count on a generation of scholars, activists, scholar-activists, curators, and archivists to continue to ask questions, to gently probe the stories told, and to insist on writing queer—in brown ink. More than for mere enjoyment, the pages ahead remember, recount, and reconstitute the critical junctures Latina/o LGBT activists faced in their work in the 1970s, 1980s, and 1990s. Of course, the stories we compile here are provided for readers to discuss, to dissent, and in sum to engage with—that is ultimately a radical way of making history. Enjoy these other, less told histories.

NOTES

1. I use both terms interchangeably, but while "queer" is often used as shorthand for "LGBT," they do not convey the same meanings, especially politically, as I explain later on.

2. The acronym LGBT (lesbian, gay, bisexual, and transgender) must be historically contextualized, as it is a relatively recent one. In the 1970s organizations such as the National Gay Task Force only implicitly included lesbians; meanwhile, and partly because of the sexism documented in gay-male-centered spaces and the feminist work of the decade, lesbian separatist groups emerged. Generally, the 1980s saw the initial use of "gay and lesbian"; in the early 1990s, as we see in the title of this national march, the category bisexual was included. Scholars have argued that the term transgender begins to circulate, and to more formally relate to LGBs, in the 1990s (Valentine 2007). At the time of this writing, some social-movement groups use a double T to represent transgender and transsexual or trans and travesti; some use LGBTI to include intersex; and yet others use LGBTIQ to include queer and/or "questioning" (referencing the questioning of sexual and gender identity as stable categories of identity).

3. "Women of color" and "people of color" are political concepts that denote the potential coalitional relationship between African American, Asian, Latina/o, Native American, and multiracial people in the United States (women of color have historically used these coalitional terms more than men have).

4. Puerto Rico has been a colony of the United States since 1898. Yet, as Olga Orraca Paredes dutifully notes in her chapter, a Puerto Rican national identity and a sense of Puerto Rico being a separate country operate in tandem with its colonial relationship to the United States, which permits many activists to work within LGBT Puerto Rican activism and U.S. "national" social movements. We connect Puerto Rican LGBT activism to U.S. activism because the stories are often intertwined, particularly in the late 1980s to early 1990s as LLEGÓ strengthened its capacity-building and technical-assistance programs. Yet we also recognize that Puerto Rican activists worked on issues on the island at the same time as they collaborated with other Puerto Ricans in the diaspora and other Latina/o LGBT activists, and we highlight it here to illustrate the multiple demands required in such coalitional work.

5. The preceding movement, founded in 1987 at the second national gay and lesbian march, was initially called the National Latino/a Lesbian and Gay Activists (NLLGA), becoming, months later, LLEGÓ. After successfully completing a subcontract for the National Minority AIDS Council from 1988 to 1990, LLEGÓ was able to apply for funds as one of (what the CDC called then) the National and Regional Minority Organizations. LLEGÓ was instrumental in establishing the presence of LGBT Latinas/os as leaders within the national LGBT movement, but it also depended, to a great extent, on those local movements, programs, and organizations. LLEGÓ had close to two hundred affiliate organizations (focusing on both sociocultural and political organizing) in the continental United States and Puerto Rico, and it offered technical assistance, managed a policy office, and hosted a conference every eighteen or so months until it closed its doors in 2004. We approach LLEGÓ as a significant organization, in terms of visibility, with two caveats: First, we must note that the agency changed and shifted throughout those sixteen years, encompassing differing political views, leadership, policy work, and social-change positions (in other words some, depending on when they engaged with the organization, remember a different LLEGÓ than others). Second, we focus on the work LLEGÓ did in the United States and Puerto Rico; for an incisive and important critique of the organization in terms of its dubious relationship to Puerto Rico, and a colonial one to all of Latin America, see the brilliant work by Quiroga (2000).

6. Horacio Roque Ramírez notes in the online encyclopedia *GLBTQ* that there were already groups in the early 1970s in the continental United States and in Puerto Rico organizing Latina/o LGBT people. He also notes the presence of Latina/o and Latin American LGBT activists at the first gay and lesbian March on Washington (preceded by an event at Howard University titled the National Third World Lesbian and Gay Conference); and he reminds us that U.S. Latinas were already involved by the second gay and lesbian March on Washington and with transnational efforts to bridge U.S. Latina lesbians and their Latin American colleagues through the Encuentros de Lesbianas Feministas de Latinoamérica y el Caribe (Latin American and Caribbean Femi-

nist Lesbian Gatherings). For a Latin American perspective, see also the work of Olga Careaga (a Mexican lesbian feminist academic and activist).

7. I had already been engaged with activism in Puerto Rico *as* a Puerto Rican since the 1980s, but it generally happened outside of a Latina/o identity/context. More than a personal note, this illustration is offered to convey that for many groups organizing as early as the 1970s and 1980s, ethnoracial identities were oftentimes based on national origin, national pride, or national identity (Puerto Ricans, Chicanas/os, Mexican Americans) and not based on pan-ethnic (i.e., Hispanic or Latina/o) identification. The latter nomenclature began to coexist with, and sometimes displace, nationality-based identification in the late 1980s and early 1990s in a process seldom written about in these social movements, but noted here in chapters by Agosto-Rosario, Gomez, and Medina, to mention but a few.

8. See the first pages of Muñoz's "Feeling Brown" (2000).

9. Furthermore, like queer—originally a stigmatized identification through methods of surveillance and disciplining—Brown adheres to, but also moves away from, a connection with pride and disidentification from certain structures, while calling them into account. Before 9/11, the term might have simply been related to Latin American or U.S. Latina/o people. In contemporary times, however, Brown does not only reference Latinas/os; it is used to link Latin, Latin American, black Caribbean, and South Asian and Middle Eastern groups of people, as well as international migrants (sometimes as disruptive, noncontained national bodies). For the latter, see the introduction of a special journal issue on the theme of "Deviant Brown" by Silva (2010).

10. José Sarria, of Colombian and Spanish descent, ran for the San Francisco Board of Supervisors in 1961; Sarria was also involved in founding the Imperial Court System, where performers did drag shows to raise funds for various groups. Sylvia Rivera, of Venezuelan and Puerto Rican descent, is known for her participation (along with others, like Marsha P. Johnson, who was African American) in the Stonewall Inn fights against the police in what became the birth of gayness in U.S. contemporary society; Rivera cofounded Street Transvestites for Gay Power in 1970, which later became Street Transvestite Action Revolutionaries. Jeanne Córdova, of Mexican and Irish American descent, was one of the first presidents of the L.A. chapter of the Daughters of Bilitis in the early 1970s; Córdova was also a journalist whose contributions extended to LGBT communities, and she was a key lesbian activist for the democratic party.

11. Ghaziani credits the founding of the National Latino/a Lesbian and Gay Organization (LLEGÓ) to Nicole Murray-Ramirez, despite interviewing actual founders of LLEGÓ, such as Leti Gomez (first female cochair and second executive director). In her chapter here, Gomez mentions other founders, such as Arturo Olivas (male cochair), Arcadio Torres (treasurer), and Dolores Gracia (secretary), as well as other members, such as Hank Tavera, Dennis Medina, María Limón, Brad Veloz, and Joe Perez. Gomez, Medina, Veloz, and

Esquivel (all in this book) recount that there were many Latina/o lesbian and gay activists at the table at the time of the founding, and Gomez, Veloz, and Medina in particular note that there was no one founder but rather a collective decision-making process. That Ghaziani's account reduces the founding of an organization to one member follows a common pattern in mainstream gay and lesbian studies (and perhaps in an overall "American" story), where a single activist or leader is given sole recognition of a much more complex process of discussion and negotiation.

12. Here, the term refers to being minoritized by more than a single aspect of one's social location. In "Cruising the Toilet" (2007, 366) Muñoz notes how minoritized "is meant to connote racialization in relationship to a scene dominated by whiteness." For Muñoz, disidentification is a productive form of letting go, or "dissing," identity in order to focus on identity formations that constitute added/third spaces that counter the forces of "heteronormativity, white supremacy, and misogyny" (5). While in *Cruising Utopias* (2009) Muñoz addresses multiple marginalizations more than in his *Disidentifications* (1999), even in the earlier work we see a strong foundation for this theorizing. Muñoz's *Disidentifications* was instrumental in showing the potentiality of queers of color within society: for instance, in highlighting the very public relationship between Pedro Zamora, a Cuban gay man living with AIDS who became popular through MTV's TV series *The Real World*, and his partner, Sean Sasser, an African American gay man, Muñoz captures the "worlds of possibilities for the minoritarian subject who experiences multiple forms of domination within larger systems of governmentality" (160). We also see this concept of multiply minoritized theorizing in "Feeling Brown" (2000), in particular in Muñoz's discussion of Ricardo Bracho's play, which encompasses an array of characters who are not white but who produce a sense of Brownness that goes beyond Latinidad.

13. The exception to this pattern of occasional participation seems to be the struggles in the 1960s, namely, those at the Stonewall Inn (New York City, 1969) and Compton's Cafeteria (San Francisco, 1966), which included Latinas/os and other people of color. Since the 1990s, the two main national organizations for LGBT rights, HRC and NGLTF, have engaged in "diversity work" or produced (and funded) reports on queer people of color; at the time of this writing, the latter group has a Latino gay deputy director, Russell Roybal. For a critique of "diversity work" see Ward's *Respectably Queer* (2008); also refer to Esquivel's chapter, in particular, for her experiences working at the L.A. Gay and Lesbian Center in the 1980s.

14. The Center for Puerto Rican Studies at Hunter College (City University of New York) has a special collection of oral histories taped and filmed by Lilian Jiménez on Puerto Rican gay and lesbian activists, whose work in the 1960s and 1970s included working within Puerto Rican organizations and the Puerto Rican pro-independence movement. For a particular example of

this narrative of activism (occurring alongside, but also influencing, an individual's LGBT organizing experience), see Jiménez's documentary on Antonia Pantoja, *Antonia Pantoja ¡Presente!* (2008). For an exploration of the spatial out/non-out place of Pantoja's activism, see Torres's article "Boricua Lesbians" (2007). Regarding the topic of outness and, in particular, the notion of tacit subjects, which troubles understandings of the closet, see Decena's book *Tacit Subjects* (2011).

15. Inspiration and thanks are owed to Rodríguez's (2003) and Roque Ramírez's (2011; 2008) work on queer Latinas/os (especially in the San Francisco area).

16. Roderick Ferguson's contribution in Grzanka's *Intersectionality* (2014) illustrates multiple sites of intersectionality's origins. Among those, Ferguson notes the "Combahee River Collective Statement" (a black feminist collective's 1974 manifesto, considered by many to be a significant moment of race/gender/sexuality theorizing) and Crenshaw's work. The concept is in this sense a moving target, both in terms of its emergence and its scope.

17. In the interest of full disclosure, I must note that I was a volunteer for LLEGÓ between 1994 and 1995, an employee of LLEGÓ during 1996 to 1997, and a program evaluator for one of its technical-assistance projects a few years later.

18. The MSM category has been problematized for its ability to convey behavior (the focus of the CDC's HIV prevention efforts and funding at that time) but not identity (the focus of a lot of gay-identified men's organizing in the 1980s and 1990s); in the 1990s and early 2000s implementation of MSM research and prevention services funded by the CDC included trans women, who are often identified by their genitalia at birth as belonging to the MSM category, sometimes resulting in funding for transgender programs. Having the term MSM serve as a buffer between identities such as gay and transgender offers a particular challenge to both the CDC and local organizations, in that sexual orientation and gender identity are often fluid for some of the people identified within those categories (e.g., sometimes a very effeminate man might be coded as transgender because of the gendered expression, regardless of the individual's gender identity or sexual orientation). What has been missed in a lot of these discussions of the categories "transgender" and "gay men" in HIV prevention is how the two groups share geographic space in neighborhoods, clubs, and sex-work sites in major urban centers in the United States; for more on that, see Mukherjea and Vidal-Ortiz's "Studying HIV Risk in Vulnerable Communities" (2006).

19. The Funding Exchange (FEX) was a national grant-making NGO. It was founded in 1979 and operated until 2013. FEX's program office hired Guerra to conduct the research and produce this report. Composed of over a dozen local or regional grant makers whose operations were based on their relationships with donors, the network was critical in offering emergency

funding, seed funding, and technical assistance and training. The Funding Exchange charged three activist-led boards with the work of recommending funding to various applicants based on their commitment to social justice, gender parity, sexual diversity, race, and other social markers. The three advisory boards were the Robeson Fund (focused on media), the Saguaro Fund (focused on people of color), and the Gay and Lesbian Fund (focused on LGBT groups). The report was done primarily in consultation with technical-assistance providers from communities of color, although, as usual with the programming of the organization, most projects evidenced an intersectional lens in their philosophy and implementation.

20. I have addressed the experiences of queering a racial binary in the United States as a Puerto Rican; for the reader interested, please see Vidal-Ortiz, "On Being a White Person of Color" (2004).

21. For an important dissertation addressing Puerto Rico's formation of a "gay city" see Laureano Pérez, "Negociaciones espectaculares" (2011).

BIBLIOGRAPHY

Alexander, M. Jacqui. 2005. "Remembering This Bridge Called My Back." In *Pedagogies of Crossing: Meditations on Feminism, Sexual Politics, Memory, and the Sacred*, 257–286. Durham, NC: Duke University Press.

Berger, Ronald J., and Richard Quinney. 2005. *Storytelling Sociology: Narrative as Social Inquiry*. London: Lynne Rienner.

Bérubé, Allan. 2001. "How Gay Stays White and What Kind of White It Stays." In *The Making and Unmaking of Whiteness*, edited by Birgit Brander Rasmussen, Eric Klinenberg, Irene J. Nexica, and Matt Wray, 234–265. Durham, NC: Duke University Press.

Cantú, Lionel, Jr. 2009. *The Sexuality of Migration: Border Crossings and Mexican Immigrant Men*. Edited by Nancy Naples and Salvador Vidal-Ortiz. New York: New York University Press.

Chauncey, George. 1995. *Gay New York: Gender, Urban Culture, and the Making of the Gay Male World, 1890–1940*. New York: Basic Books.

Cohler, Bertram J. 2008. "Life-Stories and Storied Lives: Genre and Reports of Lived Experience in Gay Personal Literature." *Journal of Homosexuality* 54 (4): 362–380.

Collins, Patricia Hill. 2000. *Black Feminist Thought: Knowledge, Consciousness, and the Politics of Empowerment*. New York: Routledge.

Crenshaw, Kimberlé. 1991. "Mapping the Margins: Intersectionality, Identity Politics, and Violence Against Women of Color." *Stanford Law Review* 43 (6): 1241–1299.

Decena, Carlos Ulises. 2011. *Tacit Subjects: Belonging and Same-Sex Desire among Dominican Immigrant Men*. Durham, NC: Duke University Press.

D'Emilio, John. 1983. *Sexual Politics, Sexual Communities: The Making of a Homo-*

sexual Minority in the United States, 1940–1970. Chicago: University of Chicago Press.

Duberman, Martin Bauml, Martha Vicinus, and George Chauncey Jr., eds. 1989. *Hidden from History: Reclaiming the Gay and Lesbian Past.* New York: NAL Books, 1989.

Faderman, Lillian, and Stuart Timmons. 2006. "Glitz and Glam." In *Gay L.A.: A History of Sexual Outlaws, Power Politics, and Lipstick Lesbians,* 231–255. Cambridge, MA: Basic Books.

Ferguson, Roderick A. 2004. *Aberrations in Black: Toward a Queer of Color Critique.* Minneapolis: University of Minnesota Press.

Gallo, Marcia M. 2007. *Different Daughters: A History of the Daughters of Bilitis and the Rise of the Lesbian Rights Movement.* Emeryville, CA: Seal Press.

Ghaziani, Amin. 2008. *The Dividends of Dissent: How Conflict and Culture Work in Lesbian and Gay Marches on Washington.* Chicago: University of Chicago Press.

Gopinath, Gayatri. 2005. *Impossible Desires: Queer Diasporas and South Asian Public Cultures.* Durham, NC: Duke University Press.

Grzanka, Patrick R. 2014. *Intersectionality: A Foundations and Frontiers Reader.* Boulder, CO: Westview.

Guerra, Luz. 1999. "Technical Assistance and Progressive Organizations for Social Change in Communities of Color: A Report to the Saguaro Grantmaking Board of the Funding Exchange." (PDF available by contacting the author.)

Guzmán, Manolo. 2006. *Gay Hegemony/Latino Homosexualities.* New York: Routledge.

Hames-García, Michael, and Ernesto Javier Martínez, eds. 2011. *Gay Latino Studies: A Critical Reader.* Durham, NC: Duke University Press.

Hamilton, Paula, and Linda Shopes, eds. 2008. *Oral History and Public Memories.* Philadelphia: Temple University Press.

Janesick, Valerie J. 2007. "Oral History as a Social Justice Project: Issues for the Qualitative Researcher." *Qualitative Report* 12 (1): 111–121.

———. 2011. "Reinventing Oral History for the Qualitative Researcher." In *Oral History for the Qualitative Researcher: Choreographing the Story,* 1–42. New York: Guilford.

Jiménez, Lilian, dir. 2008. *Antonia Pantoja ¡Presente!* Film.

Katz, Jonathan Ned. 1992. *Gay American History: Lesbians and Gay Men in the U.S.A.* Rev. ed. New York: Meridian.

Latina Feminist Group. 2001. *Telling to Live: Latina Feminist Testimonios.* Durham, NC: Duke University Press.

Laureano Pérez, Javier E. 2011. "Negociaciones espectaculares: Creación de una cultura gay urbana en San Juan a partir de la Segunda Guerra Mundial hasta principios de los 1990." PhD diss., Universidad de Puerto Rico.

Lima, Lázaro, and Felice Picano, eds. 2011. *Ambientes: New Queer Latino Writing.* Madison: University of Wisconsin Press.

Luibheid, Eithne, and Lionel Cantú Jr., eds. 2005. *Queer Migrations: Sexuality, U.S. Citizenship, and Border Crossings*. Minneapolis: University of Minnesota Press.

Moraga, Cherríe, and Gloria Anzaldúa, eds. 1981. *This Bridge Called My Back: Writings by Radical Women of Color*. New York: Kitchen Table/Women of Color Press.

Mukherjea, Ananya, and Salvador Vidal-Ortiz. 2006. "Studying HIV Risk in Vulnerable Communities: Methodological and Reporting Shortcomings in the Young Men's Study in New York City." *Qualitative Report* 11 (2): 393–416.

Muñoz, José Esteban. 1999. *Disidentifications: Queers of Color and the Performance of Politics*. Minneapolis: University of Minnesota Press.

———. 2000. "Feeling Brown: Ethnicity and Affect in Ricardo Bracho's *The Sweetest Hangover (and Other STDs)*." *Theatre Journal* 52:67–79.

———. 2007. "Cruising the Toilet: LeRoi Jones/Amiri Baraka, Radical Black Traditions, and Queer Futurity." *GLQ* 13 (2–3): 353–367.

———. 2009. *Cruising Utopia: The Then and There of Queer Futurity*. New York: New York University Press.

Patton, Cindy, and Benigno Sánchez-Eppler, eds. 2000. *Queer Diasporas*. Durham, NC: Duke University Press.

Pérez, Emma. 2005. "Gloria Anzaldúa: La Gran Nueva Mestiza Theorist, Writer, Activist-Scholar." *National Women's Studies Association Journal* 17 (2): 1–10.

Plummer, Ken. 1995. *Telling Sexual Stories: Power, Change, and Social Worlds*. New York: Routledge.

Quiroga, José. 2000. *Tropics of Desire: Interventions from Queer Latino America*. New York: New York University Press.

Ramirez-Valles, Jesus. 2011. *Compañeros: Latino Activists in the Face of AIDS*. Urbana: University of Illinois Press.

Retzloff, Tim. 2007. "Eliding Trans Latino/a Queer Experience in U.S. LGBT History: José Sarria and Sylvia Rivera Reexamined." *CENTRO* 19 (1): 140–161.

Rodríguez, Juana Maria. 2003. *Queer Latinidad: Identity Practices, Discursive Spaces*. New York: New York University Press.

Roque Ramírez, Horacio N. 2005. "Latina/Latino Americans." In *GLBTQ: An Encyclopedia of Gay, Lesbian, Bisexual, Transgender & Queer Culture*. http://www.glbtq.com/social-sciences/latina_latino_americans.html.

———. 2007. "'¡Mira, yo soy boricua y estoy aquí!': Rafa Negrón's Pan Dulce and the Queer Sonic Latinaje of San Francisco." *CENTRO* 18 (Spring): 274–313.

———. 2008. "Memory and Mourning: Living Oral History with Queer Latinos and Latinas in San Francisco." In *Oral History and Public Memories*, edited by Paula Hamilton and Linda Shopes, 165–186. Philadelphia: Temple University Press.

———. 2011. "Gay Latino Cultural Citizenship: Predicaments of Identity and Visibility in San Francisco in the 1990s." In *Gay Latino Studies: A Critical Reader*, edited by Michael Hames-García and Ernesto Javier Martínez, 175–197. Durham, NC: Duke University Press.

———. [2015]. *Queer Latino San Francisco: An Oral History, 1960s–1990s*. New York: Palgrave Macmillan.

Roque Ramírez, Horacio N., and Nan Alamilla Boyd. 2012. "Introduction: Close Encounters: The Body and Knowledge in Queer Oral History." In *Bodies of Evidence: The Practice of Queer Oral History*, edited by Nan Alamilla Boyd and Horacio N. Roque Ramírez, 1–20. Oxford: Oxford University Press.

Ruiz-Junco, Natalia, and Salvador Vidal-Ortiz. 2011. "Autoethnography: The Sociological Through the Personal." In *New Directions in Sociology: Essays on Theory and Methodology in the 21st Century*, edited by Ieva Zake and Michael DeCesare, 193–211. Jefferson, NC: McFarland.

Silva, Kumarini. 2010. "Introduction—Brown: From Identity to Identification." *Cultural Studies* 24 (2): 167–182.

Smith, Andrea. 2007. "Introduction: The Revolution Will Not Be Funded." In *The Revolution Will Not Be Funded: Beyond the Non-Profit Industrial Complex*, edited by INCITE! Women of Color Against Violence, 1–18. Cambridge, MA: South End.

Stein, Marc. 2012. *Rethinking the Gay and Lesbian Movement*. New York: Routledge.

Torres, Lourdes. 2007. "Boricua Lesbians: Sexuality, Nationality, and the Politics of Passing." *CENTRO* 19 (1): 231–249.

———. 2014. "Compañeras in the Middle: Toward a History of Latina Lesbian Organizing in Chicago." *GLQ* 20 (1–2): 41–74.

Valentine, David. 2007. *Imagining Transgender: An Ethnography of a Category*. Durham, NC: Duke University Press.

Vidal-Ortiz, Salvador. 2004. "On Being a White Person of Color: Using Autoethnography to Understand Puerto Ricans' Racialization." *Qualitative Sociology* 27 (2): 179–203.

Ward, Jane. 2008. *Respectably Queer: Diversity Culture in LGBT Activist Organizations*. Nashville, TN: Vanderbilt University Press.

LUZ GUERRA

Dancing at the Crossroads:
Mulata, Mestiza, Macha, Mujer

Luz Guerra, of Dominican and Puerto Rican descent, was born in New York and grew up in that city's Lower East Side—"Loisaida"— and in California. In her essay Guerra recounts the racism, sexism, classism, and homophobia she experienced during her childhood and reveals how such episodes moved her to challenge some of the inequalities that divide U.S. society. She then examines the challenges she faced as a Latina lesbian mother, as well as her involvement in cultural and political activism. For more than thirty years Luz Guerra has worked extensively, both across the United States and in Puerto Rico, with organizations such as the Austin Latina/o Lesbian and Gay Organization (ALLGO), New Bridges, the Indigenous Women's Network, the American Friends Service Committee, and the Esperanza Peace and Justice Center, and she has offered consulting services to national NGOs (nongovernmental organizations) including the Funding Exchange and the National Latino/a Lesbian and Gay Organization (LLEGÓ). As a former consultant and training facilitator for LLEGÓ, Guerra offers a lucid analysis of that organization's evolution and its contributions to Latinas/os. Her essay closes with a reflection on the limitations of terms such as "Hispanic," "Latina," and "LGBT." It is important, she concludes, that she honor her family, her community, and her own life experiences as a mixed-race woman.

STORIES ARE IMPORTANT. MY MOTHER USED TO tell me the story of my birth, which took place at home in Loisaida, with my father and two midwives attending, on the first day of spring. Loisaida, as the poet Bimbo Rivas christened the Lower East Side in his 1974 love poem to our barrio, was where my young parents lived in the 1950s. They'd first moved to Puerto Rico to raise a family, but my Nuyorican father couldn't overcome his anger about racism within the family or his inability to be the dominant voice on account of his halting Spanish. My mother had fled Alabama, where her own family was broken and her mixed-race marriage was illegal. I grew up hearing a lot about race, about the violence of racism, and the importance of the civil rights movement to my family.

When we rented briefly in Queens in 1963, someone scrawled "nigger" on the wall of our home, and I hid behind the couch with my mother and brothers as my father stood guard by the window because our neighbors were throwing rocks and making threats. Maybe that story will help explain why I inherited my Puerto Rican and Dominican father's "obsession" with race and why he taught his children that a mixed-race identity was a black identity, that being "colored" would define our futures.

Just as my father inspired me to know my history, my mother fed me books and poetry. She gave me Martin Luther King's "Letter from Birmingham Jail" and the poetry of Nikki Giovanni. She read me *The Hobbit* and sang folk songs and ditties while baking in the kitchen. We spent hours at the public library, which had no books by Puerto Rican or Dominican authors, nor any on the history of the Caribbean islands. Cultural markers from the islands came from my *abuela* and *tía abuela*, who taught me Spanish and the songs of their childhoods, made *sofrito* (and spaghetti), and showed me how to do fine needlework.

My philandering father abandoned my mother when I was seven, but my siblings and I were bounced between them long after that. My mother had come to New York at sixteen to act in off-off-Broadway productions and join the Beat artistic scene in Greenwich Village. Now she was twenty-four years old with four small children and no financial resources or even a high school diploma. I can tell you how I hated waking up hungry to an empty refrigerator and doing my homework in the stairwell because we hadn't paid the electric bill on time. Or how as a young girl I often had to step over junkies (a common term for heroin addicts in the 1960s and 1970s) in the hallway on my way to school and walk around winos (people, especially homeless, who drank excessive amounts of cheap wine or other alcohol) sleeping in the streets because they had overflowed from the Bowery shelters and soup kitchens. These stories may help explain why I overfill my refrigerator and like a well-lit work space, and maybe even why the first poems I wrote were about junkies and winos. But these are only pieces; they are not the whole story.

The stories of my mother and the women I looked up to were the stories of workers: waitresses, seamstresses, cooks, prostitutes, maids, secretaries, social workers, and teachers. Mirta was just a few years older than me but she was already working; she'd stand on the stoop in the morning and give me the bus fare: "Go to school, don't be like me." Mom gave me the gift of literacy, so prized and respected. Doña Fela would send her sons to get me when she needed a letter or document read; she taught me how to use herbs like *manzanilla* and roots like *jengibre* for healing and how to cook for two hundred people, and she told me to become a lawyer so I could do things for the people. I learned from my mom and the other women in my life that every day you get up in the morning and go to work, no matter how crappy you may feel.

The two things that made me feel alive when living with my father in the 1960s were exploring the woods when my dad took us camping and exploring the streets of New York, where something was always happening. When I was older I'd follow the sound of congas to Tompkins Square Park and follow older students breaking out of school to join antiwar protests and teach-ins. I found the streets, the protests, and the counterculture to be so much more interesting than school. My junior high school had the most integrated student body in the city, but that didn't mean we all got along. Every day there were fights in the girls' locker room—I got into so many fights that I was spending more time in detention than in the classroom. My father, who had a disciplinary role even when I lived with my mom, saw my fat lip and torn clothes one day and told me if I lost another fight he'd beat me up himself. "You've got to make them sorry they fought with you, even if you have to use a baseball bat," he said. Instead of using a baseball bat I learned to cut with my sharp tongue and fast talk, but I'd punch a guy out for calling me half-breed.

I started hanging out with the kids who partied and did drugs—for whom race didn't matter and with whom I could be crazy and wild. I dreamed of romance, Motown style, but my fantasies of love were shattered when I was raped by two older Italian boys. I had a crush on one of them, and I thought his offer of a ride was a date. I kept the rape a secret, but that year I dropped out of school. My friends started dying from drug overdoses and suicides, and I was crazy with rage and grief and had no tools to deal with what was happening to me and around me.

My father was moving to California with my brothers, and it was decided I would go along before I got into too much trouble. A year later my mother and sister followed. In California my story didn't fit very well. When I first arrived, my smart-ass mouth made the girls at my school cry—they told me I was too rough and loud. Some days I tried hard to fit into this place where there were clean beaches, redwood forests, and women who used chainsaws just like men. I learned to chop wood and make yogurt, and to gather herbs in the wild instead of buying them at the *botánica*. Other days I raged against the persistent racism with its new age veneer; "spic" was still a fighting word—the only difference was that in California it meant Mexican. By the time I graduated from an alternative high school I was already living on my own, and I decided to return to Loisaida.

A former neighbor took me in along with other friends of her children, and I slept on her couch and ate with her family during the summer of 1973. I got a job at the Church of All Nations, one of the many historic settlement houses in Loisaida and where my siblings and I had attended day care and after school programs growing up. Over the next several years I worked there as a camp counselor through the Neighborhood Youth Corps and as a secretary and office assistant. The pastor of the Spanish-language congregation, who was from the Dominican Republic, recruited me to work on a survey about housing conditions. We visited congregation members to document the crowded apartments with holes in the walls where rats and roaches came through, broken plumbing, and no heat in the winter. Standing in the hallway of the tenement that was no different from the ones I grew up in, I found a way to channel my rage and grief.

In 1973 New York City was broke and broken; the poorest neighborhoods were like a war zone, with buildings being burned and drug dealers controlling whole blocks. But it was also a time of activism and artistic production in Loisaida and all over the city. The War on Poverty provided new streams of funding for existing community centers like the Church of All Nations and Henry Street Settlement House, as well as for new cultural and social-service organizations. This was the birth of the nonprofits that employ so many activists today.

I joined a collective of young people publishing the Fourth Street *i* magazine, a publication of Puerto Rican culture with interviews of Loisaida elders from the Island, recipes for *pasteles*, poetry, and artwork. The *i* was part of a group of community-arts and organizing groups, including Adopt-a-Building, which organized tenant cooperatives to "rehabilitate" abandoned buildings. Activism inspired murals and poetry and vice versa. On the weekends we gathered at the Nuyorican Poets Cafe and other venues where the spoken-word tradition was evolving.

As a young poet I was lucky to learn how to craft words from two incredible teachers, Pedro Pietri and Bimbo Rivas. Pedro Pietri was a poet and playwright who became known for his epic "Puerto Rican Obituary" and his other poetic contributions to Puerto Rican and Nuyorican letters. Born in Ponce and brought to the United States as a child, Pedro was one of the first Puerto Rican poets writing in English to become widely known. His poetry and performance style were unique, as was his expression of nationalism. I met Pedro through a friend who had been a student activist with him at SUNY Buffalo. My friend told him I wrote poetry, and he asked to read one of my poems. Pedro gave me a lesson right there on the corner of Houston Street and Second Avenue. When he, Piri Thomas, and Shorty Bon Bon showed up at our Puerto Rican youth group to perform, they introduced themselves as *los borrachos*—and they were drunk. My anger at them merged with my anger at my father for what I judged to be his irresponsible behavior, but stewing over this experience I came to the realization that for these brilliant Puerto Rican men there were few opportunities for employment that did not degrade them. While I was disappointed in their playing to the stereotype, I also learned compassion for what they lived and how they gave to the community. Over the years I had opportunities to study with Pedro, and even shared the stage with him a few times. He always encouraged me and treated me with an old-fashioned chivalry.

Bittman "Bimbo" Rivas was another Puerto Rican poet and community activist, and the founder of El Teatro Ambulante. Bimbo used poetry and theater to educate and organize young people; he taught us street theater, and he wrote and directed plays that were performed on local stages. I not only was able to work with Bimbo in El Teatro Ambulante, I also was the recipient of a "download" of his complete works when he asked me to type all of his poems. Like his mentor, Jorge Brandon, Bimbo was of an old tradition in which poetry is composed and performed orally. For several winter months Bimbo picked me up outside my building before dawn, and we'd pick up coffee, fresh-squeezed orange juice, and apple pie at a corner diner and then walk in the dark to the Fourth Street *i* office, where I'd type as he recited his verses. Bimbo was generous in sharing what he knew, telling me, "Never be afraid to edit your work"; and he told me to listen to country western music, "and you'll hear the soul of the working people of this country." Like Pedro, Bimbo died too young; he was only fifty-two years old when he had a heart attack at the school where he was working.

In the midst of all of this activism there were still challenges and contradictions. The drug economy was everywhere; one campaign I worked on to "take back" a block from the drug dealers failed because some of our organizers had intimate connections with the dealers. I knew too many activists who were excluded from leadership by men who couldn't share power with women. Two women were raped by a *compañero* we worked with, and rather than kick him out, our male colleagues continued to welcome him while the women had to leave for their own safety. These were things I felt powerless over, and I was just as tempted by the fix of alcohol and drugs as others around me.

Staving off burnout, I went to visit my mother and siblings in San Francisco, and my life story took another turn. I was working for a temp agency, doing word processing at Standard Oil and Wells Fargo. My friend Aurora Levins-Morales, another *mestiza* Puerto Rican poet and activist, was translating the questionnaire for a big research project on sexual violence headed by Diane Russell. She recommended me for the job of typing the questionnaire in Spanish and English, and we both continued on the team as interviewers—knocking on every other door in the Mission and again gathering stories of survival.

Some twenty-five women worked on the rape study—lesbian and straight, white, Latina, Asian, and black. Many of the women were poets and writers, including my friend Aurora, Cherríe Moraga, Sandra Butler, and Kitty Tsui ("Kit-Fan"). The two-week training was an intensive course in the skills needed to interview strangers about their histories of sexual violence, as well as on the politics of sexual assault at that time. I was young and a bit naïve, so the flirtation and banter amongst the women at first went over my head as I tried to keep up with so much new information. One day I took my lunch break with another *puertorriqueña*, and we traded stories about a particular Puerto Rican nationalist organization. It wasn't hard for me to disagree with the party stance on women's liberation ("after the revolution"), but in my eagerness to be accepted I uncritically repeated the party line that only white people (with "bourgeois values") could be gay. Barely an hour later the ridiculousness of that statement came to me in a flash when I looked at the woman sitting across from me at work and thought the words, "That's the person I'm going to marry!" I had to laugh, thinking that the Creator had a great sense of humor to give me such an immediate lesson in truth. I don't remember which one of us made the first move, but by the end of the summer Kit-Fan and I were living together.

As women of color, Kit-Fan and I shared a common language of activism. In 1978 state representative John Briggs introduced Proposition 6, which would have banned gays and lesbians from working in public schools in California. Through Kit-Fan and Aurora I was introduced to the Bay Area women's community, and I began organizing against the antigay Briggs initiative (it was defeated), joining political actions at Alcatraz—an annual observance of Indians of All Tribes' occupation of the island in 1969 to 1971—protesting the Diablo Canyon nuclear power plant, and working with Kit's Asian women's support group. Realizing that I could love a woman was easy for me. Though my parents expressed their doubts about my sexuality, my family did not reject me. What was hard for me was the homophobia in the Puerto Rican independence movement. Kit and I both struggled with prejudice, but she had been out for much longer and felt more comfortable being out in activist communities of color. Kit and I joked that we could hold hands in the Castro District but not in Chinatown—her community—or the Mission District, my community.

In 1978 I joined the cast of Teatro Latino, which performed *Pasión y Prisión de Lolita Lebrón*, a play by the Chilean writer Carlos Baron, at the Mission Cultural Center. My personal journey—from playing the role of Lolita Lebrón as a twenty-year-old woman of the Caribbean diaspora to participating in a national meeting of people of color arguing about homophobia and revolutionary struggles in the mountains of Puerto Rico almost twenty years later—is but one thread in a story that too often seems invisible in the histories of Latina/o LGBT activism of the 1970s to 1990s.

Lolita Lebrón was a Puerto Rican nationalist who, along with Rafael Cancel Miranda, Irving Flores, and Andres Figueroa Cordero, went to the U.S. Congress in 1954 to protest the Island's colonial status. They unfurled a Puerto Rican flag and fired pistol shots in the air, wounding five people. The four were sentenced to over seventy-five years in prison for seeking to overthrow the U.S. government—charges they denied. From the time I was a young girl I had heard stories about Lolita Lebrón; her name and her image were frequently spoken and shown in the course of the multicultural arts activities and the work that educated and shaped me.

It was very exciting for me to be a part of the ensemble cast of Teatro Latino, telling the story of Puerto Rico's colonial status through verse and song in venues filled with Chicanas/os and other Latinas/os from Chile, El Salvador, Mexico, and California. At one performance we were visited backstage by a Puerto Rican *lesbiana* who'd brought her son to see the play—sixteen years later, while conducting a National Latino/a Lesbian and Gay Organization (LLEGÓ) leadership workshop, I met that little boy again, now grown up, and he remembered the play in a queer Latina/o space I could have only imagined when I was just coming out at his age.

When the rape study was over I started working at the Pacific Center, the first LGBT mental health center in the country. While it would be a few more years before transgender began to be used as an umbrella term, as it is today, and many lesbian and gay organizations were not yet including bisexuals, the Pacific Center housed support groups for transsexuals and transvestites, cross-dressers, drag queens, bisexuals, lesbians, and gay men. I had my share of mistaken notions about sexuality and gender, but working with such a diverse queer community allowed me to push beyond the stereotypes I had grown up with.

When my relationship ended I buried my broken heart in my activism and my studies, returning to New York to go back to college. While I was with Kit I had come out to my best friend in Loisaida, who couldn't accept me as a lesbian. I dated a few women back home, but I also dated and ultimately partnered with a man I'd known since I was sixteen. I was back in the good graces of my former best friend, but I struggled to articulate to her how I still identified as a woman-loving woman. I was acutely aware of the "pass" my heterosexual relationship gave me in the macho and heteronormative political worlds I now moved in, and I recognized the greater ease of working with men who had a tacit respect for "another man's woman." Once on campus, I threw myself into campus politics to preserve ethnic and women's studies and bilingual-education programs. I didn't know any other queer Latinas/os. I was happy with my partner and happy when I discovered I was pregnant. Between my political work on campus and off, my studies, and planning for the home birth I wanted, I rarely thought about questioning my sexuality.

In 1984 we moved with our newborn son to Austin where I began graduate studies. I now had three full-time jobs: mother, student, and worker. Austin was a hub of progressive political organizing—Latina/o, queer, and otherwise—with a critical mass of women of color and indigenous women activists. For instance, the Movimiento Estudiantil Chicano de Aztlán (MEChA) chapter at the University of Texas was very active. I joined the local nonprofit workforce, where my experience as an organizer and my graduate work in Latin American studies led to employment as a human-rights educator focusing on the civil wars in Central America. White solidarity organizations too often romanticized the plight of poor people and liberation movements south of the border while ignoring the realities of racism and our struggles for sovereignty and liberation in the United States. People of color working in the solidarity movement had a saying: U.S. foreign policy is the flip side of domestic policy. I was now one of the small number of women of color in paid positions within the Central American solidarity movement.

From 1988 to 1998 I worked in the Texas, Arkansas, and Oklahoma office of the American Friends Service Committee (AFSC-TAO). I'd been hired with the mandate to develop programs connecting the struggles of communities of color in the United States with justice struggles in Latin America. Ana Sisnett was a member of the AFSC-TAO governing committee. She and I were both Latina lesbian mothers; we'd been the only Afro-Caribbean-identified Latinas/os at UT's Institute for Latin American Studies; and we both served on the board of the Austin Latina/o Lesbian and Gay Organization (ALLGO). We shared a desire to incorporate the intersections of racism, sexism, and homophobia into our work.

My racial and working-class consciousness had been shaped by my father's experience as a black Puerto Rican and Dominican "race man." In 1989 he contacted me about a weekend workshop being taught by New Bridges (NB), a summer-camp program for youth that tackled race, gender, sexual orientation, and other areas of oppression. He'd worked as an NB camp counselor, and he urged me to attend a three-day training offered by the program. NB was part of a community of activists whose work would influence the theory and practice of social-justice activism for years. Ana Sisnett decided to accompany me, as she wanted to network with the Women's Building in San Francisco. AFSC-TAO and the Foundation for a Compassionate Society (FCS) financed our fees and travel costs.

By the end of the weekend Ana and I were excited by the potential of using the antioppression and alliance-building model in our work. "Diversity" approaches often lacked a critical analysis of the historical role of racism in the United States. New Bridges defined oppression as the systematic, pervasive, routine, institutionalized mistreatment of individuals and groups based on power imbalances in society and proposed that we can examine how this system divides us, "unlearn" our prescribed roles, and build intergroup alliances. My father was right: I wanted to do this work.

In my personal life I was negotiating a divorce, coming out as a queer single mom, battling the depression that followed the suicide of my younger sister, and going into treatment for an eating disorder. Tulalip elder Janet McCloud of the Indigenous Women's Network led a healing ceremony for women activists in Austin, which I attended. Janet was not a cuddly mentor; like my mother, she had the attitude that yeah, life is hard—now work to make it better. Janet told me the healing ceremony revealed my eating disorder so I could be of service to other women in our community. Janet's words were like the schoolyard dares to "cross this line"—they made me fight. Ana and I collaborated on an article in *The Left Hand*, a feminist and lesbian of color publication, about how coming out about my eating disorder had affected our friendship. We reasoned that the feminist adage "the personal is political" was empty if we couldn't put it into practice. Following a spiritual path became important to my sanity. Like so many others in our close *lesbiana* activist community, I continued to struggle with giving myself permission to heal and with working to the point of burnout.

The year 1989 was a busy one: we organized a New Bridges community workshop for thirty-five activists at Alma de Mujer; worked with Latinas/os and other organizers to support the Pastors for Peace (PFP) caravan to Nicaragua through civil disobedience at the Texas-Mexico border in Laredo; helped organize a Latina *lesbiana* retreat where we explored butch-femme desire, safe sex, and recovering from childhood sexual abuse; and organized a demonstration with other solidarity and peace activists within hours of the U.S. military invasion of Panama in December. Ana and I were holding hands in December's freezing cold when we were interviewed on local television along with Gilbert Rivera of Chicanos Against Military Intervention in Latin America (CAMILA). The only voices of opposition on the evening news were a black Panameña, a Chicano, and a Puerto Rican.

My son's father had argued that my being a lesbian would harm our son, but it was my antiwar activism that made my son's teachers and classmates ask why his mom was on television. Being an activist who publicly opposed U.S. foreign policy in Latin America was a part of my job; it was more than my passion—it was what paid our rent. My son often had to sleep on my lap during late-night meetings, and he either traveled with me or stayed with his grandmother when my travel interrupted his schooling. Like all working mothers, I worried that my work took precious time away from my family. When my son told me he was afraid that I would go to jail for my involvement in the Pastors for Peace civil disobedience at the border, I promised him that I wouldn't get arrested or put myself or him in danger. I also promised him I wouldn't "out" him by being a public lesbian, that I'd follow his lead on that.

The first New Bridges/University of Texas workshop in 1990 exemplified the strategic role NB played with other LGBT activists of color. Racism at UT Austin had made national headlines when a fraternity sold basketball T-shirts depicting Michael Jordan with a Sambo character head, just one in a long series of offenses. When Toni Luckett made history as the first African American, and lesbian, to be elected student body president, she arranged for a team of NB facilitators to give a workshop on racism, sexism, and homophobia for over one hundred UT student leaders.

With Latina/o LGBT activists and allies in leadership roles, NB continued to make history in local schools and universities, directly impacting queer, antiracist/antisexist, and pro-immigrant activism. We designed workshops for the UT School of Social Work, the Migrant Student Program at St. Edward's University, dorm resident assistants, and the Austin LGBT organization Out Youth. María Limón, working on a committee addressing lesbian and gay concerns in Austin schools, arranged the first homophobia workshop in the Austin Independent School District. From 1990 to 1997 over five thousand individuals participated in NB workshops, as well as close to two hundred organizations in Texas, the United States, and Central America.

The intersectional work of ALLGO predated New Bridges. The African American LGBT community was smaller and had fewer resources; ALLGO gave a home to Ebony Connection, a black gay and lesbian group, and collaborated with AIDS Services of Austin. The night the first Gulf War began we were in an ALLGO board meeting. After watching the bombings on the office television, we decided to survey Latinas/os and people of color in front of supermarkets, in coin laundries, and on the streets, asking them how the war was impacting their families. We didn't want the fact that so many *mexicanas* and *mexicanos* had been or were currently in the military to become a divisive issue for those of us protesting the war. At that point our various activist affiliations—ALLGO, CAMILA, AFSC, FCS—didn't matter. Uniting to support and care for the community while taking a strong anti-military-intervention stance was our priority.

ALLGO was a part of the National Latino/a Lesbian and Gay Organization (LLEGÓ) from its inception. My involvement with LLEGÓ came later, when LLEGÓ began providing technical assistance to the newly forming Latina/o AIDS services organizations. After I left

AFSC-TAO I worked regularly for LLEGÓ and other organizations as a consultant, first doing leadership-skills training for HIV/AIDS activists and organizational development for LLEGÓ, Bienestar in Los Angeles, and the Association of Latino Men in Action. Through LLEGÓ I began to work with a new generation of LGBT Latinas/os whose first jobs were often HIV/AIDS related. Early in the evolution of Latina/o lesbian and gay organizations parity between men and women was a foundational principle. But the new Latina/o HIV/AIDS organizations were predominantly male and primarily served gay men, men who had sex with men, and, in smaller numbers, transgender women. While ALLGO's founders had been active in progressive movements, some of the newer, younger HIV activists didn't see themselves as progressive beyond asserting their own human rights, and they didn't always see connections between LGBT rights and other struggles for human rights. Latina/o HIV/AIDS organizations were more often social-service providers, not necessarily social-change organizations.

Between its own staff and the technical assistance and HIV/AIDS programs it sponsored, LLEGÓ touched the lives of hundreds, maybe thousands, of Latinas/os. Dozens of Latinas/os who got their start in LLEGÓ are now employed in nonprofits of all kinds throughout the country. I facilitated several LLEGÓ board and staff retreats over the years, some of them at FCS's Stonehaven and Alma de Mujer. One staff retreat that I cofacilitated with Bárbara García at Stonehaven stands out in my mind. An "organizational orientation" for new staff and board members was scheduled for most of the morning—as it turned out, Bárbara and I knew more about LLEGÓ's history than its own staff and board, so we stepped in to do the orientation ourselves.

LLEGÓ staff innovated a range of technical-assistance and educational-programming efforts for LGBT communities, but as LLEGÓ became more institutionalized—holding conferences and training sessions at costly hotels—more and more attendees were those employed by HIV/AIDS organizations, in spite of LLEGÓ's generous tradition of providing scholarships for travel and conference expenses. Conference host cities were chosen as much by a desire to support local LGBT organizing as by the needs of individual political agendas. Yet local Latina/o LGBT and HIV/AIDS organizations were frequently strengthened through the collaborative work required to host a successful conference and accompanying events, as well as by the allocation of LLEGÓ funds, which were, for the most part, Centers for Disease Control and Prevention grants for educational and health programs specifically targeting LGBT Latinas/os and men who had sex with men. LLEGÓ board members were selected from different regions of the country, and serving as a "link" to LLEGÓ often enhanced their status and role in their communities and organizations back home.

By the time LLEGÓ's budget surpassed $1 million, the job of organizational governance, fiscal development, and oversight had grown beyond the capacity of its board of directors. The establishment of effective communication and decision-making processes was hindered by power struggles and competition between the executive director and board, and between the executive director and staff. I broached my concern about these growing conflicts and capacity challenges with the executive director and with different incarnations of the board of directors, but as an "outsider," albeit one with a very intimate knowledge of the organization, I ultimately had no power and no voice except in small measures when I was brought in to facilitate a board meeting. At one such meeting a board member became so abusive when I suggested a different approach was needed that I had to remove myself from the room.

Nevertheless, LLEGÓ's programs were often pioneering approaches to overcoming historical and cultural barriers to health. The program I had extensive involvement with was Cultura es Vida (CEV). Since I was brought on as a consultant I never saw the CEV grant proposals or mission statements, but I did work with the CEV Work Group, a committee of Latina/o HIV/AIDS scholars, educators, and activists who determined the focus of the CEV curriculum. During the Work Group phase of the project I worked with two male facilitators, Riad Bahhur and Juan Rodríguez. Riad came on when Juan became too ill with AIDS-related complications to continue. As a Palestinian raised in Venezuela, Riad represented the expanding diversity of LGBT people of Latin American and Latina/o birth who contributed to challenging political discussions, and sometimes these differences were irreconcilable.

LLEGÓ convened the Work Group three times, once in Miami and two times in Austin. I was engaged as the facilitator of the group process and asked by executive director Martín Ornelas to incorporate the antioppression principles of New Bridges into our work. Quite a number of the Work Group members were themselves well versed in theories of oppression, some from an academic perspective and some as queers of color HIV educators. Having a diverse group of gay men, *lesbianas*, and trans activists attempt to collaborate on the creation of a curriculum was both brilliant and challenging—and we often had to pause in the process to mediate conflicts arising from different political and cultural perspectives and to address behaviors stemming from the very issues of oppression the curriculum was aimed at addressing.

For the first time in LLEGÓ's history—and perhaps in the history of national Latina/o LGBT activism—transgender experts were included at the table. Some lesbian and gay Work Group participants had not shared power so intimately with transgender community members before, and at the first CEV training session for trainers at Alma de Mujer, trans activists approached me to problem solve around the resulting discomfort. That gave rise to the first transgender speak-out amongst national Latina/o LGBT activists. (A speak-out was a process used by NB and other antioppression/diversity facilitators where members of a group targeted by oppression could safely speak about their experiences and engage their allies.) Up to that point only one participant had identified as female-to-male; the other four were self-identified trans women. When we introduced the speak-out into our agenda, two participants whom were assumed to be lesbians came out as transitioning female-to-males and joined the speak-out panel.

Due to these experiences and ongoing conversations and work with trans activists Adela Vázquez and Sebastián Colón Otero, I began to understand gender as well as sexual orientation as evolving spectrums of expression rather than static categories. Combined with the activist, theoretical, and narrative contributions to concepts of transgender by people like Leslie Feinberg and her partner, Minnie Bruce Pratt, I was challenged to examine my own queer femme identity and desire. My identity as a femme, two-spirit woman changed and grew during the CEV process.

The topic of ensuring participant safety harkened back to the early facilitator discussions at New Bridges stimulated by Jesse Johnson's concern about incorporating ethical standards of behavior for ourselves and any facilitators we trained. CEV was intended to address the multiple oppressions LGBT Latinas/os experience in our communities and personal lives. The CEV Work Group proposed that HIV/AIDS education include an acknowledgement of, as well as ways of exploring and healing from, the ways we internalized the oppression we had experienced as LGBT Latinas/os. Everyone agreed we were not going to be effective in preventing the spread of HIV in our communities if we were unable to address systems of oppression. The experiential aspects of the CEV curriculum were envisioned by the Work Group to be distinct modules that could be adapted to the needs of different communities and employed by organizers and organizations as part of a long-range strategy. The group members and LLEGÓ staff were emphatic in our belief that our cultures can be a source of pride and life-affirming traditions if we can root out the self-hatred and self-defeating behaviors that result from multiple oppressions.

Work Group meetings became, in practice, a laboratory where we confronted how internalized oppression operates within the nonhomogeneity of a group of LGBT Latinas/os. That was not a stated intention, but when a group gathers to address contradictions of power in society, sooner or later those same or intersecting contradictions of oppression arise within the group. As was the custom, the Work Group generated a list of agreements for our collective interaction and for situations when one or more members perceived someone's speech as sexist; we navigated in two languages the dynamics of our different cultures and gendered power relations.

Within the sex-positive framework established by this community of queer HIV activists—a community in which flirtatious banter and bilingual double entendres were the norm—there were still misunderstandings and transgressions of personal boundaries. One individual in particular was brought to my attention by several people, including the executive director, because he did not respect the boundaries of those who declined his sexual advances.

In an intensive training in which participants share personal histories of oppression and sexuality there are always revelations of trauma and sexual assault. Professional standards for antioppression facilitators do not exist, but the practices I'd learned for doing antioppression work had evolved in community organizations dedicated to gender justice and the elimination of sexual violence. The ground rules I established for the first national training of CEV facilitators reflected that tradition. One ground rule, actually a policy of the Alma de Mujer retreat center where the training took place, was that participants refrain from using drugs and alcohol during the training at Alma. The other was that participants refrain from seeking sexual hookups during the course of the trainings out of respect for the very intimate and vulnerable processes we were engaging in. This particular ground rule was challenged by LLEGÓ staff during preparatory conference calls, as it seemed to contradict a sex-positive agenda. When I referenced the example of sexual harassment during Work Group meetings, there was disagreement over the use of that term. Bound by confidentiality I did not reveal all of the details and personalities involved. As my contractual agreement with LLEGÓ empowered me to establish the ground rules as I saw fit, we went forward without staff consensus about the ground rules; however, the staff members assigned to work with me were supportive and open, even if they disagreed with some of my policies.

I had hoped to help LLEGÓ establish some professional standards that would protect individuals during workshops that included difficult conversations about experiences at the intersections of oppression; I likewise recommended that the agency establish a process for the mentoring of new trainees by a team of experienced facilitators and that "certification" of CEV trainers be based on a measured evaluation of their skills. This would help ensure the success of the ambitious CEV community-organizing project in Latina/o communities around the country and in Puerto Rico—but more importantly it would establish an organizational culture where facilitators would not be sent out unprepared, thus being set up for failure and endangering participants.

I worked with LLEGÓ staff to conduct the first three CEV training sessions for trainers, and I personally trained between forty and sixty people, including LLEGÓ staff members who were to coordinate CEV. But from CEV's inception to the point of rolling out the campaign, there had been an almost complete turnover in LLEGÓ staff. The last time I met with LLEGÓ staff in their Washington, D.C., office, dissension and dissatisfaction with organizational leadership were palpable. Everyone was frustrated; most were looking for other work. In spite of this, the Cultura es Vida training sessions continued, and staff were working on revisions—some based on their facilitation experiences in the field. In the best of cases, CEV took on a life of its own. Former staff person Carmen Chávez went on to work for Asociación Comunitaria de Dominicanos Progresistas, a multiservice agency in New York. That entire organization participated in an organizational retreat where the CEV curriculum was incorporated into their strategic-planning process. I assisted Carmen with this training—and that experience broke my heart wide open with gratitude and with hope. To have a tool designed by and for LGBT Latinas/os be adapted and given life within a "mainstream, heterosexual majority" agency that worked with LGBT youth and the large and growing population of Dominicans at risk for and living with HIV was a validation of so much of what was envisioned by CEV's creators. It was also, in a very personal sense, a validation of my life's work dedicated to intersectional activism.

I have now seen a new generation of activists addressing race, class, sexual orientation, and gender in the Dominican and Puerto Rican communities of my home city. I've seen human rights workers in Guatemala and Nicaragua building on the seeds that were planted by myself and other activist trainers over twenty years ago and developing programs and new perspectives that now teach me. I have met queer youth of color who do not identify as lesbian, gay, bisexual, or transgender, who have a sense of their sexual and gendered or nongendered selves that was beyond my comprehension at their age. Today there are more LGBT Latinas/os equipped with an intersectional analysis of oppression working in nonprofits and academia than ever before. To the extent that those individuals continue our task of identifying, defining, and dismantling the structures and institutions of oppression, working toward a long-term goal of human rights in the United States, Puerto Rico, and the world, we can claim those as victories.

I was part of a generation of feminist *lesbianas* who came of age at a time of great hope. We engaged in decolonization, liberation, and sovereignty struggles in communities in the United States and around the world that were still sexist, homophobic, and racist. We often found ourselves to be the only visible lesbians and the few women, indigenous individuals, or people of color in the room. Years after I played the role of Lolita Lebrón in a space where my coworkers had a "don't ask, don't tell" attitude about my sexuality, I found myself in Puerto Rico listening to a presentation by Rafael Cancel Miranda at a coalition gathering of people of color who worked with the American Friends Service Committee (AFSC). Even though AFSC's written policy was to challenge heterosexism and embrace diversity, only three of us present were "out" about our sexual orientations. When Rafael used language that one ally questioned as being homophobic, all hell broke loose amongst the heterosexual members of the coalition, who started accusing the openly queer members of pushing a "gay agenda" and disrespecting Rafael's position as an elder in the movement. In fact, Rafael was true to his reputation for being committed to ongoing dialogue about intersecting oppressions and was open to discussion. Our coworkers were not, and when the meeting closed the words "gay" and "dykes" were still echoing as epithets that followed us back home and to the workplace.

The first queer activists I knew were people of color actively involved in the struggles for human rights in their own and sister communities; they were Puerto Rican, black, Chinese, Lakota, Chicana, Filipina, and Panameña, and together and individually we pushed and pulled and struggled. Our presence in every social-justice movement for change in the past forty years helped create the space for the many queer Latinas/os today who are able to stand completely free of the closet as activists of all kinds. It is important for me that the history of Latina/o activism embrace the legacies of LGBT and two-spirit activists who challenged all forms of oppression, that the term LGBT Latina/o activism not be limited to our participation in LGBT organizations and campaigns for LGBT rights.

Shortly after returning from that difficult meeting in Puerto Rico, my straight AFSC coworker handed me a newspaper article about the first Puerto Rican independence organization to include the eradication of homophobia in their political platform. It had been thirty years since I had questioned how to reconcile being a lesbian and working in a movement that dismissed the struggles of women and queer people.

Where I grew up one of the greatest offenses was for someone to "call you out your name." The curses most frequently aimed at me were "Spanish," "spic," "nigger," and "bitch." To be called "Spanish" in the 1960s and 1970s was a multilayered insult. Puerto Ricans and Dominicans are not from Spain; our islands were invaded by the Spanish. "Spic" and "nigger" deny that one is even a human being. "Bitch" defines woman as animal—in combination with a racial epithet it carries a particular type of violence. I learned to fight back when anyone called me out my name on the street, and I challenged any situation where I was told what "category" of human being I was. I became an activist in response to the discrimination I experienced as an Afro-Boricua woman. I became an activist because I believed we could change the systems of social oppression that determined the conditions of life—and death—I had witnessed growing up in Loisaida, New York.

I've never felt that the terms "Hispanic," "Latina," and "LGBT" were adequate to situate me and my life. I was a college student when the U.S. Census Bureau made the term Hispanic "official" in 1980. We had a number of long discussions about it in our Latina/o student organizations. Many argued that Latino was more accurate because it could refer to anyone from Latin America, including Haitians and Brazilians. Others thought that Latino emphasized the colonizer rather than the majority indigenous, black, and mixed-race peoples. For me, both Hispanic and Latino are vague melting-pot terms that erase our histories—for example, a *Monthly Review* reissue of Pedro Pietri's "Puerto Rican Obituary" refers to the Young Lords as "an anti-imperialist Latino youth group." By that definition, the reason for the founding of the Young Lords as a Puerto Rican activist organization and the reason Pedro wrote the poem are lost to history.

LGBT has also been a difficult term for me to embrace. It is a convenient umbrella term that emerged from valid coalition politics, but it implies a homogeneity and a unity that don't exist. It glosses over the lived experiences of lesbians as women in a masculinist and patriarchal society and simplifies the nuances of how gay men, bisexuals, and transgender people are likewise defined by the dominant masculinist and patriarchal social order.

I resist the term Latina LGBT because it is imprecise. You could say I've been called out my name so long I'm tired of explaining who I am. I will answer to Latina LGBT because it is an arguably useful shorthand—*dime con quién andas y te diré quién eres.* I am always proud to say whom I walk with and to celebrate our many stories. But it is also important for me to honor the history of my *familia*, my community, and my life experiences as a mixed-race Boricua and *dominicana*, daughter of a white mother who celebrated my birth in Loisaida by naming me *luz*.

CHAPTER WRITTEN BY LUZ GUERRA.

DENNIS MEDINA

We Are a Part of the History of Texas That You Must Not Exclude!

Dennis Medina was born into a family of activists in South Texas. Following his involvement with Mexican American groups during college, Medina started a career as a Latino LGBT leader in Houston, where he became one of the founding members of Gay and Lesbian Hispanics Unidos (GLHU) and the editor of GLHU's newsletter. Medina was also a founder of the Austin Latina/o Lesbian and Gay Organization (ALLGO) and the National Latino/a Lesbian and Gay Organization (LLEGÓ). In this oral history–based essay, Medina reflects on his childhood in an all–Mexican American community, the social landscape of Houston in the 1970s—particularly the contradictions within LGBT organizations—and the ways in which different local urban cultures were fundamental to expanding the scope of Latina/o LGBT organizations. Toward the end of the century, Medina's focus turned to his studies, family, and work; the decision to end his involvement in activism at that time was influenced by the loss of so many friends to AIDS.

*I*WAS BORN IN KINGSVILLE, TEXAS, AND RAISED IN the Lower Rio Grande Valley of South Texas. My family lived out in the countryside—and in small towns like La Joya and Los Ebanos—where our closest neighbors would be five miles away. Those isolated and underdeveloped areas were kind of the end of the earth in terms of U.S. politics, culture, and history. My mom used to joke and say ours was the last house in the United States. It felt like that sometimes.

I went to a rural, all-Mexican school in a migrant community. Even though I grew up around migrants, my family did not follow the migrant stream, because both my parents were teachers. So we stayed in South Texas all year round. And South Texas was about as far from gay and lesbian politics or identity as you could get. Still, I had that little internal metronome going, "tick tock, tick tock." I didn't know what to call it; I didn't know what it was. In the eighth grade, about 1968, I read an article in *Life* magazine about two men who were living together as a same-sex couple in Michigan or Minnesota. I remember picking it up and being sort of fascinated by this idea of two men sharing a life together as something more intimate than cousins, which was inconceivable to me at the time. Yet even though I felt an affinity toward these men, they were about as far from my life as anyone could be. I could not recognize myself in them. I didn't conceive of that story being me or a part of me in any way, but it was a glimmer of hope for something else out there.

Growing up in a Mexican community is sort of a funny experience. There's almost a duality about your sexual life, because you can do anything you want, but you can't tell anybody. That's the biggest sin—to talk about it. So I messed around sexually with male classmates and cousins, but it had no name, and there was no recognition of anything happening. It was just experimentation. Many did it and then moved on. But to me, I was always stuck with that, or the idea of that. It was much more significant for me than it was for them. But still, I didn't come out. I was pretty closeted, very sheltered, innocent, and provincial. I didn't come out until after I graduated from college. I went to Texas A&M University in College Station, a very conservative campus. So there was no gay liberation there, even though it was by this time the mid-1970s. The closest thing to any gay/lesbian activity was the science fiction club. Unfortunately, I hated science fiction.

I was born into activism. Both of my parents were migrants in their early years, and they had worked in the fields and worked their way through college—and received degrees. They were the first generation in their families to attend college and graduate. That was a period in Mexican American history when there were many strides and advancements; for instance, all of my aunts and uncles went to college, coming from a migrant family. And so they were, for most of my life, professional and middle class in the sense of being educated. And because they had to fight to achieve what they did, I grew up around activism. I heard table conversations about what they had to go through, so I just assumed that it would be the same for me, that I would have to fight for whatever I wanted to achieve, just like they did. My parents were both involved in the League of United Latin American Citizens (LULAC), which is terribly conservative nowadays, but in the 1960s it was a bit more radical. They were both activists not just in terms of Mexican American civil rights but also in terms of education and community.

At Texas A&M, there was no social or political or cultural outlet for Mexican Americans, and we, a small group of students, started the first organization specifically for Mexican Americans on campus around 1973. It was called the Committee for the Awareness of Mexican American Culture (CAMAC). That's how I became involved personally in activism. CAMAC became my social, cultural, and political outlet, and its members became my family, in a sense, because we had many commonalities that drew us together. The organization revolved around Chicana/o cultural activities and political activism. For example, we organized the first exhibition of Chicana/o art on the Texas A&M campus, which I personally curated. I contacted Chicana/o art students from UT Austin and said, "Hey, would you like to show off your work somewhere?" And so I got a trial-by-fire introduction to art exhibitions.

Similar student initiatives were happening at other universities. Groups at different campuses began talking to each other and meeting, and we would organize big conferences. God knows how we did it, because we didn't have any funding or support. For instance, we would all decide to meet one year in Lubbock, and so we would go out to Texas Tech and meet people from out there. It was a big shock to me that there were even Chicanas/os in Lubbock. We traveled around having our conventions and making lists of demands and declarations, such as that the university should provide more recruiters, scholarships, and academic support for Mexican Americans.

We got our hands slapped a couple of times. Once, we, the three co-chairs of the group, sent a letter to the registrar saying that the university needed to immediately add four recruiters for Mexican Americans. The Texas A&M administration responded in a letter that said, "You stick to your business and keep your nose out of ours." Then we got called in to the office of the director of student activities and received a little lecture about how we were to focus on cultural activities and not get involved in college recruitment, because it was none of our business. So they slapped our hands, but I really liked the attention. "At least somebody is shaking some trees," I thought. "*Si los perros ladran . . .*"

When I graduated I found myself in the big wide world discovering what to do. I finally decided, "OK, this is a fresh start. I'm starting from square zero. This time I'm going to start off gay." The summer after my graduation I drove around to all my friends' houses, and I told them that I was coming out. It was a very limited coming out, but I lost a few friends. I went to Houston and had some really intimate experiences with other gay men—some of my first openly gay sexual encounters.

After that summer I went back to Corpus Christi, where my parents were living at the time, but I had decided to live my own life. I got a job with a social program in a hospital where we would interview patients and their families. The hospital was performing heart surgeries for a low-income, predominantly Mexican American population. There were many kids with Down's syndrome and heart problems. Their parents were migrant workers with low educational attainment. Many times the doctors would be frustrated because the patients or their families would not comply with the medical regimen. So they created this elaborate research study to figure out why. My part was to interview people in their homes. My immediate boss was a Spaniard. He was a real eye-opener for me: an ex-priest in self-exile from Franco's Spain and very radical, politically.

I was coming out at the same time and was doing a lot of sexual experimentation. I started keeping a list of everyone I slept with and wrote down little notes about what we did and if I wanted to sleep with them again. And when the list got up to one hundred people, I said, "I am going to quit writing the list now." That was within the first six months. So I was definitely pushing boundaries. Then, my job, the research study, came to an end. So there I was without a job, and I told myself, "I'm on this path. And the path is leading to Houston."

In 1979 Houston was sort of a mecca, the Third Coast for gays and lesbians. At that time Texas was in the middle of an oil boom, and there were a thousand people moving to Houston every week. I became one of those thousand. I went with my lover at the time, but the relationship didn't last long because Houston was just so full of temptations. The Montrose area was a hotbed of gay activity. Gay radical activist Ray Hill was there. The year before I moved there he had an infamous confrontation with the city council, when gay and lesbian activists stormed a city council meeting. The issue was over an anti-cross-dressing regulation. At that time a woman couldn't wear pants with a front zipper. When I moved to Houston in 1978, I had just missed the first town hall meeting, which was a big convention called to gather gay men and lesbians because Anita Bryant was doing her antigay campaigning, and one of her stops was Houston. So the community organized protests. And out of the protests came this big conference about what we wanted as gay and lesbian citizens of Houston, of Texas, and of the world. I had missed that conference because I was just doing the things that I thought I had to do to have fun, like going to bars and meeting people for sex. Then I met Arthur. He said, "You should come over to the house and meet some people. I think it will be really interesting, and you'll like them. You have many things in common." That's where it all started, and there was no stopping it after that.

Bars have traditionally been important for the LGBT community because that's where we would meet. In Corpus Christi the question was never, "What are you going to do this weekend?" No, you would ask, "Are you going to the bar?" Houston had a lot more bars than Corpus Christi, so it was merely a matter of establishing which one, or in what order you were going to be visiting, or what time you were going to arrive at which bar, and just take it from there. So the bars were where you did everything. That was your only outlet. There were no organizations, clubs, or organized churches where you could meet people outside of the bar scene. That was your universe, especially when you were young, good looking, and coming out. The bar scene is where I met Arthur Cordova in 1979. We figured out right away that we would have to recruit members from the bars, so we'd go in with push cards. We would say, "Hey! You look Chicano! Here's a card! Come to a meeting!" Or, "We're having this event." That began my life with the Gay Chicano Caucus.

In 1980 I attended a town hall meeting—a follow-up to Houston's first gay town hall. The gay Chicanos at that meeting said, "The mainstream gay and lesbian groups seem to have a list of priorities, and ours are not included." For instance, Latinos were getting carded at the bars more than other people. They'd ask us for more than one ID. Then we'd get hassled and sometimes even turned away. Because some bars were so crowded, there was a doorman who would allow people to come in or not. We discovered that we got the "nay" more often than other people. So we felt discriminated against in this LGBT community that was supposed to be open for everybody and where we were supposed to shed ourselves of prejudices like racism. So we decided that we needed to make a separate list of priorities to present to the larger gay and lesbian community. And out of that town hall meeting we became the Gay Chicano Caucus.

There were several people involved at that time. Alice Torres, her brother Richard, Larry Bagneris, Arthur and his lover Richard Orozco, Ramiro Marín and his brother, and a few others created kind of an ad hoc committee called Stand Up Now! (STUN). It was formed to address issues of prejudice on the part of the Houston police force. That was the time when gay and lesbian activism was burgeoning. At the same time, the Houston police threw a young Chicano named José Campos Torres into the bayou and drowned him while he was in custody. The police said that he was trying to escape and that he must have tripped and drowned. But this incident just pointed out a bigger problem, which was how the police treated not only gay men and lesbians but also other minority groups in Houston. There were a lot of reasons to be angry and to organize. After the town hall meeting we decided that we weren't going to get that much satisfaction from within the greater gay and lesbian community. They had their own concerns. They were overwhelmed. We had to strike out on our own and do it ourselves if we wanted anything done at all about our concerns. Out of that consciousness grew a new gay and lesbian identity, at first Chicana/o but later Latina/o or Hispanic. At first we called ourselves Gay Chicanos, but later we changed the name of our organization to the Gay Hispanic Caucus, and later to Gay and Lesbian Hispanos Unidos (GLHU). For us it was the first organization for gay and lesbian Latinas/os. But then we found out a few years later that in Los Angeles they were doing exactly the same thing.

Around 1981 we started a newsletter. I was its first editor, and soon we began to hear from different groups in the United States and even from Latin America. In large part, the newsletter was my own leadership project. Once I met a guy from Chile. He told me about political problems such as the *desaparecidos*. So I put information about Chile into the newsletter. I also began to publish letters that people wrote about gay and lesbian organizing efforts in Brazil, or poetry from a lesbian who had fled her native Mexico. I met a woman who was arrested and put in jail in Corpus Christi because the police there thought that she was Comandante Ana María, a leader of the Salvadoran rebels. But it was this poor woman who was a church worker and an undocumented Salvadoran immigrant. When the police finally figured out that she wasn't Comandante Ana María, the woman was released, and she ended up in Houston. She was pretty angry about that whole business, and she was writing poetry. Then she came to me and asked, "Would you please translate my poetry? I want people to know what I've been through." So I translated her poetry the best I could, and I published some of her poems in the newsletter. In brief, I was mixing all of these other activisms together because we always had broader issues than just our LGBT identity. We couldn't be liberated as gay men and lesbians if we were oppressing people in El Salvador or if people in Brazil were suffering. We believed that it affected everybody when the Houston police threw a young Chicano into the bayou and drowned him while he was in custody.

Thus, given our local challenges and the United States' complicit role in the troubles in Latin America, I reproduced some of those stories. I also made little cartoons to make fun of President Reagan. Of course I did get in trouble for making those kinds of links. Once we had a big meeting just to discuss "my" newsletter. Other gays and lesbians didn't worry about this other junk. So they said, "Focus on the organization, focus on what we are doing," and I'd tone it down for a little while and then start sneaking the other stuff in again. It was just my modus operandi.

At the time, the LGBT community began to develop its political strategies. I remember hearing a heated discussion about whether we should say that we have a sexual preference or a sexual orientation. So the gay and lesbian movement was strategizing and moving toward "orientation," but we Chicanas/os were not part of that leadership. That was the issue for me. We were not part of the inner circle or part of that strategizing. That was all fine and good, because we always found allies, but the larger gay and lesbian movement just did not incorporate us as leaders. And so it was like, "Forget them! We're going to do our own thing. We don't need them to validate us at this point."

I remember the first *bailes* that we organized. We wanted to have our own separate Gay Pride event. So we organized a couple of backyard parties at houses borrowed from our "dates"— friends or lovers, often older white guys who liked Latinos—because they were the only people we knew who owned their own homes. But the parties were getting so large that the backyards we were borrowing to hold them in were spilling out at the seams. Then we decided to rent a hall and move the *bailes* indoors, but we couldn't afford anything in the gay community proper. Finally, Arthur found an event hall, called Noche y Día, on North Main, which was right smack in the Mexican part of Houston. Some people were like, "Oh man, people are gonna get their tires slashed!" Or, "Oh, you're gonna be attacked with clubs and knives." They were adamant. They thought that nobody would come there because the hall was deep in the North Side.

In spite of the concerns, we went ahead with the *baile*. And it was successful beyond even our own expectations. That first night, the owner came over to talk to us because he was also kind of nervous. We had insisted on being open about who we were. If there was a contract, it had to say "Gay Chicano Caucus" or "Gay and Lesbian Hispanics Unidos." That was very important to us. So he was nervous about it and showed up after the event. I remember we were all sitting around exhausted. He looked around at all of the beer cans and said, "Boy, you sure all know how to party." I said, "Yes we do." He said, "Now clean it up." So that was the start of the *bailes*, around 1981. The *bailes* were successful because they were an alternative to the bar scene. Also, it was that special space for gay Latinos and lesbian Latinas. We did not play only disco music. We played Mexican music—polkas, and *cumbias* too. It was our music, and you would get that nowhere else. There was nothing or nobody in the gay and lesbian community who was offering that. We gave people what they were yearning for, in a sense. With the success of those events, we gained respect from the gay and lesbian community as well as from the Mexican community.

The *bailes* were also important in the sense that they spread a message, but the biggest significance was to carve out a space to create an identity. You could be gay, lesbian, and Latina/o in the same sentence. They allowed people to be everything they were, express all of who they were. Most of the people just wanted to dance and have a good time, but out of that group one or two would be interested in being involved in activism. So we were able to broaden our sphere and to broaden our circle of friends, broaden our family, and bring more activists in. And so, to our way of thinking, the organizing that we did back then—the first in Texas, actually—somehow led us to the formation of the National Latino/a Lesbian and Gay Organization (LLEGÓ).

Michael Alfaro, a GLHU officer, had moved to Austin because of his job. Then in 1985 I moved to Austin to go back to school. By this time I was getting tired of Houston, tired of *la política* and the people. I wanted to go beyond, so I thought graduate school would give me the opportunity to do that. Joe Perez, who was one of my best friends in Houston, took over the newsletter and edited it for several years after I left. In Austin, Mike and I decided to organize another group like GLHU, so we went to the bars to meet some people. Coincidentally, there was a group of Chicano men in Austin who had been struggling with the idea of forming a group for Latina/o gays and lesbians. Mike and I got together with them, and we said, "Look, this is what we did. We started a newsletter, rented a P.O. box, registered our name, and organized a *baile* to recruit members." And Austin followed our model. We just had to realize that the audience was slightly different—the average Austinite, even a Latina/o, was somewhat more educated than the average Houstonian, so we tailored the message a little bit more. Soon we founded ALLGO, the Austin Latina/o Lesbian and Gay Organization. Among the first chairs were Nazario Saldaña, Saul Gonzalez, and

Manny Quiroz. Our very first event was a Valentine's Day dance, which is still one of ALLGO's signature events. Both in Houston and in Austin we depended on our allies a lot to help us out with resources. Other ALLGO events—backyard parties—were in Bill Drummond's backyard. He was a white man with a Chicano lover.

Some differences between Austin and Houston became evident. Houston had the Montrose, which was established as a gay ghetto. But Austin was so small that it did not have a concentration of gays. So we didn't have one place we could go to; it was always a lot harder to contact and meet people in Austin. Also, many of the people in ALLGO were college educated, so much more than in Houston. At the same time there were more activists involved, which meant more egos and broader concerns. ALLGO wasn't as focused on social activities, or just on identity; they also wanted to address other issues, such as marching with the farmworkers. Something like that would have caused controversy in Houston. We would have had to discuss it endlessly, but in Austin there was no question. You couldn't even speak against it. Austin was just so much more of a politically charged environment, politically aware, politically correct, if you want to say, than Houston was. So it was challenging in that way. I don't know how easy it would have been for a working-class person, though, to fit in to Austin's group. That was a big difference between Houston and Austin. When we got together, it was evident that Houston was working-class while Austin was college educated. And sometimes those two environments clashed. But in the end we had more in common than we had differences. Even those college-educated folks came from working-class backgrounds, so it wasn't so foreign to us. We recognized it; we knew what it was. And we all came from there. We all graduated from there.

Austin's broader base of Latinas/os was something more challenging. You had Colombians and Puerto Ricans, or people who grew up in Mexico their whole lives and then came to Austin as adults. Because of the variety of Latinas/os in Austin we had to deal with individual national politics—whereas in Houston all Latinas/os sort of merged into the broader Mexican American community because it was much larger—and it was easy to become overwhelmed by that. Having a much smaller Mexican American community in Austin meant more diverse voices to be heard. We had to adjust our politics to accommodate a broad array of national politics as well, not just Chicana/o. Just think about our terminology. In Houston, when we broadened, we became Gay and Lesbian Hispanics Unidos. And that was because in most places in Texas, we used the word "Hispanic." But in Austin we became the Austin "Latino/a" organization. So we were Latinas/os in Austin and Hispanics in Houston.

It was a challenge to incorporate everybody, to try and please everybody, to appeal to everybody's agendas. But I don't think that anyone had the luxury of being so singular in his or her outcome. Mainstream gay and lesbian organizations struggled with incorporating minorities and women. They had all gone through the struggle of being diverse enough, yet focused enough, to be able to proceed forward. We had the same challenges. The only difference was that ours were particularly Latina/o. We never worried about trying to incorporate non-Latina/o allies. If they wanted to come along for the ride, they were welcome. But we weren't going to waste our time trying to convert people. We had enough challenges within our own community—just defining it broadly—that we could not worry about any other things. Incorporating the women was the men's challenge at the beginning, because we did not have women in leadership positions in GLHU. So that struggle came later, actually after I left, when women started asking for positions of leadership. ALLGO was a little bit more open to that, so it was not so much of a struggle there, but in Houston it tended to be boys versus girls. As a consequence, for some time women formed their own groups, and they did their own organizing separately from the men both within and outside of GLHU and ALLGO.

Pretty soon we found out that there were people in Dallas trying to do the same kind of organizing. So Arthur, Richard Torres, Galo Reyes, and a couple of other Houston GLHU members piled in a van and drove to Dallas. They met with Jesús Cháirez, Joe Perez (no relation to Joe Perez of Houston), and Rey Anthony, partied with them, and told them what we had done and how we had done it. Then Gloria Ramirez and Graciela Sánchez came up from San Antonio to a meeting in Austin. They were organizing the Esperanza Peace and Justice Center and wanted to do work around gay and lesbian issues. At that point worlds started to converge, and we began to think, "Well, we should have a Texas network." So we had a first meeting of all the Texas groups: GLHU, ALLGO, Esperanza, and Dallas. We called it the Gay and Lesbian Tejanos, and in 1986 we had its first convention in Houston.

We first worried about Texas, but at the same time we were aware of other groups such as Gay and Lesbian Latinos Unidos (GLLU) in Los Angeles, a more political organization than GLHU or ALLGO. So we invited GLLU representatives to come as speakers and workshop presenters to our second convention, in Austin in 1987. Arturo Olivas came first, and later we invited Laura Esquivel, both from Los Angeles. In this way ALLGO started to make connections with the activists and groups outside of Texas.

In the summer of 1987 I moved to Washington, D.C., and didn't come back to Texas for seven years. Joe Perez of Houston had met Brad Veloz at the League of United Latin American Citizens (LULAC) national conference in Houston that year. Brad was from San Antonio but was living in D.C. at the time, and after talking to Joe I contacted Brad and his partner Mike Rodriguez. I met them for dinner; then I called Joe, and the first thing I said was, "I can't work with them. They are too bourgeois." I was not impressed at first. They lived in Virginia in a nice house. My plan was to live in D.C., in Chocolate City, as someone called it, and experience as much of the "real" city as I could. But after that initial bump, it turned out that we worked very well together. As a matter of fact, Mike, Brad, and I became close friends. Letitia Gomez moved up there in 1987 as well. So we just went from there and joined a group that we infused with the activities of the Texas model we knew; that group would be named ENLACE, the Washington, D.C., Metropolitan Area Coalition of Latina/o Lesbians and Gay Men.

So we, the Tejana/o activists, gained a reputation in D.C. We did like to party, and we encouraged ENLACE to do the same. One of the first activities was presenting the Grito de Carnaval de ENLACE, which was a big, very nice party around carnival time in February. It seemed like every time I moved, the organizing had to encompass bigger and bigger agendas. In Houston, Mexican Americans dominated. In Austin, it was sort of a mix, but we were still primarily Mexican American. But in D.C., nobody had an edge. If we were going by demographics, we should have been predominately Salvadoran. They were the largest Latina/o population in the area, followed by Ecuadorians. And so we had to broaden the organization's agenda. I even had to learn better Spanish in Washington, D.C.!

Just like in Houston and Austin, I started a newsletter in Washington, D.C. If you have a newsletter, you have to have a membership list. So I compiled a membership list. The newsletter was called *Noticias de ENLACE*. I don't know if my idea of what a newsletter must be had evolved so much; I was evolving as a person, but maybe I tried to minimize my role in organizations. The older I got, the less I wanted to be running things. In Houston, I wanted to be right up there telling people what to do. But by the time I got to Austin, I had gotten tired of fighting with people. I asked other people to take the lead in Washington, D.C., but I felt like I needed to show them how. I found myself much more involved in terms of implementing people to do organizing rather than doing it myself. So I tried to get away from the nuts and bolts and to teach people how to do it. That was a whole LLEGÓ model—to give people the tools to organize in Chicago or Denver or wherever they were.

How did we start LLEGÓ? It seemed like the natural next step. That was because, for the first time, I felt like it wasn't me doing it. Now we had a network. We could pick up the phone and call other people and say, "You can do this." And so we each had a little piece of the burden. Truly and honestly, I think that is one accomplishment that we can point to: not needing to credit any one person for having done everything. One person didn't start LLEGÓ. It really took all of our collective effort. It came out of those concentric circles of Houston and Austin, expanding into Texas and bringing in California and D.C. And honestly, that's why I can't remember one person starting LLEGÓ, because it was not one person.

We were doing ENLACE, and at the same time we were doing LLEGÓ. So in essence we had split personalities. In D.C. we had the reputation of being both ENLACE and LLEGÓ. Sometimes people had trouble separating the two, as opposed to other organizations, where people worked on very localized issues. Some people thought that we— gay and lesbian Latinas/os—should focus only on our local issues, but we were not that organization anymore. I knew that I was not as parochial as I had been in Houston. I had grown, the issues had grown, my consciousness had grown, my knowledge had grown, and my experience had grown. We were in a different world now. So I wanted to focus on larger issues.

The first event that our nascent national network did (for a brief period of time that network was called the National Latino/a Lesbian and Gay Activists) was the March on Washington in 1987. Even though LLEGÓ was not formally organized yet, many of the same founders of the organization were involved in the march activities. Washington, D.C., was looked at sort of as the "host" of the march. So it was just an easy matter of coordinating people to come to D.C. and to have a visible presence in the march; and we had a meeting that weekend of gay and lesbian Latinas/os. So it was easy, plus we had a lot of shoulders that could share the burden. More importantly, LLEGÓ couldn't be just ideological; we had to create a structure. People emerged who could take leadership roles here or there. Letitia Gomez, Arturo Olivas, and many others were instrumental in putting all the pieces together. In my particular case, I offered to do whatever the new leaders wanted me to do. I did not want to be the head of anything. I did not want to leave the fight, but to be just the foot soldier and do whatever was necessary at the time.

I became more of a mentor, although I didn't see myself that way because I never thought that I knew enough. There was always something new to learn; wherever I went, there was always a new challenge. I had to learn as much as I had to teach, and the challenge was balancing the teacher with the learner. And I had my own mentors along the way, because we were each other's mentors. For instance, when Arturo Olivas came to Austin and Houston, I was in awe of him because I could not even imagine trying to organize anything like GLHU in L.A. Unfortunately, a lot of the people that we mentored then have now passed on. And that's what really challenges the organizations more than anything. I think that we could have accomplished anything we wanted, but people just started dying left and right. The AIDS epidemic affected all of the people that I have worked with. Perhaps one out of ten is still alive. And that was just devastating, not only to the organization but also to me personally. It took a toll almost to the point that I did not want to do it anymore. I did not want to remember it either. The memory was dying too. At some point I felt that everything I had expected to happen was not going to come about now, because the people in whom we had invested time, energy, and love were gone. And so everything just sort of vanished. It also affected our focus and our goals. Instead of working on political issues, we began to work on AIDS issues. We began such a critical project that we did not have the luxury anymore to worry about "political stuff." We just had to worry about how to overcome AIDS. And so it just completely shifted our focus.

The AIDS epidemic had started to hit the community as early as before I left Houston, to tell you the truth. I remember as clear as yesterday: There was one GLHU member we called Roberto "La Negra." One day somebody told me, "You know, Roberto is in the hospital." I asked, "What's the matter with him?" "Meningitis," I was told. I wondered to myself, "What the hell is meningitis?" So I looked it up, and the medical dictionary said that it could be contracted from using infected intravenous needles or being scratched by a cat. Then the next week I asked how Roberto was doing and was told that he had died. I said, "What? He just went into the hospital a few days ago. How could he have died of this disease that no one has even heard of? Who the hell dies from a cat scratch?" Roberto "La Negra" was my first close friend to die of AIDS.

AIDS was already becoming a crisis by the time I moved to Austin. By then people were getting sick or coming down with HIV. It was a big mystery at first. When it first came out, we didn't know what to call it, so they called it the gay disease or GRID (gay-related immune deficiency). We didn't even know what it was or how to respond to it. When I got to D.C., it was already becoming a major focus for our organizations. ALLGO got their first AIDS grant in 1987, the year that I moved to D.C., and María Limón was in charge of that grant. It's interesting that ALLGO is now trying to turn back the clock (with their funding crisis that came a few years ago) to where they can drop the AIDS service component and now really focus again on cultural activities, which was always our intention. It was never our intention to focus specifically on health, or especially on AIDS. We always wanted to be working in the area of culture and identity, but we had to deal with AIDS first. Because of its impact, we were forced to.

I moved back to Austin in 1992 to attend graduate school. At this point, I didn't have to be an organizer, so it gave me the luxury to be part of the ALLGO board. The organization was almost exclusively AIDS focused at that time. By then they also had staff and funding. A lot of our services were related to AIDS. As a matter of fact, even our client base caused some controversy among ALLGO members, because it was predominately straight when we were supposed to be serving the LGBT population. ALLGO had some gay-focused projects—for example, the Gay Men's Project, where gay Latino men would get together and discuss issues of interest to them, such as AIDS, but also issues related to sexuality, identity, and culture. It was sort of a consciousness-raising, or a support group for gay Latino men. But in terms of ALLGO, or its AIDS project, Informe SIDA, the majority of our clients were straight Latinas. But we were committed, so we had to continue to raise funds to keep Informe SIDA and to do some other things as well. I think there were some years when ALLGO did not do a *baile*. Yeah, the organization was a little bit different, but it was not a shock for me, because we were doing the same in D.C. and in other places. We had to focus on AIDS. We were organizing less than we wanted because of the pull of AIDS services. We wanted ENLACE to be more focused on culture and identity, so we worked with SALUD, which was a separate Latino AIDS service organization.

I left Austin to come to San Antonio in 1999, but I did not seek gay and lesbian organizing as an outlet. I was at the time trying to finish my PhD. I also had a job in a library, and it took a lot of my energy. I met "the rest of my life" here in San Antonio and started a new relationship with him. There were a lot of other things to occupy my time here. Plus, I had to recognize that there was a lot of pain in losing people. I did not want to be there any more; I could not be there again. But it was also a different world. I came to San Antonio and could no longer say there was no space for gay and lesbian Latinas/os. In a sense, we all were gay and lesbian Latinas/os. You could go to the gay bars and they played Mexican music.

During my years as an activist, the gay and lesbian Latina/o organizations faced several conflicts. The incorporation of women into leadership roles was a struggle for us all the time. Sometimes it created a lot of friction, to the point that people didn't talk to each other for years. When I was in Austin in the mideighties, Linda Morales became president of Houston GLHU. She said women needed more leadership roles in GLHU, and she was determined to be one of those leaders. It caused a lot of consternation among the men. Some were willing to sit down and say, "Yeah, we're all men. How come? Are we doing something wrong?" Others would say, "Well, we're doing it. You're not." So it split the men between those who were willing to admit and say, "Maybe we're not doing enough," and those who were just not willing to entertain the idea that they were sexist. It was never our deliberate intention to be sexist. There was never at any point any deliberate intention to be exclusionary. It was just a matter of whom you were with. You know, we were the boys. We liked playing with the boys. So incorporating the women was a big struggle.

Another big issue was AIDS funding. One problem was the division between those who didn't want us to be pulled in that direction—they saw it as a distraction—and those who saw it as a crisis that needed to be dealt with immediately. When Linda Morales was GLHU president she led a lawsuit against the state of Texas to release funding for AIDS services to gay and lesbian organizations. Sodomy was illegal in Texas, and gay and lesbian groups were therefore considered "illicit." For some strange reason, Texas believes that it can do anything on its own, and it doesn't need federal money because that only makes us Texans beholden to the federal government. And we were so proud that the lead plaintiff in the court case against the antisodomy statute was a Hispanic: *Morales v. Texas*. We also had other kinds of problems with particular people who would come into the organization and seemed to have their own agendas as opposed to a broader kind of idealistic issue with oppression.

Nowadays, things are very different, but I think the legacy of those organizations is unmistakable. We have a different mind-set than we did when we began. It takes me right back to that *Life* magazine article from the 1960s, when I looked at it and said, "That's not me." And now it's a world where I can be who I am, Latino and gay at the same time. And it took little tiny steps to get us there. I don't have to worry about someone coming up—a young Chicana/o—and saying, "I can't find my-self there"; because we're all around now. I remember when I addressed the National Association of Chicano/Chicana Scholars (as the NACCS was known at the time) in Houston during the early 1980s. As far as I know I was the first Chicana/o to come out publicly at a NACCS con-ference. Teresa Gutierrez, a friend of mine, was scheduled to present a workshop, but she said, "I want to give you half of my presentation time. I want you to come and tell NACCS what you're doing with gay Chicanos." So I remember going there and thinking to myself, "I don't know them. No big deal. I'll never see them again in my life, so I don't mind coming out." So I talked about the difficulty of being gay or les-bian and Latina/o. We dragged NACCS kicking and screaming out of their complacency. Now NACCS is one of the biggest supporters of gay and lesbian issues. To me, it was just creating that space that was impor-tant—just changing the way we think about what it is to be gay or les-bian and Latina/o at the same time.

Talking about that space for gay and lesbian Latinas/os was impor-tant, because the things that were happening around us at that time were very disturbing. I remember a story about Ramón Hernández from Austin. He was instrumental in organizing ALLGO. Previously, he had applied to the American Communist Party, but his membership was refused because of his openly gay lifestyle. So he couldn't even be accepted as "left wing" because he was such a queer. That's when you look around and say, "There truly is no space for us." But there had to be a space, a place or a crack, where we could insert ourselves. And that crack, that space, is larger now. So our change in consciousness will al-ways be our biggest legacy. I think there are some smaller legacies here and there—the history of organizing in particular places, the localities. For instance, for a long time I've been meaning to write an entry for *The Handbook of Texas*. We are a part of the history of Texas that you must not exclude.

My life today is taking place at the most exciting and exhilarating time to be alive, but at the same time it is also the most dreaded and de-pressing. You have a victory in New York—the legalization of same-sex marriage there on June 24, 2011—while, at the same time, we have shit in Texas. You can focus on the good news and say, "Look how far we've come." Or you can look at how far we still have to go. However, gays and lesbians are so embedded in popular culture, there's not even a question anymore. Kids coming out today have more choices.

The world is better now because of all those little things we did.

ORAL HISTORY INTERVIEW CONDUCTED BY LETITIA GOMEZ AND URIEL QUESADA IN SAN ANTONIO, TEXAS, ON JUNE 28, 2011. CHAPTER WRITTEN BY URIEL QUESADA.

JESÚS CHÁIREZ

From the Closet to LGBT
Radio Host in Dallas

Jesús Cháirez is a second-generation Chicano from Texas. He was the founding president of the Gay Hispanic Coalition de Dallas, which later became the Gay and Lesbian Hispanic Coalition de Dallas; the organization brought political pressure and fought discrimination in Dallas, later becoming engaged with similar groups from Houston, Austin, and San Antonio. Cháirez's activism was influenced by his artistic interests in photography and painting, passions that led him to explore life in Mexico and to reconceptualize life across the border. In addition to his work within activist organizations and as an artist, Cháirez created, produced, and hosted the influential LGBT Latina/o radio show Sin Fronteras *from 1993 to 2005. In this personal essay Cháirez narrates the links between his experiences growing up in between worlds in Texas, the discrimination he faced in both Latina/o straight and gay white spaces, and his many creative ways of overcoming adversity. Cháirez also exposes the apparent contradiction between being an activist who is out of the closet within a movement yet not openly gay with family or friends. Finally, his chapter addresses how the challenges of lone leadership and limited resources structured his experiences with local activism.*

M Y PARENTS, FIRST-GENERATION MEXICAN AMER-
icans, grew up in the small segregated community of Lockhart, Texas, and dropped out of elementary school to pick cotton. Wanting a better life for their children, they moved us to Dallas, saying *adiós* to the barrio so my four brothers, two sisters, and I could get a better education and live in an English-only environment. The first day of school, I got the English name of Jesse instead of Jesús and was put

into speech classes, where I learned to pronounce English words correctly—like chair instead of "shair" and shoes instead of "choos"; it was an era long before bilingual education. Growing up without Latina/o role models was effortless in the sixties; this was a time before Spanish-language television, and in Dallas there was only one Spanish radio station, a radio station I never listened to. As a child I would cringe when, while watching television at a gringo friend's home, a Frito Bandito commercial would come on and everyone would laugh. My siblings and I never identified with being Latina/o. Our birth certificate said "white," but we ate homemade tortillas at home—tortillas were not available in our neighborhood supermarket.

Growing up, I was the creative one out of the boys; I loved to draw and color, and my work was admired by my art teachers, but this only resulted in me being called a sissy. I wasn't encouraged to pursue my creative abilities. I stopped bringing art projects home or staying late for art classes because I was told that it was stupid. My father called me *mosca muerta*—dead fly—while my little brother was referred to as "the Champ." I was never bullied by other kids in school for being a sissy, because I had three older brothers—perhaps my peers thought they might have to answer to them. I didn't play sports much, if I could help it, because if I fumbled the football or didn't catch a fly ball, I would suffer the consequences: getting yelled and screamed at or being punched or slapped on the head by my older brothers. So when it was time to play sports, I backed out when I could and would find sanctuary at the neighborhood library. Wanting so badly to escape, I often fantasized about just running away from home, though I never did. I manifested my negative home experiences into poor self-esteem, which resulted in stuttering. I would get laughed at when I stuttered, so I became quiet and reserved.

In junior high school, however, I was very popular and started to be antiestablishment. I ignored my attraction to boys and didn't have girlfriends. I also started smoking cigarettes and marijuana and drinking alcohol. I grew my hair long and began marching and protesting against the Vietnam War. Because I still lived in an all-gringo neighborhood, I almost made it through high school without seeing other people of color. Well, that was until busing came into being in my senior year. My parents were ahead of their time: they knew the good schools and new books always went to gringos first, and so did the courts. The courts thought that busing minority and gringo students around town to each other's schools would guarantee equal education.

It was in my senior year of high school that I really knew I was gay. I went to visit a friend of mine when her parents were not home. While we were watching television, she excused herself and returned to the sofa totally nude and wanting to be intimate. Though we had sex, I didn't care for it. Then it happened again when another girlfriend whom I was visiting got nude while her parents were not at home. This time nothing happened, and I got scared. I thought I was one of those guys, a queer! I tried to "pray the gay away" and to fix the pain of being homosexual. I joined the Jesus freak movement and stopped visiting girlfriends when they were home alone. My being a Jesus freak made my mother happy; she bought me a bible—for a while she had actually thought I wanted to be a priest—but then she became afraid I would leave home and join a Jesus community. About this time, my eldest brother had joined the Chicano movement while in college and was active in La Raza Unida Party. He wanted me to participate, but I didn't see a need.

I began my career with the federal government immediately after graduation from high school in 1973, accepting a job as a mail clerk. I took the bus to work and met a beautiful young lady who had also graduated from my high school—she had been a majorette. She was into Jesus too, so this made for a convenient relationship: church, no premature sex—just hugging and kissing. We got engaged. As the marriage date drew close, I knew I couldn't go on living the lie of pretending to be heterosexual, so I broke the engagement—opting instead to contact the gringo at work who had given me his telephone number. My coworker and I began a six-year relationship, renting a two-bedroom apartment—and appearing to all to be living as roommates.

Going from being antiestablishment at school, I became establishment at work. There were some Latinas/os in the federal agency where I worked, and because of affirmative action and my eye for detail, I moved up the ladder quickly. I was promoted to a job recruiter position for the federal government, a highly visible position in the Federal Job Information Center located in Dallas's main federal building.

While I was in my office at the walk-in job center, a couple of Latinos entered, speaking only in Spanish. I tried to be of assistance. However, even though I could understand what was being said, I found it hard to communicate, being unable to build the sentence structure needed to convey total ideas about federal hiring. Unknown to me, I was being set up. One of the men was Hector Flores, local president of the Intergovernmental Mexican American Government Employees (IMAGE, a Latina/o advocacy group for federal employees). Having failed the "enchilada test," I was told, in English, by Flores—who would later become the forty-fourth national League of United Latin American Citizens (LULAC) president on June 29, 2002—that I was a disgrace to my race and that I shouldn't be in my position if I couldn't speak Spanish to help recent immigrants who had just become American citizens find federal employment. I was stunned; I had never encountered such hostility from the public before. If he was looking for allies, this was not the way to do it. So I avoided IMAGE and any Latina/o organizations—why bother? I was doing fine.

After getting a lover, I found that life was simple: going to work, coming home, cooking dinner, sleeping on the sofa after watching TV—and no advocacy. We didn't go to gay bars and pretty much stayed home and hung out with friends. We lived the married life, but as roommates to the world. After six years of living together, my partner and I went our separate ways on December 31, 1979. For the first time in my life I started a new decade on my own.

In August 1980 I moved out of what was our old love nest and into the "gayborhood," Oaklawn, a place I thought would be a sanctuary. But within a month of moving into the hood, I was asked for my identification as I entered a gay bar—strange, for I had never been asked for identification before. Turned out the one driver's license I had was not good enough identification to enter the bar, because I had no other picture ID. Denied entry, I didn't think anything about it. I was walking out the door when I heard the cashier tell his coworker, "That's another Mexican down." I was horrified. I walked back to the cashier to challenge him, but he was not having any of it; he told me to leave and got security. I felt awful because of the way I had been treated. I knew that the gay bars would sometimes ask people of color for multiple identifications, but I had never experienced that until now. That one incident brought a different perspective to my life: I did a lot of thinking that evening, thinking how I had been foolish to believe I was special because I was assimilated and to not consider myself Latino. I then realized that the only person thinking I was not Latino was me—not a disgrace, but most certainly naïve.

The following day I approached the Dallas Gay Alliance (DGA; now the Dallas Gay and Lesbian Alliance) for assistance. I spoke to Don Baker, president of the DGA, an ex-schoolteacher who had lost his job in Dallas for being gay. (Baker had also filed a lawsuit to repeal section 21.06 of the Texas Penal Code, known as the Sodomy Law: "A person commits an offense if he engages in deviate sexual intercourse with another individual of the same sex.") But Mr. Baker wasn't interested in my troubles. He suggested that I speak with the manager or owner

of the club. I thought to myself, "Why?" The employees were only en-
forcing management and owner policy. After realizing the DGA was
not interested in my cause, I didn't know where to turn. I wasn't involved politically, and I didn't know any gay or politically active Latinos—a consequence of never getting involved. In October I found a
League of United Latin American Citizens (LULAC) chapter and became a member. Though LULAC was not interested in gay-only issues,
I was accepted, and after a year of membership I helped form a LULAC
chapter for young Chicanos. I went from not thinking of myself as
Mexican, to now embracing my identity as a Chicano—something my
older brother was excited about, although I couldn't really be truth-
ful about the sudden change because I was still in the closet. While in
LULAC I was able to educate myself in community and political activism. Hector Flores, the man who had earlier told me that I had been a
disgrace, was around—though we never spoke of that incident; we were
now allies. By the time we first met in LULAC, I had moved on from
being a federal job recruiter and transferred to the Federal Communications Commission (FCC). Because of my visibility in the FCC and
now visible activities in LULAC, I was asked to help form a Hispanic
journalists' organization. It was the early 1980s, and I was now a founding member of Hispanic Communicators DFW, an organization where
I made media contacts and learned how to be media suave—something
that was needed in order to advocate in Dallas's gay Latino community.

In mid-1982 I was in a gay bar having drinks with friends when a gay
Latino by the name of Reymundo Anthony came up to me and said he
was on the board of directors of the Dallas Gay Alliance and that he
wanted to get more Latinos involved in the DGA. He said he had created a committee within the DGA called the Hispanic Task Force. I told
Reymundo my story about being denied entrance to a gay bar and how
the DGA had not been interested in my concerns. Reymundo was sym-
pathetic. He suggested that Latina/o involvement could fight discrimination and change the DGA—so I joined. (Reymundo Anthony would
later be a founding member of ALLGO, the Austin Latina/o Lesbian
and Gay Organization, and was elected to the LLEGÓ board in its final days).

Dallas's Latinos and Chicanos came together and became the Dallas
Gay Alliance's Hispanic Task Force (HTF). The HTF did not have officers except for a committee head, and its mission was to fight discrimination against gay Latinos, to give visibility to gay Latinos, and to build
Latino membership for the DGA. The HTF members met socially and
contributed to a DGA newsletter, and we enthusiastically held a set of

garage sale fund-raisers, giving our time, energy, and monetary contributions to the DGA. Shortly after that, the Hispanic Task Force asked for thirty dollars so we could host a Saturday afternoon barbecue, a *comida*, for the members, an event that would also be used as a recruiting tool for new Latina/o members. Our request was denied because, as one of the board members said, it sounded like a party, "and the DGA doesn't fund parties." The HTF was not really directing any policy, because the board of directors and the officers of the DGA did that for the organization. Our only Hispanic on the board, our voice, the one who had recruited all the task force members, had already left Dallas to finish college in Austin. Though disappointed in the DGA, we were not surprised—just another gringo betrayal. The denial of our funds woke us up to the fact that as the Hispanic Task Force, a committee of the DGA, we had no real power and no real Latino voice; we were only window dressing. We called a meeting of the HTF members to propose leaving the DGA. Although at this meeting the new president of the DGA, Bill Nelson, made a pitch for us to stay, we, as Latinos, wanted and needed our own voice and autonomy. So in early 1983 the HTF membership unanimously voted to break away from the DGA and to form the Gay Hispanic Coalition de Dallas.

The members of the new Gay Hispanic Coalition de Dallas were enthusiastic and highly energized about forming an independent organization. Most of the founding members were English-speaking Mexican Americans. Some identified themselves as Hispanic, some as Chicano, and then some as Mexican—though they were born in the United States. Most members had an ear for understanding Spanish but not the skills to speak or write Spanish well. None of the members had experience in leading or creating an organization, and 99 percent of the members were in the closet to family and employers.

The Gay Hispanic Coalition de Dallas initially named only three officers: president, vice president, and secretary. We were not governed by a board of directors but by majority rule of the members, and getting everyone to agree on one issue or outcome proved to be a challenge, so we would form committees. Having been elected the first president, I, along with other members, wrote bylaws and a mission statement. Membership in the Gay Hispanic Coalition de Dallas was simple; all one had to do was state an interest in the organization, and there were no dues. We held monthly Saturday afternoon meetings in various members' homes. Before every meeting, we did a discreet mailing to the members and distributed a press release to local and statewide gay weekly newspapers. The calendar listings always generated a new member or two. Though everyone was welcome, only gay Latinos could be officers. The Gay Hispanic Coalition de Dallas meetings always began formally with speakers. We always had local politicians, community leaders, and health officials discussing STDs and HIV prevention at our meetings. One of the big items the Coalition worked on was voter registration and getting our people to vote—strong HIV prevention had yet to be a mission, though safe sex was beginning to be discussed.

As the Gay Hispanic Coalition de Dallas grew in visibility, we started attracting Latinas to the meetings; we thus changed the name of the group to Gay and Lesbian Hispanic Coalition de Dallas. We never had Spanish-speaking-only LGBT Latina/o immigrants. This was understandable, because our meeting notices were sent to the gay English-language press. There were no gay Latina/o bars or clubs where we could recruit Spanish-speaking members. As the Coalition progressed, it was not uncommon to see Dallas's lone Latino city councilman, Ricardo Medrano, in attendance. Because the gayborhood was part of his district, Council Member Medrano was one of the few on the Dallas City Council who were gay friendly. We were fortunate to have him attend our Coalition meetings and *comida* socials, often with his brother, Roberto, who was an elected official with the Dallas Independent School District. Council Member Medrano recruited members of the Gay and Lesbian Hispanic Coalition de Dallas to serve on various City of Dallas boards and commissions. Because my job provided community time, I accepted an appointment to serve on the Martin Luther King Jr. Community Center's board of directors.

Dallas's Anglo LGBT activists say that it was the gay bars that were the real pioneers in creating the gayborhood. This may be true, but the gay bars were not sacred; the gay bars were also pioneers in discrimination. Before community pressure prompted a change in discrimination policies, some gay bars routinely discriminated against women and people of color. They would not allow people wearing open-toed shoes into their establishments, a tool used to discriminate against women, and they would often request three picture identifications from people of color. The Gay and Lesbian Hispanic Coalition de Dallas, along with others in the community, successfully fought those practices through political pressure. Also, in the spring of 1988 the LGBT Latina/o club Diamantes opened up, and we now had a place to go without fear of discrimination.

The only other LGBT Latina/o organization in Texas in 1984 besides the Coalition was the Gay and Lesbian Hispanic Unidos of Houston Just like that, on a late 1984 day, members of GLHU left a message on the Dallas Coalition's answering machine saying they were on the road to Dallas to meet with us. There was no formal discussion of a meeting date and time, no mention as to how many of their members where coming; they just called and said, "We are coming to Dallas," so we waited for them. The arrival of Houston's gay Latinas/os to meet with Dallas's gay Latinas/os was monumental. For the first time in Texas gay history, two LGBT Latina/o groups were meeting. That historic weekend we talked about our histories, our missions, and our community progress. We discussed strategies for the LGBT Latina/o cause and decided to build Texas's first LGBT Latina/o alliance. Our first weekend meeting went well—nothing too formal, just getting together for conversation and drinks; in the evening we continued our conversation over dinner at a gay friendly Mexican restaurant, El Gallo de Oro in the gayborhood. There were no gay Latina/o clubs in the Dallas gayborhood at this time, but there were cantinas in the barrio where Latina/o drag queens and transsexuals hung out, so we made the rounds and continued to talk business, getting to know each other on a personal level.

We would later develop a joint newsletter that contained Dallas and Houston gay Latina/o news and information. And, because Houston's organization was better established and had longevity, we held a formal seminar meeting in that city. Jointly, we invited our members and other LGBT Latinas/os from other parts of Texas—those involved in mainstream LGBT organizations. There were about fifteen people in attendance. We had people from Dallas and of course Houston at that first seminar, but also others from Austin and San Antonio. Even two Latinas from El Paso showed up! We discussed forming other groups, lending support, and building coalitions, as well as fund-raising, networking, and HIV prevention.

Later, we collectively formed groups in Austin (ALLGO), San Antonio (Ambiente), and El Paso. After forming these alliances, we held workshops—we were meeting in a central city, Austin—on gay Latina/o activism, coalition building, writing press releases, and, most of all, HIV prevention. Members of the Gay and Lesbian Hispanic Coalition de Dallas supported Houston and Austin Pride event *bailes* and jointly participated in the Houston Gay Pride Parades. In Austin we would later form a network of Texas groups named the Gay and Lesbian Tejanos. This time period must have been around late 1984 or early 1985. There were no formal ways of staying in contact. It was most difficult then, a time long before the Internet and social media.

Though I was out in the gayborhood and out in Houston and Austin, my LGBT Latina/o activism in Dallas took place in the closet. At the urging of a Coalition member, during the first week of October 1986 I did a self-awareness seminar, the Experience Weekend, an empowering community forum that was geared toward the LGBT community. It was at this forum that I learned the importance of coming out of the closet: to have self-power. So I finally came out to my mother, who started to cry uncontrollably. The first thing my Catholic mother said was, "You are going to burn in hell!" My response was, "God doesn't make mistakes, and he made me. I did not choose to be gay." My father and siblings treated it as no big deal; they'd already had an idea, but now that the word was out, they didn't like it. I was excluded from family events held at my siblings' homes, never being informed when they had one. But I didn't care, because the chains of bondage of living a double life had disappeared. I then strongly advocated to LGBT Latinas/os for the importance of being out of the closet, and I still do.

After that seminar on finding one's self, I decided to get involved in art again—something I had left behind as a child because I was never encouraged—so I took a black-and-white photography course at the Dallas Photographic Center. There I met some cool, creative gay people who were not trying to change the world, but they sure as hell were not in the closet either. They were supportive of my photographic skills and creative eye. That Christmas of 1986 a friend invited me to travel by car to my motherland, Mexico, the land of my grandparents. We drove from Dallas to Mexico City. After arriving, I spent a few days on self-reflection, and I had another life-changing experience, a metamorphosis. Having lived an assimilated life, I felt I had been lied to about what Mexico was. I was not in a place full of burros and Mexicans sleeping under a cactus, but in a major contemporary city full of life, art, and music—one of the largest cities in the world.

While in Mexico City, I visited the Basílica and learned about the Virgen de Guadalupe. I became more fascinated with Mexican art and culture and not just with gay Latina/o advocacy. All along, I was still known by my English-language, American name of Jesse, but after returning to Dallas the first week of January 1987, I was now Jesús. Though I thought I was already embracing my heritage, I returned to Dallas determined to learn more about Mexico and to speak Spanish.

So in January 1987 I pulled back from all of the organizations I was involved in and got into my art—another type of activism. By this time, the Gay and Lesbian Hispanic Coalition de Dallas was already beginning to fade away—I had stopped being an officer or going to meetings (when there was one). The Coalition had lost many of our leaders to AIDS, and with those deaths we were also losing experience. In addition, the older guard was just tired, having become burnt out. The Gay and Lesbian Hispanic Coalition de Dallas, like most organizations, had too few individuals doing most of the work. The San Antonio and El Paso groups were gone, leaving LGBT Latina/o groups in Houston and Austin. With no one wanting to pick up the pieces, the Gay and Lesbian Hispanic Coalition de Dallas died soon after the opening of Diamantes in the spring of 1988.

But once an activist, always an activist. Now an openly gay Latino artist, I was traveling to Mexico City every other month, enjoying the gay Mexican lifestyle and taking photographs of Mexico City street scenes. In Dallas I began to show my photographs locally and regionally. I was the first openly gay Latino in Dallas to curate a Día de los Muertos exhibit for the city at the Bath House Cultural Center in October 1988, where I created an altar to friends who had passed away from AIDS. Then on December 12, 1988, the day of the Virgen de Guadalupe, a lesbian Latina artist and I opened Dallas's first Virgen de Guadalupe art show at the Unicorn Gallery. The Unicorn Gallery was Latina owned and operated.

Through my new artistic advocacy, and because the Gay and Lesbian Hispanic Coalition de Dallas had faded away, I was now able to concentrate on art. The skills I had learned with the Coalition enabled me to found a Latino arts collective in the summer of 1991 called Artists Relating Together and Exhibiting (ARTE). ARTE was for all Latina/o artists, and I was its openly gay Latino founder and first president. Latina/o artists in ARTE didn't care if anyone was gay, and if any ARTE members were found to be homophobic, they would be asked to leave. I was always recruiting LGBT Latina/o artists to participate in ARTE, for we wanted to showcase Latina/o art and artists outside of just Cinco de Mayo activities.

Because I had become known first for my political activism and now as an out gay Latino artist, I was approached by the general manager of Dallas's KNON 89.3 FM—the Voice of the People—a noncommercial, nonprofit community radio station, to create a gay Latina/o radio show. KNON already had a gay radio talk show called *Lambda Weekly*, but Mark McNeal, the general manager of KNON, wanted a new gay radio show that was strictly "gay Latino." The general manager didn't give me any specifications to define the gay Latina/o radio show—that would be left up to my own imagination. I didn't know how to run the control board, had never taken a communications class, and none of the past seminars I had attended had prepared me for beginning a radio show. I was also responsible for being the news director, program and music director, and control engineer. I was freaking out, but off I went, learning and making it up along the way. *Sin Fronteras* would be the name of the radio show, because that was how I was living my life, without borders. It would be an English-language talk show mixed with music. With the *Sin Fronteras* radio show, the LGBT Latina/o community had a voice in the Dallas–Fort Worth market area, a bully pulpit that could reach the masses in North Texas.

Sin Fronteras first went live on the air from 5:00 to 6:00 p.m. on Sunday, July 4, 1993. The opening and closing theme song was "¿A quién le importa?" by Alaska y Dinarama, a song that was the national LGBT "out" song in Mexico and Latin America. The show's first guest was a gay Latino singer and poet from Monterrey, Mexico, who was now living in Dallas. The guest was gay and out in the gayborhood; however, he asked that I not mention that he was gay, because radio was now a means to reach beyond the gayborhood and the closet. Though I honored his request, after that first guest, I had a new rule: no more closeted gay Latinas/os on the radio show. How could *Sin Fronteras* actively promote gay Latina/o pride if its guests were closeted individuals? Volunteers on *Sin Fronteras* would have to be out Latinas/os too. The show was about gay Latina/o pride, and we were not going to hide that. Those volunteering with *Sin Fronteras* were in their late teens and early twenties, a new generational voice of Dallas's LGBT Latinas/os.

Back in 1993, identifying openly LGBT people to interview for the radio show was not easy, considering that there were no LGBT Latina/o organizations around and many gay Latinas/os were still in the closet. So *Sin Fronteras* pulled artists, community leaders, and politicians into the studio. We broadcasted shows on health issues such as HIV prevention or brought in Latina/o drag queens and transsexuals to discuss their careers, sexuality, and fashion tips. We aired annual National Coming Out Day specials, bringing young LGBT Latina/os on the air to discuss being out, and we produced special shows showcasing Latina/o pride for Cinco de Mayo and National Hispanic Heritage Month. We also did interviews with gay Latina/o activists in Mexico City.

Sin Fronteras would often invite Grupo Latino to the studio. Grupo Latino was an informal LGBT Latina/o Christian group formed at the Metropolitan Community Church around 1994—they would minister to the LGBT Spanish-speaking Latina/o community. When the group was on the air talking about how God loved our LGBT community without fail, *Sin Fronteras* would get calls from people who wanted "equal time," something they confused with the old FCC Fairness Doctrine. But because LGBT Latinas/os were in charge on *Sin Fronteras*, right-wing Christian callers were not put on the air—they had their own channels for that purpose.

Every three months without fail, *Sin Fronteras* asked for donations during a pledge drive to keep the show on the air. *Sin Fronteras* was required to meet a goal of donations, or pledges, to help with KNON's daily operating costs. Listeners would donate five, ten, or twenty dollars to meet our goal. Local rock en español bands came into the studio, did live interviews, and donated their CDs for the show's pledges. Drag queens did fund-raisers in taquerias, and there were two local gay Latina/o bars to help raise pledge funds. It was a real mix of people, straight and gay, something that had not been seen before in the Dallas–Fort Worth market area.

Around mid-1995 the Lesbianas Latinas de Dallas (LLD) was formed by a Dallas lesbian couple, one originally from Chicago and the other from Puerto Rico. Lesbianas Latinas was formed to build bonds between Latina women outside the bar scene and also to let the Dallas community know that Latina *lesbianas* existed. *Sin Fronteras* was a big fan and supporter, always leaving a door open for these Latina women. The organization's officers would come in to invite listeners to their meetings or their community workshops. Because Dallas now had more Latina/o immigrants, LLD also helped with immigration issues. *Sin Fronteras* also worked with Lesbianas Latinas de Dallas on some cultural events; LLD members sang and did poetry readings in Dallas's first gay Latina/o art space, Artefacto. Then in early 1997 Lesbianas Latinas de Dallas hosted a community *baile* at a nice hotel in downtown Dallas. The event got great community support and was very well attended. Men and women from all around the Dallas and Fort Worth areas attended. Lesbianas Latinas de Dallas gave *Sin Fronteras* an award that recognized its role as an "'Outstanding Non-Profit Organization' proudly serving the LGBT Latino community." But by late 1997 Lesbianas Latinas de Dallas had faded away; as one of the founders once said, nobody wanted to do the work, something I could relate to deeply.

The popularity of *Sin Fronteras* quickly grew, and KNON provided an additional hour of airtime, so the show moved from five to six in the late afternoon to the ten to midnight slot. It was a national first: LGBT Latinas/os on the air with a two-hour FM radio show and streaming live on the Internet; we were not only reaching local LGBT Latinas/os but also an international audience.

At the beginning of June 2005, as I and the other volunteers were discussing plans for *Sin Fronteras'* twelve-year anniversary celebration, I realized my heart was just not into it. I had been in the LGBT Latina/o *lucha* for at least twenty-five years. When I first started in gay activism, I was one of the young ones, and now I was the oldest, being referred to by a younger generation of LGBT Latina/o activists as the "godfather" of Dallas's LGBT Latina/o movement. During most of the last twelve years I had not really had a vacation, because the weekly radio show was live; I was always working on news items, buying music for the radio show, thinking of the next guest, and most of all working on funding to keep the radio show on the air. All the funds collected for *Sin Fronteras* went to a general operating fund for KNON. I was not getting paid, and no funds were allocated toward producing the radio show. This isn't by any means a complaint but rather a fact: one often needs to sacrifice for a cause, spending one's time, energy, efforts, and own funds to meet objectives—something I gladly did, because this was a part of a universal form of giving and receiving and my form of tithing. Instead of thinking of a twelve-year celebration for *Sin Fronteras*, I decided to retire. The volunteers didn't want to take on the responsibility of producing a radio show, so the time slot was offered to a new LGBT Latina/o group formed in 2004 called Valiente, but their president declined. *Sin Fronteras'* last radio transmission was July 3, 2005, and on the air I announced that this was it, the end of the show had finally come. We got lots of calls, and some listeners dropped by the studio to say goodbye. The last caller was an emotional gay Latino teenager who brought tears to my eyes when he said that he looked forward to the *Sin Fronteras* radio show every Sunday night because, "When I listened to you, I knew I was not alone, and now it will be gone."

After the show ended, as I was loading up my car in the still, quiet midnight darkness of the radio station parking lot, I felt not only a sense of relief, but also a big sense of loss. As I drove away from KNON, I tuned to the radio station and listened one more time, knowing that I wouldn't be on the air any longer. Though our LGBT Latina/o equality fight was not over, the era of LGBT Latina/o radio for North Texas had come to an end.

Reflecting on what has transpired in my life to this point, I see remarkable changes: I went from being closeted and assimilated, not speaking Spanish, and not wanting to get involved politically to being out and bicultural, speaking in Spanish, and in the middle of the

LGBT Latina/o political fight. The one incident of being denied entrance to a gay bar because of the color of my skin ignited a fire of activism that could not be extinguished. Though I didn't have any gay Latina/o groups to join in the beginning, or anyone to help me advocate for LGBT Latina/o causes, I helped create them. It was immensely rewarding to meet and build alliances with people I had only heard about or seen in the news. I then became one of them. Advocacy not only opened doors for me, but it also helped me cut through red tape when helping LGBT Latinas/os who didn't have anywhere to turn. Because of my outreach in the LGBT Latina/o community, I learned to speak Spanish, lived in the barrio, and became aware of issues faced by the undocumented LGBT community. Sometimes I meet LGBT Latinas/os who say, "I don't speak Spanish, and I don't see a need to get involved." In those situations I remember that I, too, was once there. And I hope that their moment of enlightenment will come soon, for the fight for LGBT Latina/o equality is always ongoing.

CHAPTER WRITTEN BY JESÚS CHÁIREZ.

LAURA M. ESQUIVEL

An East L.A. Warrior Who Bridged the Latina/o and the Gay Worlds

Laura M. Esquivel is a third-generation Mexican American from Los Angeles. She experienced racism and classism throughout her early childhood, which she spent living in a white middle-class enclave. In later years, she voluntarily worked alongside farmworkers picking tomatoes, lived with a gang member, and served time in juvenile hall. In 1980 after going back to school she joined Gay Latinos Unidos (GLU), later known as Gay and Lesbian Latinos Unidos (GLLU). That was the beginning of an intense leadership experience not only with that organization but also with other groups, such as Lesbianas Unidas and the National Latino/a Lesbian and Gay Organization (LLEGÓ). In this account, based on an oral history expanded by Esquivel, she revisits a period of time when feminism and civil-rights awareness interwove with the struggles against sexism, racism, and classism. The result was a burgeoning and eventually solidified and integrated sense of Latina/o LGBT thought and action. Esquivel also critically reflects on the contradictions and limitations of some of the LGBT organizations of the 1980s and 1990s and the successes of the Latina/o LGBT movement.

I WAS BORN IN EAST LOS ANGELES IN THE LATE 1950S. My mother had planned to leave my father not long after my sister was born—then she found out she was pregnant with me. At the time, access to abortion was not readily available. As soon as I could toddle, my mother divorced my father and married my stepfather, Lloyd Hackett. My "Daddy Lloyd" was a tall, blond Anglo of Swedish descent—that kind of tall and that kind of blond. My mom, my nearly three-year-old sister, and I moved away from East L.A. and my father's extended family to South Pasadena, an all-white, upper-middle-class community. It was barely thirty minutes north of East L.A., but it was worlds away from what I had been born into.

My father picked us up every Sunday, and we returned to East L.A. to visit a noisy extended family who lived in close quarters under the same roof in a lively neighborhood where all the kids and old people were known by every neighbor. My father eventually remarried, and soon our visits included spending time with our young brothers. I had no idea what "bicultural" meant, but I knew the places where I divided my time as a child were worlds apart. I soon learned to function in both. In East L.A. I learned to love menudo and *lengua*, played with kids who looked like me, and regularly heard Spanish (my Mexican grandparents did not speak any English). We moved to South Pasadena, where I spent the majority of the next ten years, because it had one of the top school districts in the country. My sister, Tina, and I were the only children of color that I can remember at our elementary school. In my first-grade class there was a Jewish girl, a boy who was a Jehovah's Witness, and a girl who lived with a single mother (and was rumored to have been born "out of wedlock"). We were the "different" ones. But my sister and I were the only ones who *looked* different. Although our family owned a home, we had one of the few mothers who worked full-time, and the majority of our friends came from much wealthier families. In fact, if I saw other Latinas/os in South Pasadena, they were likely to be nannies or housekeepers for my friends' families.

I loved going to East L.A. when I was little. However, as I got older East L.A. was no longer a safe, welcoming haven. At home I was praised for being at the top of my (gifted) classes. My friends in East L.A. would tease, "Why are you talking white? Why are you acting white?" Other things were different too. Why did my sister and I get new bikes every Christmas, go on field trips, attend summer camp, and eventually get our own bedrooms—and my friends back in my father's neighborhood did not? I sensed at an early age that I should keep these things to myself when I visited and not brag about winning the latest spelling bee.

At first I was just confused. Then I became angry. Things weren't just different when I was in East L.A. They were different when I was home too. There were many differences, both large and small, but one stands out in particular, one that I have carried with me all my life. My mom had signed my sister and me up for swimming lessons (another class privilege I hadn't grasped at the time). My mom dropped us off so we could go in while she parked the car. When she got there, we were still outside. They wouldn't let us in—swimming lessons or not—because it wasn't Wednesday. As they explained to my mom, Wednesday was the day they cleaned the pool, so that was the only day "colored kids" could swim. This was not the South—this was Los Angeles in the sixties! My Swedish stepfather showed up in his police uniform (he was in the police reserves), and instead of arguing that the policy was wrong he explained to them that we weren't "colored." We didn't have a problem swimming after that.

When my stepdad was alive he was a good buffer and a passionate defender of his little (very brown) girls. When I was in second grade, my beloved Daddy Lloyd, after suffering for years from schizophrenia, shot himself in the head with his service revolver. In addition to dealing with the trauma from his suicide, we were left to fend for ourselves—in more ways than one. That's when I became really angry. I was angry at my mom. I was angry at all the people at school. I fought constantly with my sister. And I was bereft about my stepfather leaving us. I was only a child, and it was impossible for me to untangle all these things from one another.

I was angry at my mom for taking me away from my Mexican culture, for not teaching me Spanish, for trying to "make us white." It wasn't until I was an adult, and a parent myself, that I was able to understand and to really appreciate what had motivated her. My mom wasn't trying to be white instead of Mexican. She wasn't ashamed of who we were or who her parents were (also immigrants from Mexico, although they came here as teenagers). It was my mother's way of trying to ensure we had opportunities and weren't discriminated against. My mother had once carried the shame that made her and my aunt covertly eat the burritos they took to school for lunch. She didn't teach us Spanish because she didn't want us to have an accent, because people who talked with an accent had a harder time getting work. This is why my mom has always been proud of her impeccable English (and to this day corrects me if I get sloppy!).

I became bored in school and eventually incorrigible. I was an angry, wounded, confused female child growing up in a racist, sexist, classist, stratified world. I was also highly gifted, which, in its own way, contributed to my feeling of not belonging anywhere. Not from South Pasadena, not from East L.A. Not Mexican, not white. *Ni de aquí, ni de allá.* Neither from here nor from there.

It was by now the seventies, the waning of the hippie era. We lived by a park where disillusioned, middle-class, counter-culture white kids hung out smoking pot and making daisy chains. I got kicked out of the sixth grade, was hanging out with older kids (including the ones in the park), sneaking out of my room and staying out all night, eventually running away for weeks or months at a time. I started drinking regularly, smoking cigarettes and pot, and experimenting with drugs. I was twelve years old.

When I got kicked out of South Pasadena schools my mother enrolled me in nearby Highland Park, which was already beginning to turn heavily Latina/o. That was my first exposure to Latina/o gang life. I wasn't yet in a gang, but I was finally back in a primarily Latina/o environment, and I wanted to fit in. We had long since stopped going to East L.A. to visit with my father; as we got older we wanted to spend weekends with our friends instead. I was very confused about my identity and where I belonged. All I knew was that I wanted to feel like I belonged somewhere. If being in a gang, talking with an accent, dancing to oldies, and getting tattoos was being Mexican, then that's what I wanted to do.

Around that same time I started being sent to juvenile hall. When I wasn't in juvenile hall I was a runaway. I was given "one last chance" and sent to live with my father, stepmother, and young brothers. My stepmother had also wanted to move out of East L.A. as soon as possible. They had moved to a modest home in El Sereno, which was around the fringes of East L.A. but still heavily Latina/o and working class, and had enrolled my brothers in Catholic school. They were literally "altar boys," and it was with much trepidation (and to their credit) that my dad and stepmother let me live with them.

They enrolled me in seventh grade, but I don't think I ever went to class. I can't picture the inside of a single classroom, but I can picture the inside of the girls' bathrooms because that's where I met my "homegirls." I still listened to rock music and didn't crease my pants, wear my makeup, or dress like a *chola* yet. But by then I had been around some gang members back in Highland Park, so I knew (or thought I knew), more or less, how to act. They made fun of me a lot, but they were also willing to have me be part of the group and, eventually, part of their families. I was elated and threw myself into fitting in.

I became very close to three girls: "Caco," who was my age, her big sister, Debbie Cordero, and another girl, Rachel Cisneros, "Smiley"— she and I started telling people we were sisters. The four of us were rarely separated whether in or out of trouble. The drug use and drinking escalated, and by then I had been in and out of juvenile hall a couple of times. One time I ran away, and Debbie and Caco's mom let me live with them and even hid me from the police when they came to look for me. In the summers the whole Cordero family, including younger siblings, would pack up and head up north to work in the fields. The summer I turned fourteen the police and my parents were looking for me because I had run away from one of my placements again. So the Corderos took me with them to a little town in the Central Valley called Mendota, where we worked in the tomato fields and I was part of the family.

We were picked up in the dark at 5:00 a.m. every morning, with our makeup on *y todo*. By then I had shaved my eyebrows, wore thick false eyelashes, and my accented English was peppered with slang words. It was pretty funny because we were these badass *cholas* from L.A. picking tomatoes alongside migrants from Mexico, many of whom didn't speak English. It was awful, hard, exhausting work. It was during that time that I started learning how to cook really good Mexican food. I was accepted, and for the first time felt like I belonged somewhere, and in a lot of ways I was happy.

This was another formative experience that exposed me to a whole other world of disparities, even between the way we lived in El Sereno (with four kids to a room in the Cordero house) and how these (mainly Mexican) migrant farmworkers lived and were treated. But we also got paychecks. From that time on, whenever I wasn't locked up, I worked. When summer was over, we went back to L.A. so the kids could go back to school. But I never went back to school, not until I was an adult in my twenties.

By then I was identifying as a lesbian. In juvenile hall, when I was thirteen, I had met lesbians for the first time, and I was very excited. I had been dating guys but just knew I was a lesbian too. My parents were among the first people I told. My mom cried for a week, and my dad said, "Well at least you won't get pregnant." It never even occurred to me to not be out. I was fourteen.

"Cutie," the nineteen-year-old sister of Debbie and Caco, was my first "girlfriend." She didn't live at home, but she would come around and get high with us. I soon dumped my gang boyfriend, started openly dating Cutie, and stayed involved in my gang. The Cordero sisters had earned their respect among our homeboys and homegirls—including Cutie, who was a super-cute butch and was not afraid to fight anyone. So everybody knew that I was with Cutie, and that was that. Their mom liked me better than Cutie's other girlfriends because I was well mannered and didn't (really) speak like the other girls, in spite of my best efforts. In fact, Cutie's older sister, Loretta, was also a lesbian. It was never an issue in the family, for me or for them. The whole family was fiercely loyal to each family member—including me. Cutie was also in and out of jail and had a girlfriend who was older than her (and used to come looking for me to beat the crap out of me). Eventually we went our separate ways and just saw one another intermittently.

When I turned sixteen I was at the age when it wasn't illegal for me to not be in school. By that time I had been in a number of placements and "girls' homes," which I kept running away from and going back to El Sereno. They could keep locking me up, but they knew I wasn't going back to school.

I got my first serious girlfriend, another Latina named Cindy. When I met Cindy her mom was paying for her to live in a boardinghouse filled with men. She was very butch and looked like a teenage boy. Her mom had a new husband and a young daughter at home, and it was more convenient for them to not have Cindy around. We were both sixteen. She was not in a gang and was not from El Sereno—she didn't like my homegirls and didn't like me hanging around there. Cindy loved me, and my mother loved Cindy. We joked that I was working to put Cindy through high school, and we even lived with my mom for a little while. Cindy loved having a mom who accepted her and acted like a mom— cooking dinner, making her lunches, and encouraging her in school. My mom has always accepted me, and I am very grateful for that. I bounced around in a variety of jobs, Cindy graduated high school early, and we soon got our own apartment, a cute little single in East Hollywood. My mom even took us apartment hunting. We were seventeen years old. We broke up when we were eighteen.

I renewed my friendships with my homegirls and met Lupe, the "love of my life" at the time. I got a job through the federally funded Job Training Partnership Act (JTPA) program and was placed in The East Los Angeles Community Union (TELACU), a nonprofit whose mission was economic development in the Latina/o community. Lupe was also working, and we got a nice one-bedroom apartment in Alhambra, not too far away from her family, who lived in East Los Angeles. Although Lupe grew up in East L.A, she had gone to Catholic school and had never been a gang member. But our close circle included my friends, who were nominally members of a gang at that time. By then it was more of a cultural affiliation—the makeup and the social environment—as opposed to active gang activity.

Lupe and I promised we'd be together forever and talked about having a family and growing old together. In the 1970s and even 1980s there were few lesbians choosing to have children. The lesbians I knew who had children were mothers who had left straight marriages or relationships. Needless to say, services were not widely available to help lesbians become parents. Nonetheless, Lupe and I decided we wanted to have a family together. Besides, I had always known I wanted to become a mother—in spite of being a lesbian from an early age. I never saw that as a deterrent. I rarely saw anything as a deterrent to what I wanted to do in my life.

Although we were working and supporting ourselves, this was, unfortunately, during some of my heaviest periods of drinking and drug use. By nineteen I was pregnant, and we were over the moon about it. We had to move out of our apartment because our lease prohibited children. We moved to El Sereno for a little bit (where our apartment became the party house). We moved in with my mom for the last month of my pregnancy so she could help me, and though she wasn't crazy about Lupe she was wonderful to us and excited about her first grandchild. After my daughter was born, Lupe and I moved into the house behind her family's main house in East Los Angeles. Our relationship was tumultuous, and I knew Lupe was cheating on me. She left me when my daughter was three months old. Her family, who had never been supportive (they were appalled that I got pregnant and opposed Lupe acting like a coparent), sent her to Mexico and encouraged her to stay there for a while. All of a sudden I was a single mother—something I had never intended—and was deeply in trouble with drugs.

Eventually I hit bottom, and it took me over a year to get my life back on track. Being a good mother became the most important thing in the world to me. I knew that in order to do that I had to start over and put everything, and everyone else, behind me. I put everything I could in the trunk of my car and headed north to the white, mostly middle-class enclave of North Hollywood. My Tía Nena (my mom's younger sister) had also married an Anglo, my wonderful Uncle Bill. They saw how wounded I was, opened their arms and their home, welcomed me into their family, and loved me unconditionally. They had two teenage kids at home, my cousins Lisa and John, and it was like having a little brother and sister. They were all happy to have me there while I worked to get my "crap" together, as they say.

I got a job and soon had, yes, another girlfriend, Joanne—also a Latina. Joanne and I got our own apartment in North Hollywood, and the three of us settled in nicely. She was amazing with my then almost two-year-old daughter. In 1980 I got a job with the U.S. Census Bureau, and within two weeks I was a supervisor. I had always been confident of my abilities and intellect, regardless of the level of formal education I'd received. But I realized that there were many jobs where that wasn't going to be enough.

We lived across the street from Los Angeles Valley College, and I decided to enroll. Federal student aid was plentiful and there was a high quality day-care center on campus that was free to full-time, low-income students like me. I spoke up in my sociology class when the subject of homosexuality came up, and soon my professor asked me to come speak to his other classes. My friend Bob May and I started a Gay and Lesbian Speakers Bureau, even though we were the only two speakers! That created visibility on campus, and soon we had formed what I believe was the first gay student group on campus. Bob and I became the first cochairs. We organized a field trip for the student club members to the Los Angeles Gay and Lesbian Services Center, which was just over the hill in Hollywood. During the tour I met another Latina lesbian named Geneva Fernandez, who worked in the youth department. Geneva recruited me to attend a meeting the following week for a recently started group called Gay Latinos Unidos, which met in a room at the Center.

At my second meeting elections were being held and I was nominated for president. I wasn't ready to be president, and it felt like more their need than mine. There were very few women involved at the time. I did accept a position as vice president under the incoming president, Oscar de la O. The group's first president had been David Gonzalez. The following year I became the first female president of the growing group; the incoming vice president was Rolando Palencia. By then "lesbian" had been included in the name: Gay and Lesbian Latinos Unidos, or GLLU, as it became widely known.

I was just twenty-one when I realized that I was capable of being a leader. It wasn't like I set out to do that. I didn't even know that the world of nonprofit advocacy existed, but I did become aware of my potential as a leader. I couldn't explain either why it was so important to me to be out with everybody. I already knew what it felt like to be treated like I wasn't as good as other people. I just wasn't going to let people do that to me anymore—not about being a Latina and a Chicana and not about being gay. I had never been shy, and my willingness to speak up meant that people listened.

Race wasn't as much of an issue for me in college, but sexism was. It was the early 1980s. It didn't take too long for me to consider myself a feminist. Feminism motivated me to enter the Miss Valley College beauty contest so I could denounce it from the stage! I was so earnest. The school magazine did a profile of me as a lesbian mom, which, as I said, was somewhat of a novelty back then. Around 1986 I was asked to be on the first nationally broadcast television program about lesbian parents for the Geraldo Rivera Show. It was the first time I had ever been to New York. More importantly, it meant that I had now come out nationally.

I was always asked questions like, "Don't you think you're going to hell?" Or, "Who is the man, and who is the woman in bed?" Or, "Doesn't being a mother mean you are straight?" I was good at dealing with it, did not get hostile, and encouraged people to ask questions. It was important to educate people, but more important to me was for any gay people in the audience or the classroom, who may have been living in shame or in fear of being found out, to see someone who felt positive about being gay. The response I received, usually privately, was extremely gratifying.

I was soon offered a job at the L.A. Gay and Lesbian Center as a youth caseworker. By then I had learned about all the gay kids who were runaways and "throwaways," kids whose families threw them out because they were gay. These kids came from all over the country, hitchhiking or taking Greyhound buses to Hollywood, where they thought it would be easier. They were young, wounded by their families, society, and churches, and easily preyed upon; many—both male and female—resorted to "survival sex" out of necessity.

With a few semesters of community college under my belt I moved with my daughter to Hollywood to take the job (it would be quite a few more years before my next attempt to go to college). I loved my work. I knew what it was like to run the streets of Hollywood, getting high, often being sexually assaulted. My youth, experience, and visible gang tattoos gave me a kind of credibility that no middle-aged social worker would ever have. I felt like I was making a difference. I started appreciating my mother and the rest of my family for their support and love. I had left home because I wanted to, not because I wasn't wanted. Thus began my long journey in nonprofit work and in working for social and familial understanding for, and ultimately acceptance of, gay people. My fight for gay rights had begun.

Disparities based on race were as apparent to me at the Gay and Lesbian Center as they had been in South Pasadena—and I wasn't the kind to just let it pass. The years of horror of the impact of AIDS on gay men were beginning. But there were no staff or programs to do outreach and education or to serve men of color in the programs at the Center, and our gay brothers were being very hard hit. I even became a peer counselor, because there were no people of color on the staff of the counseling department. And it wasn't just a problem at the Center. The gay movement and the institutions that were springing up and being nurtured by a growing donor base and by the beginnings of federal funding were devoid of people of color—and women for that matter (AIDS Project Los Angeles being an example).

GLLU provided an opportunity and a platform for people of color to have a political voice and to exert external pressure on the Center and on the white gay movement. We tried to make sure that GLLU, our issues, and LGBT Latinas/os themselves were visible in the gay media and started reaching out to, and developing relationships with, policy makers—especially the growing number of Latina/o elected officials. California state senator Art Torres was one such early supporter.

For me there was no conflict between working for the Center and wearing the hat of GLLU. If anything, my working at the Center gave me the credibility to criticize its policies. Ultimately, the thing that gave the Center the most heartburn was my effort to help organize a union. After my summer contract was up in the youth department I was let go. The irony was that after a leadership change I was eventually hired back at the Center in a management position, so I never had a chance to be in the union! However, the L.A. Gay and Lesbian Center, still the largest such agency in the nation, became the first gay and lesbian center to be unionized. It has been a union shop ever since, with great benefits and working conditions—a far cry from when I first started. I think of the thousands of Center staff, and the tens of thousands of clients who have gone through there in the last thirty-plus years, and I feel good about the contributions I made back then. The intersection of these issues—race, class, sexism, labor, and homophobia—became clear to me early on from working at the Center and as a result have always informed my organizing and advocacy.

For me GLLU was as much a cultural home with a feeling of *familia* as a political/activist home. It was the first place that I felt accepted and understood as 100 percent Latina and 100 percent gay, and that changed so much for me in terms of the strong development of my own identity as a Latina lesbian with an integrated, honest identity. It truly was the first time in my life that I had found someplace where I felt like I really, finally "belonged." There was just no place to be my "whole" self until GLLU.

The feminist, lesbian separatist movement was picking up steam, but we faced no such issues in the early years of GLLU. I am not sure how much of it was attributable to culture, but I do know that the majority of the men in GLLU were just as feminist as I was. There were no issues about power, and it was one of the few places where I felt respected and supported as a lesbian and as a leader. It was not a fight we needed to have internally, though it was raging all around us. Lesbians were walking out of the Center and were resistant to joining other gay groups that were so male dominated.

The early years of GLLU were so great. A lot more women joined. We went through a lot of birthing pains, writing and rewriting the bylaws and debating whether non-Latinas/os should be allowed to serve on the board. There were other gay people of color groups being founded, like Asian/Pacific Lesbians and Gays (APLG) and Black and White Men Together (BWMT). But these groups were male-dominated and often sought and encouraged white gay men to join their leadership and membership. GLLU decided our leadership would always be Latina/o and cogender.

In addition, there was tension between people who wanted the mission and activities to be more social and people (like me) who wanted them to be more political. That was the biggest issue to be worked out in the beginning. We ended up being both, and there were some people who only showed up for the dances, but there was a large core group of people willing to do the work to grow the organization. Our main priorities were to create supportive environments where people could explore or just experience what it meant to be both Latina/o and gay or lesbian and to become advocates for LGBT Latinas/os. And we had a lot of fun doing it. GLLU really fed me personally, in large part because of the support for my development as a leader and activist, but also because of the cultural context. Everything we did was infused with our culture, our music, our art, and our food. It was so affirming. It was home.

The Center, on the other hand, didn't have people of color—or women—in leadership positions. In 1985 Steve Schulte, the handsome longtime executive director, resigned and the search began for a new ED. Del Martinez, the only Latina board member and Latina lesbian applied for the position. Del was a social worker who already ran a mental health center and had raised money while a board member at the Center. The Center had a long history of pushing out women and excluding them from leadership. All of the lesbians at the Center supported Del, and there was a big showdown. She was not hired, and the perception was that the primarily white, male, wealthy board members and donors were not comfortable with a Latina or a lesbian in leadership. There were very public charges of racism and sexism. The image of the Center as an organization that is run by wealthy, white, primarily male donors is an image it has never quite shaken to this day.

In 1985, after the decision to not hire Del, the majority of the women walked out of the Center for, I believe, the second time in its history. These women started a new organization called Connexxus/Centro de Mujeres, and it was the first organization in Los Angeles created to specifically serve lesbians and nurture the development of the lesbian community. Although I was still extremely active in GLLU, I soon joined the Connexxus board. It was an all-white, lesbian board except for me and Del. I had a lot of respect for the executive director, Lauren Jardine, who had headed the women's programs at the Center while I was there.

Although there were some women in GLLU who were critical of my decision because they felt I should be putting my energy into GLLU, I argued that it was a potential opportunity to direct resources to serve Latina lesbians. Connexxus became the first agency to create Latina lesbian support groups, which I occasionally ran. Because the agency was located in predominantly white West Hollywood, the support groups were held at a partner agency in East Los Angeles.

In the mid-1980s GLLU formed committees and started organizing retreats and workshops. Louis Jacinto and I were the cochairs for GLLU's first retreat. We rented a facility in Big Bear in the mountains north of Los Angeles with cabins and a central hall. It was a space that groups like the YMCA and the Boy Scouts rented. About two hundred people attended a three-day weekend filled with cultural activities and workshops on racism, sexism, and classism. We bought and prepared all the food ourselves (everyone signed up for a shift to contribute), and some of my best memories are of doing all that cooking with everybody. It was thought provoking, and healing, for so many people.

There was much debate about whether to allow white people to come—some of the GLLU members had white partners—but ultimately we did not. Those of us who argued against it were very protective of our space and our right to claim it. It was just like when I first joined GLLU and we wrote the bylaws to exclude non-Latinas/os from board positions. The argument was that there were other leadership opportunities for them and so few for us. I don't remember if we had another cogender retreat or not. The first one was very, very successful, but it was so much work!

For a long time men and women were equally involved, and we had committees that people were very committed to. We held fund-raisers, like our first awards gala dinner. At the time, I had been reaching out to

Latina/o elected officials. They were already on the city council, in the state assembly, and in the state senate. So at our first awards dinner we honored a Latino senator, Art Torres. He came, and that was a big deal. Soon after that I received a commendation from the state assembly, also a big deal. In this way we began building our own political power that the white gay community wouldn't be able to dominate.

The GLLU women started having our own parties. It's not that we weren't part of the organization; there was just a real feminist/separatist consciousness. Like feminists of all stripes we were engaged in our own consciousness raising. Lesbians of color were publishing things that spoke to us. Cherríe Moraga and Gloria Anzaldúa had published *This Bridge Called My Back: Writings by Radical Women of Color*, which was seminal. During that time being a radical feminist was a good thing. We were radical, feminist lesbians of color, and we wanted our own space. We started doing our own retreats with between 80 and 120 Latina lesbians. There was space within GLLU for us to be there as separatists. The men got it. We didn't fight with them. They respected the women and supported us, so we didn't have to leave. Over time GLLU became less active, while Lesbianas Unidas was going strong. Lesbianas Unidas continued as a freestanding organization after GLLU ended and for over fifteen years provided the foundation for the development of a strong Latina lesbian identity and community in Los Angeles. Lesbianas Latinas continued with the tradition of retreats in the Big Bear retreat years. The tenth Lesbianas Unidas retreat for Latina lesbians was held in 1992.

In addition to Lesbianas Unidas, several groups and organizations came out of GLLU. GLLU's AIDS committee evolved into Bienestar. Lydia Otero was the force, along with Oscar de la O, behind the formation of Bienestar, an organization that grew to become a leader in Latina/o community services with over six locations throughout Southern California. For nearly thirty years Bienestar has been providing culturally competent HIV testing, mental health services, counseling, support groups, and well-being outreach for the LGBT and Latina/o communities. VIVA, a group started by Rolando Palencia in 1987 to support Latina/o LGBT artists, was originally a GLLU social committee. Most of the historical documents from these groups can be found at the University of California, Los Angeles's Chicano Resource Center.

Because GLLU didn't have an office we would meet at each other's homes, where there were usually food and drinks. This contributed to the feeling of family and, in itself, was a very culturally Latina/o way to organize. GLLU was very active in challenging the lack of treatment, access, and resources that were going to LGBT Latina/o and people of color communities. The Rev. Carl Bean, an openly gay African American minister, the founder of the Unity Fellowship Church Movement, and the eventual founder of the Minority AIDS Project (MAP), came to some of our early gatherings. We were meeting to discuss the lack of HIV/AIDS services going to minority communities. By then AIDS Project Los Angeles (APLA) had started and was receiving large federal grants; it became the main service provider to the gay community. This was the beginning of the professionalization of services to LGBT communities, and we were being completely excluded. We were starting our own organizations, but we didn't have wealthy donors, health professionals, or access to federal funding.

We held a meeting at my apartment to discuss what to do about the fact that gay men of color were getting sick and dying and were not being serviced by APLA. And few people of color were being hired by APLA; for example, they had a large hotline, but it was not bilingual. We decided to picket APLA. GLLU issued a press statement publicly criticizing APLA. However, we realized that it was important for us to create our own organizations and not just continue to fight to get others to care about our people. So Carl went off and founded the Minority AIDS Project in 1985, and Bienestar soon followed.

At some point Lesbianas Unidas was the only group in GLLU organizing activities and raising money. Though most of the women were engaged more in Lesbianas Unidas activities than with GLLU, we did not see any reason to formally break off from the organization. Then a new board was elected to GLLU. The new board declared that the money Lesbianas Unidas was raising was actually GLLU's money and could be allocated by the board. The new president, a Latina lesbian named Cecilia, was a lawyer who had never been involved with Lesbianas Unidas. Most of us didn't know who she was. She and the new board bought pagers and GLLU business cards for themselves with what was basically Lesbianas Unidas money. It was ridiculous—there was never going to be any GLLU emergency that they needed to be paged for.

I knew the bylaws because I had helped write them, so we challenged the board. They got an attorney to go up against Mercedes Marquez and me. But we got them kicked off the board—and they did not know what hit them. I don't know what they were trying to do. These were all people who didn't have a history with GLLU. Frankly, I think they saw GLLU as an opportunity to further themselves politically. So we had a big showdown with them; we took Latinas Unidas's money and formally broke off from GLLU. That basically gutted the organization since the lesbians were the most active members. GLLU didn't have much of a profile after our heyday of the 1980s to early 1990s, but Latinas Unidas did. It continued and so did Bienestar. However, the majority of the men who left GLLU did not get involved with Bienestar, and Latinas Unidas eventually tapered out as an organization. Latinas did not have the same needs, because there were other places they could go and be openly gay, and we continued to have big Latina lesbian events. It didn't mean, though, that there was less of a need for advocacy.

By the early to mid-1990s I was burnt out. Starting and sustaining an organization was hard work. After nearly eight years of pretty much dedicating myself to the Latina/o LGBT movement I decided I had to start thinking about my own future. I had been active for many years, and there were still great women involved, like Lydia Otero and Irene Duran, and more women coming in—people like Elena Popp, Bridget Gonzalez, and Yolanda Retter. I remained visible in other parts of the gay movement to make sure that we would be there and be recognized. Lesbianas Unidas had become more social than political. They weren't out on the picket lines anymore; the priority had become creating social support for Latina lesbians. I still went to all the events, but I wasn't one of the organizers anymore. My daughter was growing up, and I wanted to provide for her. I finally started thinking about going back to school.

In 1987, following the International Lesbian and Gay People of Color Conference held in Los Angeles at the Ambassador Hotel (some of the main organizers were former GLLU members, including Louis Jacinto and Lydia Otero), a handful of people strongly felt the need for a California Latina/o lesbian and gay organization or a national one, but there was no momentum. Hank Tavera, from Northern California, pushed for a statewide organization. GLLU was fairly inactive. I became part of those conversations, and we just couldn't get anybody in L.A. to be serious about the possibility of that state or national organization, though Hank was working hard from Northern California to get something started. Lesbianas Unidas was very active, but they didn't really have a desire to start talking about a national organization.

Right about that time I received an invitation to be a keynote speaker at the Gay and Lesbian Tejanos (GLT) conference in Austin, Texas. Arturo Olivas encouraged me to use the opportunity to discuss the idea in Texas. GLT was a statewide network of Latina/o lesbian and gay organizations in Texas, and many of those groups had started after GLLU and were still going strong. At the GLT conference, Arturo and I talked to people about the idea of a national organization. After the conference we had a meeting to talk about organizing Latinas/os at the National March on Washington for Lesbian and Gay Rights being planned for October of that year.

We came up with a plan that included fund-raising and organized a meeting in D.C. to actually found a national Latina/o LGBT organization. Letitia Gomez and Dennis Medina were moving to D.C. from Texas, and they became the lead local organizers along with the new Latina/o LGBT group in D.C. called ENLACE (Washington, D.C., Metropolitan Area Coalition of Latina/o Lesbians and Gay Men).

I met Cesar Chavez behind the stage that weekend on October 11, 1987. He was the first major civil rights leader to publicly speak out in support of gay rights. I have always been so proud of that. GLLU had supported and participated in the boycotts of grapes and lettuce organized by the United Farm Workers (UFW), founded by Chavez and Dolores Huerta. And in the 1980s members of the UFW had often marched with the GLLU contingent in the L.A. Pride Parade to show their support. I wore my UFW sweatshirt for the March on Washington and was wearing it when I spoke to Cesar.

I spoke with Cesar about the pressure we often felt as LGBT Latina/o activists to be one or the other—Latina/o or LGBT. We were committed to both but faced so much resistance from both Latina/o and LGBT communities when raising the issues. At the time, gay issues were not perceived to affect Latinas/os, and the gay community was as resistant to addressing issues of race as the larger society was and is. Even though we had GLLU there were very few gay organizations of color. I told Cesar about the meeting we were planning to have in D.C. and about starting an organization for lesbian and gay Latinas/os. He was so incredibly sweet. I don't know that I remember his exact words, but he told me that we deserved to be all of who we were and that we should have our own organizations. I started crying. It made a huge difference to me. From then on I did not have any conflict about being a Latina and a lesbian activist, even when people challenged us, particularly in the gay community. They would say, "Why do you need to have your own organization? Why do you want to be separate? Why don't you want to be part of our groups?" After that conversation—my only one with him—I felt like I had no more need to apologize for what we were doing or to even try to get people to understand. My work for the next twenty years was dedicated to educating and even forcing the issue—discrimination against LGBT people is an issue that affects Latina/o communities; and discrimination against Latinas/os is an issue that impacts LGBT communities. I have to say that addressing the former has been way more successful than addressing the latter. Growing numbers of Latina/o communities and organizations across the country are embracing the fight for LGBT rights. In regard to Latina/o rights, the same cannot be said of the majority of LGBT communities or organizations.

The meeting that weekend in Washington, D.C., drew LGBT Latinas/os from dozens of states. There was agreement about the need for a national organization but much discussion about the strategies and goals of such a group. My feeling was that the organization should provide the technical assistance and support to increase the number of local Latina/o LGBT groups around the country. But to me our strength was coming from the grassroots, our communities, and nobody could do the work on gay issues in Latina/o communities but us. We also needed to have a voice and a seat at the table with other national LGBT groups to press our issues, and we needed a platform from which to do that. The strength and number of local grassroots groups would in turn provide the basis for a strong national group that represented them.

The National Latino/a Lesbian and Gay Organization, LLEGÓ, evolved from that first meeting and was based in D.C. Dennis Medina and Letitia Gomez, in particular, tirelessly invested the time and energy needed to bring a national group to fruition. I returned to Los Angeles and went back to school, this time serious about finishing. By that point I had decided that I was going to make my daughter and me the priority—not Lesbianas Unidas, not GLLU, and not LLEGÓ. It was clear that there was excitement and energy behind the movement, and I felt like I could step back and the work would still move forward.

I went to school full-time at night and on weekends and worked full-time during the day. In two years I had earned my associate of arts degree from East L.A. College. Of course I had also become an active part of MeChA (Movimiento Estudiantil Chicano de Aztlán) while there. I transferred to California State University, Dominguez Hills, and continued with the same schedule until I received my bachelor's degree. At the time I was working as a paralegal, writing appeal briefs for social security disability cases. I also worked as a legal secretary for a criminal lawyer. After a break I enrolled at Cal State L.A. and obtained my master's degree in political science in 2001. Ten years later I graduated from the Harvard Kennedy School with a master's in public administration.

LLEGÓ moved forward, becoming a nationally recognized voice for

Latina/o LGBT people. Unfortunately, the reality for many gay organizations of color was that they did not have a wealthy private donor base and soon came to rely on federal funding to do HIV/AIDS education and outreach in Latina/o communities. Many of us were in our twenties and early thirties, and we didn't have the experience around the table for writing proposals or interacting with funders. While federal AIDS money allowed the organization to grow in size (at one point it had up to fifteen employees and a $5 million budget), it restricted the growth in terms of issues.

By then I was working in Los Angeles politics on the same issues, but I had a different focus: I was acquiring the experience to do policy and professional electoral work. I worked for the first openly lesbian member elected to the Los Angeles City Council, Jackie Goldberg, who represented a heavily Latina/o area with a significant gay population. In 2000 I ran my first campaign for a lesbian candidate and won. Although I wasn't involved in LLEGÓ, I was continuing the work I had begun in my early twenties, just using different strategies.

Thinking about all those years in *activismo*, I think GLLU really had an impact on the LGBT movement that reverberated across the country. For one thing, Los Angeles is a big pond where there was a lot of money and attention for the gay community—and there were a lot of Latinas/os. GLLU helped set the stage for our expectation that we were going to be at the LGBT movement table. GLLU also supported the early development of people who became important activists. It was an incubator for Latina/o gay and lesbian activists who have had a big impact in their communities: Rolando Palencia, Oscar de la O, and Elena Popp are just a few of those activists. GLLU left a legacy at both the individual and societal levels. It was one of the earliest organizations of its kind, and its members' willingness to be publicly visible was really important in helping to change the conventional wisdom and stereotypes. Lesbianas Unidas impacted individual Latina lesbians on a personal level. It was a place where women who were made to feel ashamed about being Latina lesbians found strength to continue on and be who they were. I think that was really important to our kids too. And being Latinas/os, our children were always welcomed and nurtured. It was great for my daughter to be around other kids, to be around this whole loving tribe of Latina lesbians. I'm really happy she had that.

I do feel my greatest legacy has been the work I've done bridging the two worlds I come from through my LGBT activism in the Latina/o community. I feel really proud about the part I played in changing that whole narrative. Now nearly every major national Latina/o organization, as well as Hispanic members of Congress, includes the support of LGBT rights in their platform. That is astounding to me considering where we started so long ago.

ORAL HISTORY INTERVIEW CONDUCTED BY LETITIA GOMEZ AND SALVADOR VIDAL-ORTIZ IN WASHINGTON, D.C., ON SEPTEMBER 18, 2011. CHAPTER WRITTEN BY LETITIA GOMEZ AND EDITED BY LAURA ESQUIVEL.

BRAD VELOZ

A South Texas Activist in Washington, D.C., Houston, and San Antonio

Brad Veloz comes from a family of social activists from Corpus Christi, Texas. His personal journey took him to Washington, D.C., where he participated in the National Marches on Washington for Lesbian and Gay Rights in 1979 and 1987. The year following the second march, he became one of the founders of LLEGÓ, the National Latino/a Lesbian and Gay Organization. In 1988 Veloz moved to Houston, where he was elected president of Gay and Lesbian Hispanics Unidos (GLHU). His last LGBT leadership position was as cochair of the San Antonio Lesbian and Gay Assembly (SALGA) from 1992 to the organization's dissolution in 1998. In this chapter, based on an oral history, Veloz pays homage to his parents, who were always involved with the community. He also reflects on the AIDS epidemic and its devastating consequences on the Latina/o LGBT movement. Finally, Veloz tells the story of the tensions between Latina/o and Anglo LGBT activists that led to the dissolution of SALGA.

I'M A FIFTH-GENERATION TEJANO FROM CORPUS Christi. My family has been in South Texas for five generations before me (Canales, Ojeda, Ortega, Carvajal, and Veloz) and continues to be part of South Texas. Of eight siblings, I am the only one who is openly gay. To me it's interesting to see, just within my own family, the development of the Latina/o LGBT experience. I have nieces and nephews who are also openly gay, but they seem to have had a totally different, more open and accepting, experience than what I went through.

I think I've always been a closeted activist, really. My parents were activists—not in the sense of taking to the streets, and so on—but, for example, my dad was very active in the Democratic Party and the democratic process in South Texas. He chaired precincts in South Texas, and he was the Nueces County Democratic Party chair for twelve years. He always talked to us about the importance of voting. He became a citizen at age seventeen, and so the vote was very important to him. He and my mother were part of a Latina/o organization known as the League of United Latin American Citizens (LULAC), which was founded in Corpus Christi in 1929. I remember them having at least one meeting in my house; the women were relegated to the kitchen while the men were conducting business, but the activism was there.

My dad was involved in migrant work in the 1940s and 1950s. My parents traveled with the seasonal workers from Corpus Christi to Colorado and as far as Indiana, making a full circle when they came back to Corpus. There were several summers that my brothers, my sisters, and I spent working the cotton fields of South Texas, and I hated it. I absolutely hated it. I would always tell my mother, "Mom, cuando yo crezca, mis niños no van a saber ni cómo es una bola de algodón." *Porque*, you know, I just hated it. I just hated the hot Texas sun, and I hated that we had to pick cotton. I guess the money was helpful, but we really didn't have to do it. But my mom and my dad, especially my mom, wanted us to experience what some people really had to do. They had to follow the migrant stream to survive. Both my parents came from farms and worked in farms, so they wanted to ensure that we knew what it was to have to survive from the land. I look back now, and it was an incredible experience. I have always been grateful that I had that opportunity.

My mom, while following the migrant workers, always made it a point to come back to Texas to give birth to her children. My older sister had already been born in Waco, and my mom always told the story of my next sister, Consuelo. They were in Colorado picking cherries at the time my mom was pregnant. My mom knew that she was going to go into labor, so she told my dad she needed to go to Texas. They drove to Waco, straight to my grandmother, who was a *partera*, a midwife. So I have two sisters who were born in Waco, and the rest of us were all born in Corpus and then in San Antonio. My parents followed the crops until I was five or six years old, and then they stopped with the migrant work and stayed in Corpus. They didn't go to the fields anymore.

In high school I became involved with a social organization, a boys' club, so to speak. I was first elected treasurer, then vice president. It was an organization that at that time, the 1960s, had an impressive bank account. We had enough money to pay, for example, for trips to Mexico. We would drive to San Antonio and from there fly to Monterrey. All expenses paid for about twelve kids. It wasn't really activism per se, but it was the start of being part of an organization, and I really enjoyed that. I guess my activism didn't really start until probably the 1980s. I met my partner, Mike Rodriguez, in 1978, and we traveled to Washington, D.C., Houston, and San Antonio. In 1979 Mike and I went to the very first National March on Washington for Lesbian and Gay Rights. It ended on the National Mall, at the Ellipse. It was not anything impressive, since the march was relegated to only a couple of hundred folks on the grounds by the Lincoln Memorial, but we were glad that we saw it, and that was it. What was interesting to me—and Mike also noted it—was that there weren't any brown faces in the crowd or leading the march.

But it wasn't until the 1980s that I got involved with federal government organizations. I became involved through work—I was employed in the federal government—and I soon found myself leading, either as president or as chairperson. I remember, for example, that the government had a program called the National Council of Hispanic Employment Program Managers, which was made up primarily of senior-level or high-level Hispanic government employees. I was also part of the general membership of the League of United Latin American Citizens while in Washington. And because I'm a U.S. Navy veteran, I also took an interest in the American GI Forum. Not an active role, but I was involved with that organization.

By 1987 I was still pretty closeted about being gay, especially at my job with the U.S. Department of Defense. I had a close circle of friends who knew that I was gay and that I was in a relationship. I didn't know who I was, because sometimes I would be asked, "Are you gay? Are you Latino? What are you?" And I'd go, "I couldn't separate being Latino and being gay." A little before 1987, a young Latina *lesbiana* from San Antonio came to Washington, D.C., to do an internship with the Department of the Navy. She had been involved with organizations, so she was already prepared to take the lead. Mike and I were living in Arlington, Virginia, at that time, and she stayed with us. The young Tejana Latina *lesbiana*—Letitia Gomez—Dennis Medina, and others were working on the National March on Washington for Lesbian and Gay Rights in 1987. And I thought, "Wow, that's incredible! There are people actually involved with the march, and they're making sure that brown people and their voices are heard and seen." I really liked that idea. Leti asked us if some friends coming to the march could stay at our place. So we housed about twenty-five lesbians from all over the country. It was wonderful. The energy was just incredible. I think about it, and I still get goose pimples, because it was an experience and an awakening.

This time the march was totally different, because I really felt empowered. I felt for the first time that I knew who I was and wanted to come out. I came out in 1987 to my family, at work, to my friends, and so it was a very moving time for me, personally. My family told me that they had known about me since I was five years old, but they hadn't wanted to say anything. They said they respected my privacy and my life, and they never would say anything. But they were waiting for me to tell them that I knew who I was. So they continued to support me and love me, and they still do to this day. For them it was no big surprise; neither was it at work. OK, they said, we already knew.

The group also wanted to form a national organization of Latina/o LGBT folks. By this time Leti, Mike, Dennis, John Gomez, and I, among others, had gotten involved in local LGBT Latina/o efforts and in ENLACE, the Washington, D.C., Metropolitan Area Coalition of Latina/o Lesbians and Gay Men. ENLACE was asked to host a meeting of LGBT Latinas/os from all over the country, and we said, "Sure!" We—or more precisely, I—invited some non-Latina/o gay friends, but Laura Esquivel, along with some other folks, announced that the meeting was about Latinas/os for Latinas/os. If you were not Latina/o, you needed to leave the room, because this was going to be about us. We were going to talk about us and learn about us, Latinas/os as Latinas/os. I didn't expect that to happen, but I knew that it was right. So I just asked my friends to wait for us outside, and they did. They were kind of taken aback. So the meeting proceeded, and a movement to create a national organization was born: The National Latino/a Lesbian and Gay Organization, known as LLEGÓ. I was very proud to be part of that effort. At ENLACE, I was just a member. For LLEGÓ, I was on the board of directors. And so the LGBT Latina/o activism just exploded.

In December of 1987 Mike and I spent a few days in Houston with LGBT Latinas/os whom we had met at the Washington march. Dennis Medina invited us to a New Year's party that the organization known as the Gay and Lesbian Hispanics Unidos (GLHU) sponsored. We had never been to a Latina/o event like that before, held by and for Latina/o LGBT folks. I told Mike, "If I ever get transferred again, I want to come back to Houston," because we liked the people there, we liked what we saw, and we figured that it would be a good place for us. Well, it happened. A job was offered to me in Houston, and I immediately took it. I left Washington in 1988, and Mike followed shortly after. Soon we poured ourselves into GLHU, which by that time had already been ten or eleven years in existence, so they had already built a reputation in the gay and lesbian Houston community. We got involved as members and then ran for office in 1989. First I became vice president, but later on, when Juanita Bustamante decided not to seek reelection, Felix Garcia and I ran against each other. I got elected president and he vice president. Mike became the treasurer.

GLHU sponsored a *gran baile* for the Gay Pride celebration in Houston. People would come from all over for this dance. In 1989 or 1990 we had almost 3,200 people jam-packed into the Astro Village Hotel, which later became the Sheraton. We had Tejano entertainment, such as Gary Hobbs, Elsa Garcia, and mariachis. It was a very successful event. It really provided GLHU with money to help AIDS organizations and individuals and to provide scholarships for LGBT Latinas/os. We partnered with other organizations and allies, and LGBT business people would also seek our endorsement. I remember early on making connections with Annise Parker, who in 2010 became the mayor of Houston. Annise and her girlfriend had a bookstore. We would always try to help both her and her business, and she would help us, so we built those alliances with other LGBT folks in the Houston area. GLHU was a very well-known, well-respected organization.

Many people attended the *bailes*, because it was a good time to get together, see old friends, and make new ones. A lot of them did become members of GLHU, and others continued to support the organization without being members. We had a mailing list and monthly newsletters that continued to go out to all these folks. We would reach as many other folks as we could. And so our membership did grow. It was just such a time to be in Houston and a time to be part of the pride celebrations in Houston.

By the time Mike and I got to Houston, AIDS had already wiped out a lot of gay men in our community. We had experienced that in Washington, D.C., somewhat, but by the time we moved to Houston it was already an incredible pandemic. GLHU was involved with efforts to help with the AIDS epidemic. We would volunteer, for example, as "buddies" to help people with AIDS at home and in the hospital with whatever their needs were. Sometimes we would provide funding if they needed it. GLHU had drag shows. Drag queens would come out in numbers to support our efforts to raise money that would go back to AIDS organizations and especially Latina/o AIDS organizations. We could always depend on drag queens. They were very successful in helping us fight the AIDS epidemic and always came out to help. That way we would make sure that our people with AIDS were being helped.

There were times when GLHU was put in the position of having to defend Latina/o LGBT efforts. The tensions that existed in Houston and South Texas between the Latina/o and Anglo communities were also found in the LGBT community. GLHU had people from not only South Texas but also Mexico, Puerto Rico, Cuba, and other Latin American countries. At one Gay Pride Parade we wanted to carry as many Latina/o flags as we could find and show that there were other LGBT Latinas/os who were part of GLHU. At the beginning we ordered just what we thought we were going to need, three or four flags—Puerto Rico, Cuba, Mexico—but it turned out we had representatives from all over. It was a global picture of these flags. I thought it was just incredible! It was an opportunity for people to see that the Latina/o LGBT folks were not just from Houston. We had to present that idea to the Gay Pride committee. There wasn't outright opposition, but it was subtle, like they thought, "Well, we're all gay; we should be carrying the gay flag." For us, we were gay but also Latinas/os. There were some discussions before the committee voted to accept our flags idea. In the end we got approval, and it was a visual experience to see all those flags, carried by representatives of each country, in the parade.

The greatest impact of GLHU in that period of time was helping people with AIDS in our community. The organization was also mirrored in other parts of the state and the country, such as Austin, Dallas, California, Illinois, and Florida. Because of that, I would say that GLHU was helpful in establishing a national, unified voice. For instance, in Austin we had a retreat that brought together Latino men from the Austin area, but also from Dallas and even El Paso, to talk about AIDS in our community, organizing, leadership, and relationships.

By 1990 Mike and I had already become a part of GLHU. I was president from 1990 to 1992 and also a member of LLEGÓ's board of directors. LLEGÓ approached GLHU to get help with bringing a national conference to Houston. I presented the request to the GLHU board, and they said, "Sure! We'll help." So in 1992 we had the first Latina/o LGBT national conference. I believe this was the first time that LGBT Latinas/os in a global network had gotten together in South Texas. There were people from Mexico and Puerto Rico, of course, but also from Cuba, and maybe other countries. GLHU was responsible for the day-to-day planning of this event and working with Martin Ornelas, who was in Washington, D.C. We also decided to have the conference coincide with Gay Pride in Houston. As I said before, during Gay Pride we held El Gran Baile, and that year it took place at the Hyatt Regency Hotel in downtown Houston.

LLEGÓ took the lead in putting the conference together as far as speakers and workshops. Topics included everything from relationships to AIDS in the community to building alliances to lesbian issues. Because I was involved with GLHU, I wanted to make sure that the *baile* had a good attendance. And it was super packed. Some people asked what does a *baile* have to do with the conference, but that was our contribution. At the *baile* we also elected a Mister and Miss Baile, which had been a tradition. They represented GLHU and did a lot to promote the organization.

Mister and Miss Baile—and even the idea of El Gran Baile itself—started in somebody's house or garage, where people would come to party. They would name the most popular people. A panel of judges usually elected these representatives—not only of the organization but also of the Latina/o LGBT community at large. We would ask attorneys, judges, and local folks in politics to pick and to judge the Mister and Miss Baile. It was a contest that would bring out an incredible amount of talent and bring great energy to GLHU. The contest also attracted people with AIDS and activists working on lesbian issues.

There were some internal issues at GLHU. Women led the organization for the most part, starting in 1978, when Linda Morales became the first president; Juanita Bustamante also led it. But within GLHU there was some resistance, some friction between gay men and lesbians. Some men didn't want to work with women. I saw it happen even outside of the Latina/o LGBT community, where gay white men would freak at the idea of having women in leadership roles or just having women involved. I would try to make it an agenda item for discussion. We needed to talk about it and put it out in the open. I didn't know if what was happening in the gay and lesbian community outside was being mirrored in GLHU in terms of leadership and in the lack of women in other organizations in Houston. In the end, those men would not get as involved, but they would still help financially or in some other way.

In 1992 Mike and I moved to San Antonio, and we brought our Latina/o activism with us. We immediately got involved with two organizations: the Esperanza Peace and Justice Center and the San Antonio Lesbian and Gay Assembly (SALGA). Through the Esperanza Peace and Justice Center, we met other Latina/o activists, including a young woman, Dulce Benavides, who was an officer. There was nothing Latina/o about SALGA. Mike and I found that the organization was predominantly white, with a few exceptions: Dulce—who I think was secretary—a Latino male cochair, and maybe one other person. After the first meeting Mike and I attended, they had a little reception. I was meeting and greeting people like I usually do. Then I came across this young man. I introduced myself, and he did the same. He had the last name of Huerta. I thought, "Oh wow, Huerta!" And I asked him, "Are you any relation to Dolores Huerta?" And he went, "Who's that?" I thought he was kidding. I couldn't believe it. That guy didn't know about Dolores Huerta, the Latina activist and cofounder of the United Farm Workers, and he shared the same last name as her. So I looked at Mike. He just rolled his eyes, and I thought, "Oh my God, what are we getting into?"

I joined the board of directors of the Esperanza Peace and Justice Center, and then, through Dulce, Mike and I became involved with SALGA. I sat on the Esperanza board for not very long, maybe not even a year. In the meantime Mike was finishing his degree at Our Lady of the Lake and doing an internship at the Esperanza Peace and Justice Center. San Antonio was different from Houston. For me, it was very noticeable in the struggles not only in the LGBT Latina/o community but also outside of our own community. I remember the resistance against Latina/o LGBTs. I'm not sure if it was because we, Mike and me, already came with a totally different frame of mind, but when we got to San Antonio it was like a brick wall. So the Esperanza Center kind of helped us fill that void. I want to quote something about the Esperanza. It says, "The people of Esperanza dream of a world where everyone has civil rights and economic justice, where the environment is cared for, where cultures are honored, and communities are safe. The Esperanza Center advocates for those wounded by domination and inequality—women, people of color, lesbians, gay men, the working class, and the poor. We believe in creating bridges between people by exchanging ideas and educating and empowering each other. We believe it is vital to share our vision of hope." That's their mission statement, and I really identified with it, and so I was honored that I was asked to be part of the board of directors.

On the other hand, I felt that SALGA was not really talking about issues that were affecting the Latina/o community at large, or more specifically the Latina/o LGBT community. I found myself challenging folks in SALGA about what was happening, and then, when election time came around in 1992, I decided to run for cochair with Dulce Benavides. We were elected, and so for the first time two Latinas/os led the organization, but there was resistance to that. Some gay white men really took issue with being led by Latinas/os. Why? Just racism and internalized homophobia I think, but no one would ever be that open about it. Never. I think collectively they represented all sorts of individuals. For example, one of them was a physician and had a newspaper. One was a professor at Trinity University. Another one had chaired the Pride events in San Antonio, and the other two were involved with other organizations. They were pretty well connected, not only with the LGBT community but also with people outside of the community. So they had influence.

SALGA sponsored an annual conference. They brought people from other parts of the country to talk about several issues, but rarely about Latina/o issues. So Dulce and I thought, "We need to talk about LGBT Latina/o issues, we need to make sure that Latina/o LGBT voices are heard, and we need to be part of it." We began to experience very harsh resistance from those gay white men who felt that the annual conference was not about Latinas/os and that we shouldn't be talking about anything Latina/o.

Then they threatened to leave the organization or to not support any events that the SALGA cochairs decided to take on. SALGA always sponsored an annual Pride Picnic in San Antonio. The first picnic that Dulce and I organized was very successful. We even made some profits that, as usual, returned to the community, not only to AIDS organizations but also to others within the LGBT community. By the time the second year rolled around, the resistance had really manifested into accusations of financial mismanagement by Dulce and me, allegations that were all false. Those accusations were publicized mostly in the gay newspaper owned by a gay white male, becoming an issue outside of SALGA. People found out that there was turmoil within the organization led by "those two Latinos." And so the LGBT community decided to have town hall meetings to talk about what was happening with SALGA. When the very first meeting was held, Dulce and I were blasted with such hate that it was incredible. We could not defend ourselves from those gay white men who just bombarded us not only with questions and allegations but also with all sorts of notions that we were doing something illegal.

In spite of the attacks, Dulce and I continued to move within the organization. I felt like, "Why aren't people coming to help us? Why aren't our white allies coming to support us and to tell these guys to fucking back off?" In reality, a lot of SALGA members just stood by and watched as Dulce and I were torn to shreds. Our reputations were on the line, and those white men really made it their goal to ruin our lives, not only personally but also professionally. To this day, I think I'm still bitter over it. I've never gotten over that experience. It had just a negative impact on my life.

For the second town hall meeting, they hired an impartial mediator who happened to be a white lesbian. Her partner was Latina. The mediator was pretty well respected in the community, but she didn't get what was happening between the LGBT Latinas/os and those gay white men. When Dulce and I arrived, there was a quietness that was just eerie, and it was not a very good feeling. Within minutes after the mediator started explaining the process that was going to take place and what her role was, the gay white men, in different locations of the room, stood up and started bombarding her with issues and questions. Dulce and I just looked at each other and went, "This is not going to work." She and I and a couple of people that were with us just got up and walked out. Because we left, I think, a lot of people decided to back off and not do anything to help us. I wish that we would have had white allies or Latinas/os from the organization supporting us, but no one would. Nobody came to our rescue.

For 1994 Gay Pride, two Pride Picnics were held. Some people asked what was going on, but others just thought, "There are two different events." We had our Pride Picnic at the Sunken Gardens in Brackenridge Park. The group of white men held theirs at San Pedro Springs Park, the traditional location for SALGA picnics. Ours was first, and someone was passing out flyers with captions about our event saying that the picnic was being funded illegally. They also denounced financial mismanagement. In spite of that, our picnic went on, and it was very successful. It was the last picnic Dulce and I organized as SALGA cochairs.

That same year we proposed to bring a Peruvian shaman to talk to the organization as part of SALGA's annual conference. I picked him up at the airport. When I walked up to him and shook his hand—it was the first time we had met—he looked at me and hugged me. Then he said, "You need to be careful, because there are people out there who want to harm you." I was totally freaked out. Later on, when he came into the conference room, he walked back out and said, "Brad, something is going on here." And I responded, "Yes, there's some tension, and there's stuff going on." He said, "Be careful." It really worried me that he would be that observant, that he would sense that there was something wrong.

Dulce and I both resigned in 1995, but there were no elections held that year, so we continued as cochairs until 1997. SALGA formally dissolved a year later. During those years we were threatened, and there was harassment on the phone. Members of the group that opposed Dulce and me also published articles in the newspaper about us. The situation involving the two different picnics became public, but without names, in the San Antonio paper. Then one of the white gay men—the one who owned the gay rag in the LGBT community—ran some articles about Dulce and me in connection with the alleged financial mismanagement and the lack of leadership. His attacks continued even after we left the organization. The conflicts in SALGA created some resentment and distance between Latinas/os and white LGBT people. People just stayed away. And that was their way of dealing with it.

What was happening to Dulce and me at the time mirrored what was happening outside of San Antonio and across the country with LGBT folks. There was a lot of hate in the 1990s, and a lot of it was directed toward LGBT organizations and the LGBT community. A woman came to speak at the Esperanza. Her name was Suzanne Pharr. I attended her talk, and it was like, "Fuck! That's what happened to us!" It was both nationwide hysteria and homophobia. Similar attacks with similar issues were happening all over the country. I thought, "Well, maybe those guys are part of that effort. Maybe one of them is leading the rest." Maybe one of them was part of a national antigay movement. It seems kind of paranoid, but it made sense to me. One of those white guys, a very wealthy one, had moved to San Antonio, gotten involved, and then just disappeared.

After SALGA was dissolved I got transferred again, but this time I wanted to leave. Mike and I headed back to Washington, D.C., and we stayed there until I retired in 2003. Then we came back home, back to San Antonio. I took the first two years after my retirement to help care for my mom, who was suffering from Alzheimer's disease. She passed away in 2008, and shortly afterward I was approached to join a children's advocacy organization. I was later elected chairman of the board of directors and stayed involved with the organization for a couple of years. That was my volunteer time, and I never really got involved again with LGBT organizations. My activism has always been about class, gender identity, culture, sexuality, and race. I see all of these issues as interconnected, and I feel in my heart that you can't really separate them. Because of my activism, I certainly see and hear things differently.

For LGBT Latinas/os, there has been a struggle. We continue to struggle. But the little bit that I helped in bringing some of those issues to the limelight, to bring some awareness to other folks, has been a personal satisfaction for me.

I have mentioned Mike Rodriguez, my partner. We're approaching our thirty-fifth anniversary. As states pass laws that will allow for gay marriages, I wonder if in my lifetime, if in the state of Texas, we will see some equality for the LGBT community. I would like to get married in the state of Texas. They say it's never too late to adopt children. We're still young enough, and we'll see how things go, but I'm glad to see that there's some equality coming to the LGBT community, and I'm happy for that. But at the same time, some states continue to disregard equal rights for the LGBT community. I am hopeful that I will get to see the day when our country recognizes our status as equal citizens.

ORAL HISTORY INTERVIEW CONDUCTED BY LETITIA GOMEZ AND URIEL QUESADA IN SAN ANTONIO, TEXAS, ON JUNE 27, 2011. CHAPTER WRITTEN BY URIEL QUESADA.

DAVID ACOSTA

The Boy in Fear Who Became a Latino/a LGBT Advocate in Philadelphia

Born and raised in Colombia, David Acosta moved with his family to Philadelphia when he was eleven years old. Several life events marked Acosta's future: He was sent to boarding school at age seven, where he discovered his romantic and sexual attraction to males and his dislike for the discipline imposed on young men at those kinds of institutions. As a teenager he was a victim of bullying, but books gave him inspiration and strength. The post–civil rights era—a period vibrant with political consciousness and activism among feminists of color and the LGBT community—helped inform Acosta's sense of self and commitment to social justice. In 1984 he started an intense activism career that has opened a path for other young Latina/o activists. In this essay Acosta recounts his early years in Colombia and Pennsylvania—key periods of time in defining his subsequent work for LGBT Latinas/os—and the founding of organizations such as the Gay and Lesbian Latino AIDS Education Initiative (GALAEI), the AIDS Coalition to Unleash Power (ACT UP) Philadelphia, and Fuego Latino. Of particular relevance are his reflections on otherness, on the influence of feminism on his own personal development, on the AIDS epidemic as a pivotal moment in Latina/o LGBT activism, and on the contributions of late twentieth-century activists to today's Latina/o LGBT movements.

I WAS BORN IN 1958 IN CALI, COLOMBIA, AND IMMI-grated to the United States in 1969, where I have resided ever since. My childhood was a pretty normal one. I came from a very large and close-knit family. Growing up, my grandparents were central figures in my universe, and in many ways they shaped and continue to shape my sense of self and sense of family. As their favorite grandchild, I spent a great deal of my childhood living with them for extended periods of time. From them, I got a sense of our family history and of the world as a kind of magical place populated by larger-than-life ancestors, including witches, ghosts, and other supernatural beings, all of which were either relations or family acquaintances. It is this magical realism in everyday, ordinary life that Gabriel García Márquez captures so brilliantly in his writing.

My family had been devout Catholics from as far back as we could remember, and the church and its rituals figured prominently in my early years and played an important role in my upbringing, including a predestined sense and an expectation from the family that I would join the priesthood. Even my first name, John, was given to me in honor of Pope John XXIII. Growing up in the church, I spent a great deal of time among saints, incense, flowers, candles, and its many rituals, which left a great impression on me and filled me with a sense of wonder and a desire to belong to it all. It was only at about the age of thirteen—as I struggled to come to terms with my sexuality—that I made a conscious decision to abandon Christianity all together, as I could not comprehend a religion that excluded me and whose teachings about love did not extend to me, at least in its organized sense.

In 1967 my grandfather died, and a large part of my universe collapsed with his death. It was the first time I had experienced such loss. I was seven, and while struggling with such grief I was sent to boarding school, going the day after he was buried. Life in boarding school was unlike anything I had known before. It was a place where every activity was rigidly structured, from our waking at 5:00 a.m. every day to our bedtime, which took place at 7:00 p.m. Showers, breakfast, lunch, classes, recess, dinner, and evening playtime were all highly organized and regulated. On our first day there, we were assigned a number and were often referred to by that number when being called out in a group. Our clothes were taken away, and we were provided with three different colored uniforms: khaki, military green, and a blue dress uniform to be worn only on Sundays or special occasions. The school was located in the mountains of Coconuco, named after the Indian tribe that inhabited the region, and was remote in every sense of the word. The school grounds spanned hundreds of acres and included a church, bread ovens, orchards, schools, dormitories, and flower and vegetable gardens. I mention this boarding school experience for two reasons, both of which would be critical to my latter development as both an activist and a gay man.

The first of these was an awareness of my interest and attraction both romantic and sexual to boys, especially the older ones. They seemed to my young eye mature, aloof, and beautiful. They had swagger and confidence, and because of their age, seemed to have an unspoken and tacit power that was acknowledged by us younger boys in the implicit pecking order that is inherent in any military or all-male institution. The second was my utter dislike for the discipline imposed on us, some of it quite harsh, including corporal punishment. I would in later years find ways to rebel against such authority, both parental and institutional.

In the winter of 1969 my family and I moved to Philadelphia, like so many others before us in search of better opportunities. It was difficult to adapt to life in a different country, away from the people and places we knew well. During the first few years we missed home terribly, especially our relatives. However, we soon began to adapt. English as a second language came easily, and with that came a new understanding of the American experience we would be a part of and would in many ways come to embrace. Despite our acceptance of U.S. culture, an important part of us remained deeply grounded in our Latin American culture and language. A feeling of being an outsider would prevail, and it defined my experience then and now. This otherness would play an important role for me as I navigated race, culture, class, and sexual orientation. This search for self and for an answer to the many questions posed by my "perceived otherness" led me to explore a wide range of reading material at an early age and eventually led to my encounter with individuals who were also on the same quest and who were engaged in changing the conditions of their environment. It is also important to note the impression that the civil rights movement, including the assassination of Martin Luther King, had left on the national psyche, which would inform much of the civil struggles that followed as other groups—women, farmworkers, and LGBT people, among others—sought both equal participation and representation in U.S. life.

Adapting to U.S. life, language, and culture came easily, and I entered adolescence acutely aware of my attraction to other boys and to men. Women never interested me in the way they seemed to interest other boys. They were, however, an important part of a universe I admired, as was the boisterous bragging of males about women as sexual objects to be conquered and discarded. Women for me were not objects of sexual attraction. They inhabited another sphere, one that was strong and nurturing. I had grown up around women—my grandmother and aunts—and from them I gleaned the quiet sense of power they held in a male-centered culture. I intuited this early at that time.

Feminism, as I understood it abstractly (and later on as a theoretical concept), was a shaping force in the way I would come to understand the world and my privileged position in it as a man.

My entrance into junior high school and the public school system would play a pivotal role in my coming out and in my activism. Mercilessly bullied both physically and verbally from the seventh grade till the ninth, I found solace in books. I had always loved reading, but books in this period took on an incredible importance, and they remain important to me to this day. Books were my route of escape, a respite from the constant harassment and violence. By the time I reached the eighth grade I was being escorted to classes by nonteaching assistants. I was given special dispensation to spend my nonclass time, including lunch period, in the school library. It was there that I began to search.

I did not know what I was seeking answers to or what the questions were. What I now know is that even then something made me feel different and set me apart from others. This feeling of otherness made me experience and see the world differently, both objectively and subjectively; it set me apart from it and made others hate me. There were words for what I was: fag, sissy, queer, homo, and pansy, among others. These were the words I heard directed at me every day. Those words meant something to the world and to my tormentors; the world had sent its messengers, and the message was loud and clear. What exactly did those words have to do with me? I didn't know, but they frightened me, and tired of being afraid, I began the search myself.

By the time I graduated from the ninth grade, I had perused the entire library at least once if not more and had read hundreds of books. I do remember books gave me a sense of self, but many of them were tragically sad, and they all ended badly. Death or tragedy seemed to be the only redemption for the characters that were the most like me, those that reflected who I was and how I felt. These books named my desire, framed both my longings and my fears, and told me I was not alone.

In those painful years between 1972 and 1975 I came to identify with others who were also marginalized and hated. This happened through reading as well as through observation. This was a heady time to be coming of age. We were coming out of the civil rights struggles of the sixties—Black Power, the Beats, the Summer of Love, Stonewall. There were struggles for greater recognition and acknowledgement of civil liberties, workers' wages, a woman's right to choose, the antiwar movement, and the environment, among others. Groups which had until then either been marginalized or unable to participate fully in the democratic process—blacks, Latinas/os, Asians, Native Americans, women, the working poor, farmworkers, and of course LGBT people—were all waging battles for recognition of their civil rights, for access and representation. There was energy in all of it and a feeling in the air that everything was possible. I wanted to work in those struggles and communities and was slowly but easily gravitating into many groups where I felt embraced and validated, at least for my political leanings and my budding commitment to social and economic justice issues. I would come to meet other LGBT people in those movements, since many worked across a wide range of social- and economic-justice issues, aware of the interconnectedness of oppression.

A lot of this activism was informed by new theoretical constructs and frameworks of thinking emerging out of feminist and postcolonial theories as well as postmodernist critiques on language, race, sex, and gender, among others. From these organizations/coalitions and the people who ran them, I found a sense of empowerment and gradual self-acceptance. In those years I became active in local chapters that supported the American Indian Movement and Big Mountain. The taking of Wounded Knee in 1973 and the imprisonment of Leonard Peltier in 1977 were opportunities for community organizing and educational efforts about the plight of Native Americans. Other events that helped to inform my sense of self and a commitment to social justice were the strikes by farmworkers in California, the antiwar movement, Three Mile Island, and the fall of Salvador Allende in Chile.

The entrance of the 1980s would have gone unnoticed except for the onset of the AIDS epidemic. The 1970s had passed, and with it, I believe, the dreams of a generation. Like many young gay men of the period, I embraced the new music and fashion. Looking back on it all now with some perspective, informed in large part by distance, it seems the 1980s were a self-centered, hedonistic period. Coming out of the 1960s and 1970s, the 1980s would be defined politically by a strong backlash against the progressive movements that preceded them.

And so we danced under the residual, liberating glow of the Stonewall Riots and the renewed activism that followed the tragic assassination of Harvey Milk in 1978. Unbeknownst to us, however, a stranger had entered our party, an unknown guest that would radically change the world as we knew it then and is still with us now. This stranger would come to be known as gay-related immune deficiency (GRID) and then AIDS. AIDS came to define my generation, changed the gay universe forever, and literally took us "out of the bars and into the streets," to quote an ACT UP chant of the period.

In 1984, still in Philadelphia, I was asked to sit on the first Mayor's Commission on Sexual Minorities, established by then mayor Wilson Goode. I was the first Latino appointed to the commission. Within that role, and because of it, I began to agitate and to question the lack of HIV-prevention efforts directed at Latino gay men. The AIDS Activities Coordinating Office was started in 1987 and came out of the need to create an office within the health department in Philadelphia that would focus solely on HIV/AIDS. Philadelphia Community Health Alternatives (PCHA)—now Mazzoni Center—had already been in existence as a clinic providing sexually transmitted disease services to gay men since 1979. In 1981 it became the Philadelphia AIDS Task Force as it sought to meet the growing need for HIV/AIDS care and prevention services. Soon other organizations came into existence. Community-initiated responses to the AIDS epidemic, in light of the federal government's lack of response to AIDS as a public health issue (not only in Philadelphia but across the United States), are by now well known. Despite the blossoming of AIDS service organizations at that time, there were as yet no HIV/AIDS organizations for Latinas/os in Pennsylvania or elsewhere in the United States, and none for Latino gay men.

In 1986 I received a call asking if I was interested in helping to start an HIV/AIDS education program for Latinas/os and, more specifically, if I would be interested in developing a similar program for Latino gay men. The first efforts to educate Latinas/os in Philadelphia would come out of Congreso de Latinos Unidos, which received the contract for start-up and was at that time the largest Latina/o community-based organization in the state. Programa Esfuerzo was born out of this effort. Led by Carmen Paris as its director (Carmen had been one of my first contacts in those early days when I was calling the health department to question the lack of HIV/AIDS education efforts directed at Latinas/os and at Latino gay men in particular), Programa Esfuerzo was located in Philadelphia's Latina/o neighborhood and from its inception faced strong community opposition. Vandalized countless times, it was eventually forced to close its doors and relocate to Congreso's larger headquarters.

My philosophical approach toward developing a program for Latino gay men would work from an asset-based perspective. This would entail developing HIV/AIDS prevention messages while speaking to Latino gay men directly in ways that saw their sexual orientation and their homosexuality in a positive light. I did not want a shame-based prevention approach, but a sex-positive one, one that included representations of safer sex messages that would be not only explicit but also erotic.

There was no other way, I believed, by which to convey the fundamental shift that AIDS presented for gay men and intimacy. Not surprisingly, this approach found resistance from the top-level management of Congreso, including its board.

Unable to reconcile our differences and continuing to believe that there was a need not only for such a program but for such an approach to HIV prevention, I began to make inquiries about where I could place it. After gaining the support of the health department, I decided to take the program out of Congreso and to start my own organization. The organization would not only be devoted to HIV/AIDS prevention and education but would seek to further both the visibility and civil rights of Latina/o LGBT people in Philadelphia and the United States. At a desk within the Philadelphia health department, I began to programmatically set the pieces that would lead to the founding of the Gay and Lesbian Latino AIDS Education Initiative (GALAEI). Founded in 1987 and incorporated in 1989, GALAEI remains the oldest of the ongoing Latina/o HIV/AIDS prevention programs in the country, alongside Bienestar in Los Angeles.

My work in the area of HIV prevention also coincided with the start of ACT UP Philadelphia in 1988 and my involvement in it. This was also the beginning of the involvement of Latino gay men not only in healthcare issues but in civil rights issues as well. For many years, Latina lesbians, trans individuals, and a small number of intrepid gay boys had been at the forefront of organizing for both visibility and civil rights issues in Puerto Rico, New York City, and the West Coast, in organizations such as Las Buenas Amigas in New York and Gay and Lesbian Latinos Unidos in Los Angeles. I believe women's position within Latin American culture and trans people's abandonment of rigid Latina/o constructs of gender roles allowed both groups to question and challenge male privilege. This challenge was seen as coming from a non-threatening place, which allowed lesbian and trans people to be subversive. I believe men had too much privilege to lose, and while there were a few queer Latino men who were involved in those early movements, the majority of us came into our own as a result of the AIDS crisis. Sadly, it was AIDS that provided us with a safe place from which to discuss, in many instances for the first time in our communities, Latino male same-sex desire. It was safe to discuss it publicly then, because it was done under the context of pathology and illness—much as homosexuality had been and continued to be viewed as an illness, even after its removal from the *Diagnostic and Statistical Manual of Mental Disorders* in 1973. Unfortunately, also concurrent with the rise of the AIDS epidemic were conservative forces working toward challenging the gains made by social- and economic-justice movements in the previous two decades.

It was against this political and cultural backdrop that the LGBT Latina/o movement in the United States and Puerto Rico gained momentum and myself and others came into our own. The air was heavy with the work that needed to be done; the threat of AIDS and our exclusion from the larger LGBT movement's agenda and from our own Latina/o community and *familia* spurred us on.

My involvement in helping to start many of the local organizations at that time in Philadelphia (and in working with those that were already established) stemmed in large part from the unique fact that I was the only LGBT Latino active in public life in Philadelphia who was out, at least publicly—my appointment to the Mayor's Commission on Sexual Minorities ensured that. In this context, my being Latino added to the diversity of these organizations. More importantly, however, my work within these organizations allowed me to voice the concerns of people of color in relationship to the LGBT movement's inclusion or exclusion of issues critical to people of color and, more specifically, to Latinas/os. Within non-LGBT Latina/o organizations, the same issue of exclusion and invisibility was a constant. This may sound hard to believe, but while there were many people in the Latina/o community whom you knew were gay or lesbian, those individuals, many of them from the old school (meaning they had been involved in community organizing), had for many years failed to articulate an agenda that was pro-LGBT within that community. It therefore fell to me to articulate those needs, especially in my appointment to a commission that was supposed to serve as a voice for the LGBT community and, more specifically, for LGBT Latinas/os. Traveling among Latina/o community-organizing groups that were working on a wide range of social- and economic-justice issues, I was able to articulate the need for viewing Latina/o LGBT struggles as intrinsically connected to larger Latina/o struggles and was able to point out the connections found at the intersections of racism, classism, and homophobia. Our "Latino-ness" within the mainstream LGBT movement excluded us from their table, and our sexual orientation excluded us from the Latina/o table. It was much later that a small group of out Latina/o individuals came together so that we could discuss community organizing around other issues that were not focused just on HIV/AIDS but on larger issues of visibility and representation.

One such example involved the formation in 1992 of a group that we called Fuego Latino. Our small group came together one evening to start an organization for Latina/o LGBT individuals in Philadelphia. The organization's founding and its development highlight one of the challenges inherent in early Latina/o LGBT organizing, at least in Philadelphia. The philosophical reasons for the group's forming meant different things to the founders and to those who would join later. For those of us who were its initial founders, the organization would serve a dual purpose. It would be a vehicle through which to organize social events and, in doing so, indirectly provide us the opportunity to conduct community organizing and to work toward visibility and furthering a Latina/o LGBT agenda—both within the LGBT community in general and within the Latina/o community in particular. The goal of queer liberation across race, class, and economics was of course a given, at least among our initial group, which included transplants from Texas and Puerto Rico.

Some individuals who later came to the group were attracted solely by its potential as a social outlet. Philadelphia at that time no longer had a gay bar or club like New York's La Escuelita. Our own local Latina/o gay bar, El Bravo, had been closed for several years. These newer individuals were mainly interested in organizing social events, which centered on Latin salsa-dance parties. The social aspect of these dances was, of course, incredibly important in that it allowed us opportunities for community organizing and the dissemination of information. In my particular case, I was interested in disseminating HIV/AIDS prevention information and safer sex messages to a community that was widely dispersed and that was not targeted for HIV/AIDS education and prevention messages by other local HIV/AIDS organizations at the time—although some of these organizations would today swear up and down that they did target the community back then. I was also personally interested in making the larger Latina/o community aware of the threat that the HIV epidemic posed to Latino gay men in Philadelphia. Part of the strategy (pressuring local white gay bars to host Latina/o specific events) was due in large part to the lack of Latina/o LGBT spaces for socializing. The Gay and Lesbian Latino AIDS Education Initiative set out to organize such spaces within community dance clubs, none of which were Latina/o. The Bravo's closing several years before had left a huge need for such spaces, so GALAEI stepped in.

While acknowledging the importance of creating Latina/o specific spaces, some of us were also cognizant of the fact that our group could push forward an agenda for visibility and inclusion in areas where we had up until that time been invisible. Thus one of the first political actions we took was challenging the committee responsible for the organizing of the Puerto Rican Day Parade. Our task was simple: we wanted to be allowed to march within the parade as an openly LGBT Latina/o contingent. In retrospect, it might not have been the case that the parade's organizing committee would have kept us out. The fact was that no one had requested such a thing before, and confronted with a challenge, the group initially denied our participation. We countered that with a challenge on the grounds of discrimination (since the group responsible for organizing the parade received taxpayer support from the city of Philadelphia, which had an LGBT nondiscrimination clause, one of the first in the country). And of course, I was still on the LGBT advisory commission set up by the mayor. Forced to confront such a charge, including potentially losing funding, the group ceded to our demand. The battle won was bittersweet, and those of us who had pushed the hardest for such a confrontation found ourselves alone—a small group of folks, just like our beginning. The loose membership that had coalesced around Fuego Latino quickly dispersed, its members, in my opinion, wishing to remain in the closet or to not be seen as publicly challenging such an august and powerful committee. One needed to remember that the committee was the old guard, activists who had honed their skills in fighting against discrimination during the 1950s, 1960s, and 1970s and to whom we were all connected in some way. They were our teachers in many respects; we, or at least I, had learned something from them, their tactics, and their struggles. We had fought the same battles and years later were still fighting them. To them I owe a great debt. Challenging them on Latina/o LGBT issues and pushing for inclusion in spaces within the larger Latina/o community while using their tactics was for me not negotiable. Many saw it as disrespectful. I begged to differ.

As we began to organize for marching in the parade, we realized there were less than half a dozen of us willing to do so publicly—certainly not enough for a contingent whose strategy was one of challenging invisibility. Faced with the prospect of a contingent so small, we reached out to Latina/o LGBT allies in New York City, many of whom agreed to march with us, and still we did not have enough people, so we asked the larger LGBT community and straight Latina/o allies in Philadelphia to join us—and many did, including then councilman Angel Ortiz and other community leaders. Because the group could not guarantee our safety, we were offered police protection, and thus, flanked by cops and holding the flags of every Latin American nation high and proud, we marched, holding hands, into history.

Looking back at my specific involvement in many of the organizations important to LGBT organizing in both Latina/o and non-Latina/o queer communities in Philadelphia and nationally, including the National Latino/a Lesbian and Gay Organization (LLEGÓ) and the National Coalition for LGBT Health, among others, it becomes clear that what may have seemed at first like disparate organizing attempts by Latina/o LGBT individuals across the country and in Puerto Rico (including the creation of our own organizations, whatever their purpose) was actually a larger unfolding strategy. Unaware of it at the time, mired in the trenches of survival, a generation of LGBT Latina/o activists (most of us propelled by the AIDS epidemic) challenged the status quo, our local communities, and the power structures that had historically defined and excluded us. That the AIDS epidemic played a key role in Latina/o LGBT organizing is undeniable for many of us and for me in particular. There are absolutely no words that can describe how our Latina sisters stepped in and made our survival their priority, relegating their struggles to our collective survival. I think, while aware of the polarizing aspects of gender-based agendas that had split white gay and lesbian movements, Latina lesbians and "we" gay boys were joined at the hip. Maybe we did not have the luxury of white privilege and of pursuing different agendas to get to the same place, but Latina lesbian women were for me, then, the only rock and anchor. They know who they are, and to them I offer my eternal love and thanks.

One wonders what indeed would have happened to the larger LGBT movement and to LGBT organizing had AIDS not interrupted their course. For many of us, the urgency of the moment was unquestionable. We were on our way long before the AIDS epidemic moved in to take so much away from us, to redirect our paths—the fork in the road. We could also argue that the AIDS epidemic gave us a unique window of opportunity from which we could organize and challenge our communities. AIDS was a costly gift from fickle forces, exacting a dear payment so that we would be invisible no more. As I write these closing words, the names and faces of countless brave Latina/o queer colleagues, now long gone, float to the surface, and I am grateful for having known them. I remain, like so many others, committed to the social-justice issues that drove us then and drive us now.

In so doing, I hope we honor their courage, their lives, their spirit, their memory, and our collective work—our common past, our present, our future. I think they would be pleased to know we are strong after all these years; that we are on the wind; that we are finally writing our story, carried on the wings of ancestors, family, and community. And more importantly, that young, brilliant, and unapologetically proud Latina/o LGBT individuals no longer have to check their Latina/o LGBT or Latina/o selves at the door, so that we might enter rooms we already inhabit, by just being. Those who come after us need not start from scratch.

The child in me looks back, no longer afraid. We need hope to spring...

CHAPTER WRITTEN BY DAVID ACOSTA.

Jesús Cháirez, circa 1999, at his studio during production of the Sin Fronteras *radio program. Courtesy of Jesús Cháirez.*

A promotional poster for Jesús Cháirez's Sin Fronteras, *the first gay Latina/o radio show in Texas. Courtesy of Jesús Cháirez.*

David Acosta, center, at a demonstration for United for AIDS Action in New York City, July 14, 1992. Courtesy of David Acosta.

Sexo Latex poster. This was one of several posters printed for a 1992 HIV prevention campaign produced by David Acosta through the Gay and Lesbian Latino AIDS Education Initiative (GALAEI). Courtesy of David Acosta.

Laura Esquivel and Letitia Gomez on the National Mall at the 1993 March on Washington for Lesbian, Gay, and Bi Equal Rights and Liberation. Courtesy of Letitia Gomez.

Lesbianas Unidas of Los Angeles at the 1993 March on Washington for Lesbian, Gay, and Bi Equal Rights and Liberation. Courtesy of Letitia Gomez.

Hank Tavera (the bearded man carrying the banner), founder of the California chapter of the National Latino/a Lesbian and Gay Organization (LLEGÓ), at the 1993 March on Washington for Lesbian, Gay, and Bi Equal Rights and Liberation. Courtesy of Letitia Gomez.

Luz Guerra as Lolita Lebrón in Carlos Baron's Pasión y Prisión de Lolita Lebrón, *Mission Cultural Center, San Francisco, 1979. Courtesy of Luz Guerra.*

José Gutiérrez at home showing some of the archival materials he has collected over the past twenty years. Courtesy of Noriega James.

Flyer publicizing a dance featuring a popular Tejano band to play to a gay audience. Courtesy of the Rare Books and Manuscripts Division at the Nettie Lee Benson Latin American Collection, University of Texas at Austin.

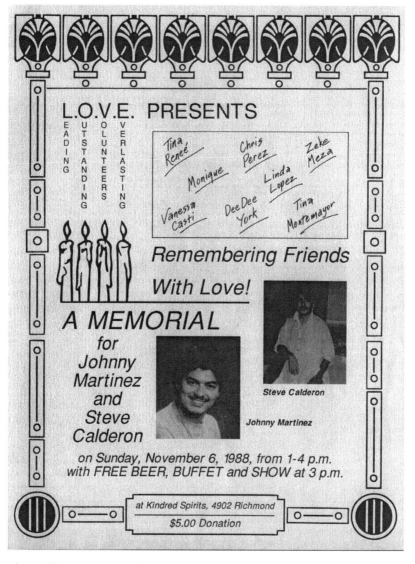

Flyer publicizing a memorial event for two members of Gay and Lesbian Hispanics Unidos (GLHU) in Houston who died of AIDS. Courtesy of the Rare Books and Manuscripts Division at the Nettie Lee Benson Latin American Collection, University of Texas at Austin.

NLLGA

National Latino Lesbian/Gay Activists
Red Nacional Latina de Lesbianas y Gays

PRIMER ENCUENTRO

A Strategy Session for a National Consciousness
Una Session de Estrategia hacia una conciencia nacional

NLLGA hopes to lay the foundation for future projects by creating a forum that will focus on the following items:

* Building a national network
* Identifying alliances
* Identifying special interest groups
* Developing a future plan of action
* Plant seeds for future growth

NLLGA espera poder desarrollar los cimientos de proyectos futuros creando un foro que enforque sobre lo siguiente:

* La creacion de una red de informacion nacional
* Identificacion de alianzas
* Identificacion de grupos de intereses especiales
* Desarrollo de un plan de accion
* Planeficacion de futuro crecimiento

This forum is happening: **Este foro tendra lugar:**

Saturday, October 10   Sabado, Octubre 10

1 - 4:30 p.m.
Reeves Municipal Center
(Office of Latino Affairs)
2000 14th St. NW
(14th & U Sts.)

For more information - Para mas informacion: NLLGA, P.O. Box 44483, Washington, D.C. 20026, tel. (202) 544-4442.

From Metro Dupont Circle (red line): exit on "Q", turn right, cross Conn. Ave., turn left on New Hampshire, about 8 blks. to "U" St., turn right , about 2 blks. to 14th St.

National Latino/a Lesbian and Gay Activists (NLLGA) flyer to convene the first gathering of gay and lesbian Latina/o activists at the 1987 March on Washington for Lesbian and Gay Rights. Courtesy of the Rare Books and Manuscripts Division at the Nettie Lee Benson Latin American Collection, University of Texas at Austin.

NEWSLETTER OF THE

AUSTIN LATINO/A LESBIAN & GAY ORGANIZATION

¡ALLGO PASA!

MARZO 1987

GENERAL MEETING
THURS., MARCH 19
7 - 8:45 P.M.
TERRAZAS LIBRARY
1105 E. FIRST

LESBIANA LATINA RETREAT

The Lesbiana Latina Retreat is a project which was proposed as a result of the Gay & Lesbian Tejanos Conference I which took place August 30-31, 1986. It was agreed that a special project bringing lesbianas latinas together for the purpose of sharing information and experiences might stimulate interest in getting involved with the Latino lesbian-gay organizations in Texas.

A committee of women from Austin, San Antonio and Houston has been organized to coordinate and plan the retreat. They have held several meetings to discuss these plans.

The statewide Lesbiana Latina retreat of 1987 has now been set for June 12-14 at Stonehaven Ranch in San Marcos, Texas. The basic purpose of this retreat is to raise the consciousness level of lesbianas latinas. A fifty person limit has been set, and child care will be provided on an "as needed" basis. Cost to participants will be minimal as the space has been donated.

The coordinating committee is working to finalize the agenda, raise the necessary funds and get everything ready. The next meeting of the coordinating meeting will be held on March 28 in San Antonio.

Anyone interested in more information or in helping us out, nos pueden llamar sin meido: en Austin, Maria 320-0293 o Clemencia 448-2346, y en San Antonio, Gloria (512) 534-3825. It looks to be the start of a great thing ... I'm scared of that.

* * * * *

"DIA DE AMOR"

Were you there? The "Dia de Amor" was an outstanding success. About 350 celebrantes danced the night away in the lovely Ramada Inn-Townlake ballroom. The lovely view added to the festive mood. Surly waitpersons did not mar the party spirit of ALLGO and their friends. The decorations were "right on time" thanks to Henry L. The music kept everyone on their feet -- and what could have been a potential problem with the turntables was quickly avoided thanks to our D.J. Mike A. and his ayudante Rick G. Our undying gratitude to those brave souls who worked the door (and I mean WORKED!) Tony, Richard, Mark, Dennis, Esther, Clem, Saul, Oscar, Nazario, Arnold, Juan, Henry, Marta and Jesse J. Special thanks for publicity to Mark for the lovely invitation design and to Domingo, Joseph, Maria, Joe G., Esteban, and Jesse R. for helping with the mail-out. A big hand to the Steering Committee of ALLGO for putting it all together. (We do apologize if we have left anyone out.) And to the rest of you, thanks for being there and adding to the festivity.

We would also like to recognize the ALLGO sponsors and contributors who made "Dia de Amor" baile possible: Nazario Saldana, Saul Gonzales, Mark Casstevens, Arnold Longoria, Bill Foster, David Nieto, Henry Castillo, Oscar Molina, Mike Alfaro, Oscar Gaytan, Virginia Raymond, Minerva Carrera, Alfred Munoz, Enrique Lopez, GMB, Henry Lopez, Glen Maxey, Paul Casarez and Jesse Carmona. Thank you, thank you, thank you.

1986 Austin Latina/o Lesbian and Gay Organization (ALLGO) newsletter describing a Latina lesbians retreat. Courtesy of the Rare Books and Manuscripts Division at the Nettie Lee Benson Latin American Collection, University of Texas at Austin.

GLHU GAY & LESBIAN HISPANIC UNIDOS
NOTICIAS

SEPTEMBER - OCTOBER '89   VOL 5 NO 11

HISPANICS CELEBRATE SEPTEMBER

Traditionally the month of September is recognized as Hispanic Culture or Hispanic Heritage month. Not only do we celebrate Mexico's Independence Day on September 16th but it is precisely during this month that eight Latin American countries gained their independence: Brazil, Costa Rica, El Salvador, Guatemala, Honduras Nicaragua, Chile, and of course Mexico.

Mexico began its long hard struggle for independence from Spain on the evening of September 15th, 1810 under the leadership of Miguel Hidalgo y Costilla, a Roman Catholic priest. On the evening of the 15th a message was secretly and urgently sent by Dona Josefa Ortiz de Dominguez to Miguel Hidalgo. The message revealed a government plot to stop a revolutionary movement that he and others were organizing. To warn his followers and to prevent intervention, Father Hidalgo rushed to his church in the little town of Dolores and rang the church bells to summon his people. He then gave the now famous cry of independence, "El Grito de Dolores": "Viva Mexico! Viva la Virgen de Guadalupe! Abajo con los gachupines!" (Long live Mexico! Long Live the Virgin of Guadalupe! Down with gachupines!, Peninsula - born Spaniards).

It is now a tradition that on the evening of September 15th the President of Mexico stands on the balcony of the National Palace and gives a new version of "El Grito de Dolores." The President shouts: "Mexicans, long live our heroes! Long live independence! Long live Mexico!" The President then rings the original bell that Father Hidalgo rang.

VIVA MEXICO! VIVA HOUSTON! VIVA GLHU!

♟ ♟ ♟ ♟ ♟ ♟

INDUCTION OF NEW OFFICERS

On Saturday, September 16th, the newly elected officers for the 1989-90 fiscal year were inducted at G.L.H.U.'s banquet which was held at Jalapeno's Restaurant. Also recognized were the outstanding members which included: Felix Garcia, Pamela Aguilar, Zeke Meza, and Arturo Cordova. Let us not forget our outstanding supporters for the year: Printex Plus, Rubio's and Patrick Media.

THANK YOU!

G.L.H.U. OFFICERS

(Pictured below L-R,Brad Veloz-President, Valentine Rodela Jr.-Vice President, Mike Rodriguez-Treasure, Not pictured L.J. Cavazos-Recording Secretary.)

Gay and Lesbian Hispanics Unidos (GLHU) newsletter featuring Brad Veloz and his partner, Mike Rodriguez, as new officers of GLHU. Courtesy of the Rare Books and Manuscripts Division at the Nettie Lee Benson Latin American Collection, University of Texas at Austin.

Dennis Medina (in gay Latino sweatshirt) marching with Gay and Lesbian Tejanos (GLT) at 1987 March on Washington for Lesbian and Gay Rights. Courtesy of Gloria A. Ramirez.

Photo showing the first of three statewide Texas Lesbiana Latina retreats, this one held in 1987 at Stonehaven Ranch, near San Marcos, Texas. The statewide organization ELLAS was born from this retreat. Courtesy of Gloria A. Ramirez.

*Gloria Ramirez and Graciela Sánchez at Laura
Esquivel's home in Los Angeles, preparing to at-
tend a Gay and Lesbian Latinos Unidos (GLLU)
dance during the International Lesbian and Gay
Association conference, November 21, 1986.
Courtesy of Gloria A. Ramirez.*

*Mike Rodriguez and Dulce Benavides at 1996 Pride Picnic sponsored
by the San Antonio Lesbian and Gay Assembly (SALGA). Courtesy
of Brad Veloz.*

Group photo at Primer Encuentro de Lesbianas Feministas de Latino-américa y el Caribe in Cuernavaca, Mexico, October 14–17, 1987. Courtesy of Gloria A. Ramirez.

Cover of Sexile/Sexilio *comic book based on the life of Adela Vázquez. Illustrations by Jaime Cortez, graphic designs by Pato Hebert. Courtesy of Jaime Cortez.*

Adela Vázquez in San Francisco, circa 1995. Courtesy of Jaime Cortez.

Cover of SalPa'Fuera, *a bimonthly publication by Coalición Puertorriqueña de Lesbianas y Homosexuales (CPLH), 1994. Courtesy of Olga Orraca Paredes.*

Cover of SIDA Ahora, *a publication of People with AIDS Coalition of New York. Courtesy of Moisés Agosto-Rosario.*

"Live long, sugar" ("Vive más, cariño") National Minority AIDS Council campaign poster featuring Moisés Agosto-Rosario and singer Patti LaBelle. The campaign promoted awareness and prevention of pneumocystis pneumonia as a serious illness for people with HIV/ AIDS. Courtesy of the National Minority AIDS Council.

LETITIA GOMEZ

No te rajes—*Don't Back Down!*
Daring to Be Out and Visible

Letitia (Leti) Gomez, a Chicana lesbian, grew up in San Antonio, Texas. Influenced by her mother's civic involvement, Gomez joined her first organization when she was a student at the University of Texas at Austin. After coming out and moving to Houston she met other Chicana/o gay activists, who were of great influence on her own activism. She participated in the Gay Chicano Caucus, organized the Latina lesbian retreats, and helped organize the first Gay and Lesbian Tejano network conference. In 1987 she moved to Washington, D.C., where she became an activist for lesbian and gay Latina/o rights, primarily with the Washington, D.C., Metropolitan Area Coalition of Latina/o Lesbians and Gay Men (ENLACE) and the National Latino/a Lesbian and Gay Organization (LLEGÓ). In her oral history–based essay, Gomez describes how her organizing efforts grew out of a need to make lesbian and gay Latinas/os visible to both the non-Latina/o gay community and the larger Latina/o community. She also discusses the early years of the founding of LLEGÓ and her role as its second executive director, as well as the challenges of sustaining a new organization.

I WAS BORN AND RAISED IN SAN ANTONIO, TEXAS, A city with a majority Mexican American population. I remember my mother telling me that in the 1950s and into the 1960s there were certain public parks that Mexican Americans and blacks could not go to. Organizations like the League of United Latin American Citizens (LULAC) worked toward breaking down the barriers that existed for Mexican Americans in public accommodation and politics by promoting civic participation. Growing up watching my mother's enthusiasm for working as a member of LULAC with other Mexican Americans for the betterment of the community, I gained an appreciation for what it was to work toward an end that was positive for the community. I saw that she was giving back to the community, making friends, and growing personally at the same time.

As an undergraduate student at the University of Texas at Austin, I became friends with a group of Chicana/o student activists from small towns like Crystal City, Texas, where in the late 1960s students walked out to protest discrimination against Mexican American students in the local schools. I was inspired by my friends' burning desire to work for justice. In early 1977, during my last semester at UT, I was recruited to help a Chicana activist who was organizing the Austin to Houston leg of the Texas Farm Workers' march to Washington. She was part of a group of activists who were trying to help organize a farmworker movement in Texas—like the United Farm Workers had been organized in California by Cesar Chavez and Dolores Huerta. The Texas Farm Workers, mostly Mexican or Mexican American, were marching for their rights to improved conditions in the fields and decent wages. When my mother learned that I was involved with the march, she remarked, "These people are radicals. You shouldn't be associated with them." I remember thinking, "Well, maybe they are 'radical,' but it's for a good cause."

During that last semester at the University of Texas, I also finally came out after falling for Diana Soliz, a coworker in the dean of students office where I worked. She invited me to join her and some of her friends to go dancing at a gay bar in San Antonio. I remember being thrilled and nervous that I finally had an opportunity to go to a gay bar with someone I knew. I will always remember the moment that I walked into the space, feeling that I was "home." And my first kiss with a woman (Diana), later that night, felt perfectly right.

After graduation I moved to Houston in June 1977 for my first professional job, working as a bilingual medical social worker at MD Anderson Cancer Center. From 1977 until 1980 I worked and just focused on having fun, going to bars, dancing, and being with Diana. However, as a Chicana lesbian, I felt very alienated in the predominantly white and male gay community of Houston. In 1981 I read an article in the local gay newspaper about a gay Chicana/o group in Houston that was hosting a movie night in a member's home. I thought, "Wow! This is great!—an opportunity to meet other gay and lesbian Chicanos." This is where I met Dennis Medina and Arturo Cordova, who were the leaders of the Gay Chicano Caucus. At one of those meetings, someone came up with the idea of a *baile*. I remember thinking, "If we organize a *baile*, we'll get a chance to dance to music that we know and enjoy, like Tejano music, and we'll get to be with other Chicanos, which would be a really great thing." We were beginning to create our own space and really identify ourselves separately from the larger white gay community.

In the early 1980s another reason for creating our own space and social events was in response to the discrimination that lesbians, Latinas/os, and blacks experienced at the bars. The most common method of discrimination was to request two (or more) forms of identification for persons of color to enter a bar, while requiring none for whites. I experienced this in Houston in 1979 and in Atlanta in 1981. I remember feeling angry about the rejection from "my own gay people," because the message conveyed was, "We don't want you."

As a member of the Gay Chicano Caucus, I could see how important it was to organize and make a space for gay and lesbian Chicanas/os. In 1981 we rented the Noche y Día ballroom in a north Houston barrio. The event was such a success that the group hosted several other *bailes* with Tejano bands. Later, these *bailes* became so popular they had to be held in large hotel ballrooms, where popular Tejano bands played for hundreds of LGBT Latinas/os. The *bailes* were an act of recovering something from our culture that had significance to us, LGBT Chicanas/os. It also became our organizing tool to enlist people in volunteering for Gay Pride events and protests and in sharing information on issues. I remember hearing Dennis Medina say, "I might not be able to get you to come out to march on an issue, but I might be able to get you to a *baile*, where I can tell you about the march, and maybe you will decide to come along."

In 1983 I decided that I no longer wanted to be around death and dying, so I left my medical social-work job and moved back to San Antonio. Soon after that, an African American woman who was senior in the agency I worked for encouraged me to get a master's degree in order to move up in any organization. I got accepted at Trinity University in urban studies, and I was lucky enough to get probably one of the last U.S. Department of Housing and Urban Development Urban Fellowship Grants for minority students to finish a master's degree program in urban studies. In spring 1987 my final semester of grad school was coming to an end. I was in the final stages of completing my master's thesis and learned that I had been accepted into the federal Presidential Management Intern Program, which would give me an opportunity to work in Washington, D.C., for two years.

On September 5–6, 1987, just before I moved to D.C., the second Gay and Lesbian Tejano network conference was held in Austin, Texas. One goal was to continue the conversation about creating a national gay and lesbian Latina/o network to support the local organizing efforts of Latinas/os that had begun at the 1986 International Lesbian and Gay People of Color Conference hosted by Gay and Lesbian Latinos Unidos (GLLU) in Los Angeles. The Gay and Lesbian Tejano network conference organizers invited Arturo Olivas and Laura Esquivel from Gay and Lesbian Latinos Unidos, who had been part of the 1986 conversation. We convened on September 7 at a breakfast meeting to discuss mobilizing gay and lesbian Latinas/os to go to the March on Washington in October and to organize a meeting of Latinas/os to occur that weekend to discuss establishing a national network. Dennis, who was in D.C. working for the Smithsonian, reported that he had found a newly formed group that was just starting to organize in Washington called ENLACE (the Washington, D.C., Metropolitan Area Coalition of Latina/o Lesbians and Gay Men). Dennis had enlisted ENLACE's help in organizing the logistics for the meeting in D.C. We wanted to get as many gay and lesbian Latinas/os as possible to Washington so we could march together, be visible, and have this meeting to discuss a national gay and lesbian Latina/o network.

In late September I moved to Washington, D.C. During the March on Washington weekend, on October 10, about seventy people representing thirteen states in the United States, Puerto Rico, and even Latin America came to our *primer encuentro*. It was very exciting. ENLACE brought food, and we spent all of that Saturday afternoon talking about what important issues the national organization would address.

The next day, October 11, I was bursting with pride to be marching with other gay and lesbian Latinas/os. Gay and lesbian Latinas/os who represented their organizations brought their organizational banners to be visible. There were ENLACE (D.C.), Gay and Lesbian Hispanics Unidos (Houston), Gay and Lesbian Latinos Unidos (Los Angeles), and others. I will always remember how very splendid I felt that beautiful, sunny fall day to be marching with my Latinas/os.

After the March on Washington, I became involved in ENLACE. ENLACE had been formed in the summer of 1987 to support SALUD, which was a community agency also newly formed to address HIV/AIDS in the D.C. Latina/o community. The founder of SALUD thought it was critical to have a gay Latina/o component for the purposes of outreach and education. Almost immediately, however, the group expanded its focus beyond the original intent of supporting SALUD's HIV/AIDS education outreach to the Latina/o community.

Through ENLACE, I began meeting and working for the first time with Latinas/os who weren't Chicanas/os, including Puerto Ricans, Salvadorans, Colombians, and Spaniards. The differences between us were not as significant as what we shared in common. We educated each other about our respective cultures, and we shared a love for music and dancing. Our organizing tool of choice was to reach lesbian and gay Latinas/os socially. ENLACE would host parties and *bailes* in hotel ballrooms, where SALUD would hand out condoms and HIV/AIDS literature. The ENLACE parties became very popular. We created a monthly newsletter, *Noticias de ENLACE*, which was sent to our mailing list numbering in the hundreds. We were intentional in our purpose to "abolish discrimination against Latina/o lesbians and gay men, develop leadership ability among Latina/o lesbians and gay men, promote our culture, and build a strong political base for our community." To accomplish these goals we set up a cultural/educational committee, a social committee, a political committee, and a membership committee. We would hold monthly business meetings and special meetings on topics of interest, such as exploring stereotypes. We collaborated with other D.C. lesbian and gay organizations on issues such as domestic partnership, sodomy law repeal, and stopping antigay violence. We hosted fundraisers for other groups that were getting started, like the Gay and Lesbian Film Festival and the Latino Civil Rights Task Force. We would invite elected officials to speak at our events, and people who were running for local office would show up to be seen. ENLACE became quite visible in both the gay community and the greater D.C. community. The reaction from the greater Latina/o community, however, was not initially positive.

In 1988 Judith Arandes, our president, was invited to a local Spanish radio show to talk about ENLACE and to respond to a statement by a local Latino DJ that in the Latina/o community, "No tenemos gays. No existe una palabra para gay en español." Over time, our straight Latina/o allies in the media came forward to invite Judith Arandes to speak more about ENLACE and provided overall positive coverage of our events in some of the Spanish weeklies.

Several of us in ENLACE decided that the organization was going to be more visible in the greater Latina/o community. During the 1990s, every July there was a Latina/o festival in D.C. that was preceded by a parade down Constitution Avenue. Every country in the Americas had a float and a marching contingent, and community organizations would also march in this parade. In 1994 ENLACE decided that we would march in this parade and carry our banner that read, "D.C.

Metropolitan Area Coalition of Latina/o Lesbians and Gays." I went to the meeting where the parade organizers accepted group applications to participate in the parade. I remember that year the lead organizer was a Brazilian man who said, "Yeah, ENLACE can be in the parade."

The day of the parade I rented a convertible and we attached our banner on the front. I remember being disappointed that there were only eight of us who showed up to march. We had invited all of our membership to come out. Our contingent was composed of three gay men, two lesbian couples with their recently adopted babies, and me and my then partner, Sabrina Sojourner. The parade organizers told us that we would be marching toward the front of the parade because the country groups were organized alphabetically, and they inserted community organizations in between alphabetically. I expected we would go in behind Ecuador.

As we were waiting around for the parade to start, the head of the Office of Latino Affairs, Carmen Ramirez, came over and said, "Leti, you just need to know there's been a lot of pressure to get you guys to not be in this parade today." I said, "Really? Is there someone I need to speak to?" And she said, "You should probably speak to the lead organizer." I went to find the organizer. He said, "No, no, no, don't worry. You're going to be in the parade, don't worry." He did acknowledge that he had been pressured to take us out of the parade. After I returned to our contingent, we waited our turn to enter the parade. When the Venezuela contingent entered, I walked over to one of the parade marshals and asked him when we would go in. He answered me, very angrily, "Go ahead and get in!" We were the last entry in the parade that day, and as a result were followed by the police contingent that closes off the parade. As we started down the parade route with our car, banner, and baby strollers, some people began yelling at us, angrily. One Latina/o couple rushed at the car yelling at us to get out. Sabrina, who was driving the car, was terrified, but the police contingent kept them away. Happily, not everybody along the parade route was antigay. We saw lots of people waving, and I remember marching by one corner where a group of gay Latino men were standing and waving at us with their hands at their sides. We finished the whole length of the parade without further incident.

It was a risk worth taking because it was important to be visible. We were part of the Latina/o community. This was our attempt at being more visible in our community, especially during a festival parade that was supposed to represent the entire Latina/o community of D.C. While I was disappointed that more of our members and supporters did not march that day, the reality was that there were still a lot of people in the closet back in the early 1990s, like the Latino gay men on the corner waving discreetly.

While I was in ENLACE we also really tried to make inroads with other gay groups, other gay organizations in D.C., and to build alliances around issues of common importance, like police harassment. In D.C. at that time you might have been harassed because you were gay, or you might have been harassed because you were Latina/o. There was some intertwining of issues that came together for us. As a result, ENLACE became the go-to point of contact for anyone wanting to include the LGBT Latina/o community in a coalition or alliance on an issue in the larger D.C. LGBT community. Leaders in the Latina/o community also reached out to us for alliances on issues that affected the Latina/o community in general. Several years after ENLACE folded in 1995, I would still get asked, "How's ENLACE doing?" because it just had become such an integral part of the community. When people thought of Latina/o lesbians and gays in D.C., they thought of ENLACE.

My involvement with ENLACE led to my involvement in other D.C. issues. On Cinco de Mayo in 1993 a Salvadoran man who had been drinking in a public park was told by a female African American police officer to stop drinking. There was an altercation between them, things got out of hand, somebody was stabbed, and a riot ensued. Metro buses were overturned, cars were burned, and businesses were vandalized and looted in the heavily Latina/o Adams Morgan and Mount Pleasant neighborhoods. The D.C. police tear-gassed the crowds, and the Latina/o community exploded in frustration over being harassed by the police. As a result, local Latina/o community activists formed the Latino Civil Rights Task Force to address issues of inequality. Community elections were held to elect the leadership of the Latino Civil Rights Task Force, and I was asked to join a slate of candidates. I was a known gay activist due to my leadership in ENLACE. This became an issue raised by the opposing slate to garner the antigay vote. My slate ended up winning, and to my surprise I was one of the highest vote getters in spite of the fact that I was the openly gay candidate. The election results told me that some in the Latina/o community had moved beyond their homophobia, and I'd like to believe that it signaled to the Latina/o LGBT community that it was okay to be visible in the greater Latina/o community.

As I mentioned before, during the weekend of the 1987 Second National March on Washington for Lesbian and Gay Rights we had our *primer encuentro*, with seventy Latina/o lesbians and gays representing thirteen states, thirty-three cities, and Puerto Rico. The group at the *encuentro* achieved consensus on five areas that the national network would focus on. One was "to build a national organization of lesbian and gay Latinas/os in order to effectively address the concerns of our communities locally, state-wide, nationally, and internationally." The second area was "to create a forum for awareness, understanding, and recognition of our lesbian and gay Latina/o identities, legal rights, relationships, and roles *en nuestra comunidad*." The third was "to formulate and sustain a national health agenda for the impact of AIDS, AIDS-related complex, HIV+, and other health concerns in our community." The fourth area was "to develop a supportive network that facilitates the sharing of information and resources nationwide." And the fifth, "to educate and sensitize ourselves as well as our Latina/o and non-Latina/o communities on sexism, racism, homophobia, discrimination, and other issues." These became our future network's goals. The group decided to create a national network of gay and lesbian Latinas/os and agreed to call it the National Latino/a Lesbian and Gay Activists (NLLGA). We agreed that we would meet in California the following February 1988 to draft bylaws and form the organization. We met at UCLA because Arturo Olivas had friends there who could provide meeting space on campus for a large gathering. Our meeting coincided with the National Coalition of Black Lesbians and Gays forum. Black gays and lesbians were also organizing nationally as a follow-up to the 1987 march.

Four ENLACE members went to L.A., all at our own expense—Dennis Medina (Chicano), Arcadio Torres (Puerto Rican), Dolores Gracia (Spanish), and me. We were hosted by Arturo Olivas and Laura Esquivel. I remember meeting in one of the university auditoriums, where there was more talk about a national organization. Hank Tavera, who had been an activist and a member of the Latina/o theater community in San Francisco, was very organized. He came to the meeting with a draft of bylaws and a proposal for how to organize nationally. Hank talked about the importance of gender parity in the leadership. He thought there should be cochairs—male and female regional representatives—on the board of directors. We decided that there would be western, eastern, south central, and north central regions. Dr. Ed Morales of San Francisco proposed that we had to change the name from National Latino/a Lesbian and Gay Activists because the acronym, NLLGA, when pronounced, meant "buttocks" in Spanish. I had personally experienced laughter at the acronym when I participated on a panel representing NLLGA. The legend of the creation of the name LLEGÓ is that Dr. Morales related to the group, "I was in the shower, and I thought of Latino Lesbian and Gay Organization—LLEGÓ, which means "arrived": "we've arrived." At that suggestion almost everyone agreed it was a great name, and so LLEGÓ was born. That weekend the group elected regional representatives. Activists elected to represent the central region included Linda Morales, Joe Luis Perez, Amparo Jimenez, and James Balcazar. The activists I recall from the western region were Arturo Olivas, Marcos Rodriguez, and Veronica Flores. Arcadio Torres, Dennis Medina, Dolores Gracia, and I were elected to be the eastern representatives to the board, and because we lived in D.C., where LLEGÓ would be located, we also became officers of the board. I was elected cochair, and Arturo Olivas was elected the other cochair. Dolores became the secretary, and Arcadio became the treasurer. Our four officers were two Chicanas/os, a Puerto Rican, and a Spaniard. That was the beginning and the founding of LLEGÓ.

The establishment of a national organization by and for Latina/o lesbians and gay men was important to many of the founders and seemed like the necessary thing to do for our communities. Many had been involved with gay organizations where they were the minority and treated as the token representatives of the Latina/o community. Many of us felt that it was important to have our own organization to address issues of importance to lesbian and gay Latinas/os, to educate our own community about these issues, and to create a national presence in the national lesbian and gay movement on these issues. Another catalyst for organizing us was AIDS. HIV/AIDS in the late 1980s was devastating for our communities. We were losing many gay Latino men and a few Latina lesbians. Not many people were talking about marriage then. We were talking about adopting children, but it was hard to do that because there was little precedent at that time. For Latinas/os, immigration was as important an issue then as it is today. I was meeting undocumented gay and lesbian Latinas/os through ENLACE, and their fears were discrimination, arrest, and deportation. The societal oppression in these areas was overwhelming, and this motivated us to speak out.

Following our meeting in Los Angeles, we did all the things that one does to establish a 501(c)(3) organization. However, it took until 1990, because we had no money. Everything we were doing was on a volunteer basis, and we were traveling around the county on our own dime to continue to meet each other and continue organizing.

We held to the concept that LLEGÓ would be a network of the various gay and lesbian Latina/o organizations in the United States and Puerto Rico and that the leadership would be egalitarian. We thought our strength would lie in the established local organizations that existed in Texas, California, New York, and Puerto Rico—groups such as Gay and Lesbian Hispanics Unidos in Houston, ELLAS in San Antonio, Gay and Lesbian Hispanics of Dallas, Gay and Lesbian Latinos Unidos in Los Angeles, Gay and Lesbian Tejano network in Texas, and Las Buenas Amigas in New York. We began hearing about new organizations forming in other cities, like Chicago, and of course in D.C. we had ENLACE. Early in our existence, we had over thirty organizations in the network, and it grew from there.

In retrospect, the extent of our organizing was admirable given our monetary and technological limitations. This was the late 1980s. We had landline telephones and fax machines to communicate and share information. We were limited to what our personal budgets would allow or what we could leverage from the organizations we worked for. E-mail did not become accessible to the general public until the late 1990s. We published a newsletter, *Noticias de LLEGÓ*, which Dennis Medina started. Our new board of directors kept meeting, and we would look for opportunities to piggyback other gay and lesbian organization meetings.

In July 1988 the Executive Committee members decided to meet in Boston during the Second National Lesbian and Gay Health Conference. Several of us went to Boston because we knew that in addition to our LLEGÓ meeting, we would have the opportunity to network with other gay and lesbian activists and Latinas/os in the Boston area, talk to them about LLEGÓ, and recruit them to help us build the network. As we attended other gay and lesbian conferences and events, we became known to the larger gay and lesbian community. There began to be interest on the part of some in national gay and lesbian leadership to include Latinas/os in certain dialogues. Where it became contentious at times was on what issues we were going to address as a national gay and lesbian community. Issues of immigration, education, and discrimination were more important to us as Latinas/os than to the larger gay and lesbian community, and so early on it was clear to us that there would be a limit to what we were going to agree to work on together.

At the Boston conference, Arturo Olivas announced that he had been approached by the executive director of the newly formed National Minority AIDS Council (NMAC) with the offer of a subcontract from NMAC's contract with the Centers for Disease Control and Prevention. Under that subcontract, LLEGÓ began developing HIV/AIDS prevention materials for gay Latinas/os. NMAC was based in Washington, D.C., and offered LLEGÓ free office space in addition to the grant.

It was an offer we felt we couldn't pass up, because it was an opportunity to begin tackling two objectives simultaneously—community organizing and HIV/AIDS in the gay and lesbian Latina/o community.

The challenge became deciding who would staff this project at NMAC. Arturo lived in California, and Dennis, Dolores, Arcadio, and I had full-time jobs. However, because we were in D.C. and I was the cochair, I took on a larger leadership role by default. It was challenging to figure out how we were going to manage our new organization without start-up money. Arturo had much more experience than I did in terms of leadership, networking, and running an organization. What I had was a burning desire to make the organization a reality and some very basic experience in the nuts and bolts of organizing, which I had learned from Dennis Medina. I was applying this experience in ENLACE, but I was still learning.

In November 1988 Arturo, Dennis, Arcadio, Dolores, and I went to Chicago to meet the men of the Association of Latino Men in Action and the women of Latina Lesbians en Nuestro Ambiente. During that trip I met Amparo Jimenez, a Mexican writer, and James Balcazar, a local stage actor. Amparo and Jim organized a reception for us to meet with other LGBT Latinas/os, members of the Hispanic AIDS Network, and the HIV/AIDS commissioner of Chicago. Amparo and James would later become LLEGÓ board members.

An even greater challenge was how to get the word out about LLEGÓ and its goals to the U.S. and Puerto Rican LGBT Latina/o communities. We were surprised, once the word did get out, that we encountered resentment on the part of locally organized Latina/o lesbians and gays. One such encounter was in New York City in 1990. Dennis, Joe Perez, and I traveled there to meet with New York Latinas/os at the lesbian and gay community center. We wanted to talk to them about LLEGÓ and had the expectation that they would be enthusiastic and supportive. How naïve we were! I remember we met in a large room with about thirty New York Latinas/os who were Dominican, Puerto Rican, and from various South American countries. Several New York LGBT groups were represented, including Las Buenas Amigas and Salsa Soul Sisters, as well as Latinas/os from AIDS Coalition to Unleash Power (ACT UP) New York. So there we were, these three Chicanas/os, talking to a group of New York Latinas/os, who questioned, "Who are you Chicanos to come here and talk to us about organizing this national Latino network, this organization?" I remember one of us said, "Well, this is bigger than just about Chicanos or Puerto Ricans; this is about lesbian and gay Latinos nationally. This is about figuring out how to move and work in the larger gay and lesbian community and how we also work within our Latino communities. And it's about being organized and visible and coming together, because we're stronger in numbers than we are by ourselves." It wasn't our intent to take anything away from them, and we really were hoping that LLEGÓ would benefit from this alliance with them. On the drive back to D.C. we discussed that it was going to be hard to keep them engaged.

In August 1989 LLEGÓ hired its first executive director, Mizzette Fuenzalida. We used funds from the NMAC subcontract. (NMAC gave a small contract to LLEGÓ and one to the National Coalition of Black Lesbians and Gays to do outreach in our respective communities.) Mizzette was of Uruguayan heritage. She had been an organizer in the lesbian and gay communities in Michigan and Ohio with her partner. We hired her to manage the grant and begin to develop support for LLEGÓ. She had a lot of enthusiasm and the skills we needed to grow our new organization. She traveled to California, Chicago, and other Latina/o urban centers, and every time she would find Latina/o lesbians and gays who were organizing in their communities.

When Mizzette went to Chicago she met Amparo Jimenez and James Balcazar and recruited them for the board. In California she met Mario Solís Marich, a young gay Latino man who was working for AIDS Project Los Angeles at the time. Mario is significant to my recounting of events because he felt really passionate about raising awareness and figuring out how to get money to help Latino gay men fight HIV/AIDS. Mizzette enlisted him in helping LLEGÓ, and he joined the board of directors in a subsequent election. After a couple of years we lost the subcontract from NMAC. Mizzette continued to work on a volunteer basis while we waited to see if any of our grant proposals were funded. Ultimately, we were unsuccessful in securing foundation grants, and we had to let her go. Losing Mizzette was a major setback to LLEGÓ because she had done great organizing in the short period of time that she was with us. Our inability to figure out how to quickly raise money to keep her on was unfortunate, but not an unusual story amongst community-based organizations. We were a group of people who were really passionate about what we were working on, but we lacked the necessary skills or the knowledge or connections to bring the resources to bear to help the organization keep the momentum going. Despite our passion about the issues, we didn't know how to successfully ask for money. Mizzette tried to coach us, teach us the nuts and bolts of fundraising, but we just weren't comfortable asking for money, and thus we were not successful. We also had no connections to funders and didn't have the skills to get started. So we resorted to what we were comfortable doing, rolling up our sleeves and working on a shoestring budget.

I remember around this time that there were a lot of doubts expressed to me about the ability for our organization to survive, because it was hard to raise money for a purely gay and lesbian cause, much less a Latina/o gay and lesbian organization and its work. There just wasn't interest among foundations in this period to support multiple LGBT organizations. LLEGÓ didn't quite fit into a niche, like only social justice or only immigration, which we tried for. Funding for HIV/AIDS prevention was the only clear source of any kind of funding because of the threat to survival in the gay community. I remember the executive director of NMAC saying something like, "Who wants to fund Latino lesbians and gays? People want to fund HIV/AIDS!"

In April 1990, after Mizzette departed, we went back to being a totally volunteer organization. We moved the office to Dennis's apartment on Eleventh Street, Northwest. This is also about the time that Joe Perez got very sick from complications from AIDS and was dying. Joe had brought a lot of enthusiasm, humor, and ideas to LLEGÓ. But probably most important was his contribution to the dialogue about the need for education on HIV/AIDS treatment for gay Latinas/os. He had spent a few months in California living with Mario Solís Marich, but had since returned to D.C. Now Joe was living with Dennis—and dying. I don't recall that we were working much on LLEGÓ during that period, because we were focused on Joe's declining health.

It was a very sad time. Joe was a young person, in his late twenties. He was an activist until near the end. I remember that he was invited to speak at an AIDS conference. Even though he was very sick and emaciated from the disease, he used the opportunity to tell the audience, "Listen, you can't give up. You've got to keep working on this issue." And it was not too much longer after that that he died. A year later Arcadio Torres also died of complications from HIV/AIDS. It was a heartbreaking and difficult time, losing friends. A whole generation of Latino gay men and some Latina lesbians died during this period.

In the midst of this HIV/AIDS crisis, our attention did get diverted somewhat. There was money available for HIV/AIDS education in the gay community. Around 1992 to 1993 Mario aligned himself with an Asian gay man, an African American gay man, and a Native American gay man, and they became the Campaign for Fairness. They lobbied Congress and federal agencies like the Centers for Disease Control and Prevention (CDC) and the Substance Abuse and Mental Health Services Administration for resources to be designated for gay men of color. Mario worked for obtaining resources that LLEGÓ could use to work on HIV/AIDS prevention in the gay and lesbian Latina/o community. The Campaign for Fairness was successful in getting some funds. It was as a result of Mario's work that LLEGÓ got the opportunity to apply for a grant from the CDC to work on HIV/AIDS prevention in the Latina/o gay community. Mario had access to a grant writer in L.A. who drafted the grant proposal for the board to review. The proposal did not mention anything about lesbians and HIV. On a conference call to discuss the proposal, Nena Trujillo, a board member, said, "Wait a minute. We're a Latino lesbian and gay organization, you have to mention lesbians." Now granted, lesbians weren't dying in the numbers that gay men were, but there were some. There was heated discussion on this point. Nena Trujillo and I argued, "We're either including lesbians or we're not submitting a proposal, because lesbians have to be included. That's who we are." In the end the board agreed to include lesbians in the grant proposal. I remember Mario telling us afterward that the grant writer told him we wouldn't be successful because we had included lesbians.

By 1993 Dennis had moved back to Texas, and the board decided that we would move the LLEGÓ office to my house, a small row house in Southeast D.C. where I lived with my partner. We lived on the third floor, and we made the second floor the LLEGÓ office. We also housed the D.C. office of the National Task Force on AIDS Prevention (NTFAP). The project officer from the CDC came to the "office" for a site visit. Mario and Joey Pons, another board member, and I met with her and walked her through our plans, talking to her about what we were already doing and what we would do if we were successful in receiving a grant. Later that year LLEGÓ was awarded a multiyear CDC grant for HIV/AIDS prevention. In order to receive the grant, we had to have an executive director, somebody in charge. I agreed to be the executive director because I was in D.C., but I had my full-time job. So I worked on LLEGÓ after my day job, after hours. Martin Ornelas, who was working for NTFAP, became LLEGÓ's project manager for the CDC grant.

Upon receipt of the grant, I decided to rent an office space a block away from where I was living at the time. We set up the office, hired a staff, and laid out the framework for promoting HIV/AIDS prevention education through organizing and tapping all the gay and lesbian Latina/o organizations that were in our network. Our plan was to reach gay and lesbian Latinas/os in communities throughout the United States and Puerto Rico by granting money out of the CDC grant to those organizations so that they could do the education and outreach locally. We were focused on delivering what needed to be delivered for the goals of the grant, but we were using the tool that we were familiar with: organizing.

LLEGÓ ultimately gave grants to several LGBT Latina/o organizations, such as the Austin Latina/o Lesbian and Gay Organization (ALLGO), Gay and Lesbian Hispanics Unidos (GLHU) in Houston, and the Gay and Lesbian Latino AIDS Education Initiative (GALAEI) in Philadelphia. By 1994, in D.C., ENLACE had folded, but there was a new LGBT Latina/o organization called Gente Latina de Ambiente (GELAAM), to which we gave a grant. What was important about LLEGÓ's method was that we accomplished the promotion of HIV/AIDS education in the LGBT Latina/o community at the same time that we were promoting visibility of LGBT Latinas/os and facilitating local organizing in the community. LLEGÓ was a CDC grant recipient until 2004.

I was the executive director of LLEGÓ from 1993 to December of 1995. In 1994 I began working part-time at my federal government job so that I could devote more time to LLEGÓ. I had initially intended to quit my federal government job entirely, but my boss (I was out at work) didn't want to lose me, so he suggested that I continue working for the government part-time and devote part-time to LLEGÓ.

In 1995 LLEGÓ hosted its Tercer Encuentro (our annual conference) in D.C. (The Primer Encuentro was held in Houston in 1992, and the Segundo Encuentro was held in San Jose, California, in 1993.) The Tercer Encuentro is memorable to me for a couple of reasons, one really good memory and one not so good. That year we planned to have a panel of Latina/o parents speak about their gay and lesbian children. It was important for us to open the dialogue and show that there were Latina/o parents who supported their gay and lesbian kids and to address the issue of how important *familia* is to LGBT Latinas/os. I asked my mother to come to Washington, D.C., to speak about having a lesbian daughter. My mother, Angelina Gomez, was always proud of me, but the day she spoke to the conference, I was proud of her. It was really wonderful for me to see many people go up to her afterward, some of them crying as they told her that they wished their parents felt the same way or that they just appreciated her being there in support of her daughter. Especially now that my mother is gone, I will always remember that day.

The sad thing about that Encuentro was that we had a board election that ultimately led to my involuntary departure from LLEGÓ. Prior to that board meeting, I announced that I planned to step down as the executive director so that I could return to my full-time federal civil-service job. The board cochair positions were up for election. The incumbent cochairs were Puerto Rican and were being challenged by two Chicanos from the western region. The Chicanos told me that they had a plan to raise nongovernment funds to stabilize the organization, and they wanted me to stay. In retrospect I should have just gone with my gut and left, but I didn't. We canceled the search for my successor, and I quit my government job to work full-time. Within months it all fell apart.

In October of 1995 our bookkeeper reported to me that we had overspent the CDC grant allotment ahead of schedule by $50,000, or 10 percent of the grant. I immediately called our outside certified public accountant (CPA), who advised me not to tell the CDC until we figured out how to address the deficiency. I was very concerned, so I faxed a memo to the board chairs telling them what I had discovered and what the CPA had advised. It didn't seem right to me, but I agreed to follow the CPA's advice. I later found out that as soon as I left the office that evening, the program director asked my administrative assistant to fax the memo to other board members, and from there it made its way outside of the organization. The board took a "no-confidence" vote in late December, and I was fired immediately.

In retrospect, I learned something from this experience—about myself and my leadership. I didn't have enough knowledge and skills to have said to myself, "You know there's a way to get around this issue, you just need to ask for help." I should have gone with my instincts and spoken to our CDC project officer and told her, "We've screwed this up, we need to fix it." Instead of looking for help, I withdrew. It was also unfair to the staff to ask them not to tell the visiting project officer what was going on. The board cochairs didn't know how to help me, and they were getting a lot of pressure from other board members to fire me. One day the program director and the staff asked to meet with me, and they asked me to quit. I told them that only the board could ask for my resignation. It was really an awful time for me, because I felt like the Latinas/os whom I'd been working with for "our community" had turned against me and were not supporting me or my leadership.

The months that followed were a terrible period for me. The story of my firing appeared in the local gay paper, the *Washington Blade*. Aside from the humiliation, I was most devastated by the fact that I had devoted the previous nine years to working on Latina/o lesbian and gay organizing and to creating this organization—only to come to this unceremonious end. LLEGÓ had been very important to me. Losing LLEGÓ was a huge loss in my life, as if someone dear to me had died. Another deeply disturbing aspect of what happened was that despite the close friendships and other relationships that I had built in the Latina/o lesbian and gay community, those friends and acquaintances, for the most part, did not support me or offer me assistance. Hank Tavera, the board cochair, to his credit, was the only one who said, "We need to support her," and a female board member asked, "How can we help her?" As I learned later, they were alone in this opinion.

After being dismissed from LLEGÓ I was devastated and went into a deep depression. It felt awful to have worked so hard, to have given so much personally and financially to the cause, to then just be sent packing in a flash. Another thing that especially hurt at the time was that it was my own people, *mi gente*, who told me to leave. That was especially hard to fathom, and I think that episode pretty much burned me out on ever putting that much of my personal energy into any community organizing for a long period of time.

I used to say that LLEGÓ was the "other woman" in my life. I spent so much time trying to keep LLEGÓ going, helping to enlist people to keep it moving forward, that I neglected my relationships with my partners. Fortunately, there was life for me after LLEGÓ. Luckily, when the people at my old job in the federal government found out I was available, they were eager to have me back. I have been very successful and am one of the top Latinas in my agency. I was sought out to sit on other LGBT organizations' boards of directors, such as the National Lesbian and Gay Health Association.

I have never again felt the kind of energy and passion that I had for ENLACE and LLEGÓ. But I will always be glad that I did this work. I'm proud of the work I did and really happy that I made some very good long-lasting friendships out of this experience. I learned a lot about myself, about my leadership, the importance of community organizing, and the value that it has for movements. I learned that I need to ask for help; I realized later that many of my peers at other LGBT organizations would have been glad to help me figure out how to address the problem with the CDC, but I was too embarrassed to ask. I would like people not to be at all discouraged by my story. It's really important to follow your passion, to surround yourself with people who are going to be supportive, and to ask for help when you need it.

I think the greatest impact of LLEGÓ was that it encouraged members of the Latina/o lesbian and gay community to be visible to each other and to our respective communities—out and proud of being a gay or lesbian Latina/o. Similarly, it was critical to be out in the larger Latina/o community in order to begin making the linkages for ourselves on issues of mutual concern, such as immigration, economic fairness, and access to health care. Beginning with our work, and through the work of other Latina/o activists that continues to the present, the mainstream Latina/o organizations have become great allies to the LGBT community. It was also important to be visible in the larger gay and lesbian community in order to gain the acknowledgement and recognition that there was this community of Latina/o gay and lesbian people in the United States and Puerto Rico and to begin to gain the support of the mainstream LGBT organizations for issues of mutual concern: equality rights, immigration, and access to health care.

I would like to think that the legacy of the movement—out of all our efforts, out of all our organizing, and all of our striving to be visible—is that it provided us the freedom to be all that we are, so none of us have to leave anything at the door. Latina lesbian, mother, daughter, whatever makes up your identity, every part of you comes through the door.

ORAL HISTORY INTERVIEW CONDUCTED BY URIEL QUESADA IN SAN ANTONIO, TEXAS, ON JUNE 30, 2011. CHAPTER WRITTEN BY LETITIA GOMEZ.

MONA NORIEGA

Creating Spaces to Break the Circle of Silence and Denial

Mona Noriega was born and raised in Chicago. She engaged for the first time with the feminist movement at Chicago's Northeastern Illinois University in the 1970s. She then became involved with Latina Lesbians en Nuestro Ambiente (LLENA), and in 1993 helped open the Midwest office of Lambda Legal. In 1995 she cofounded Amigas Latinas, an organization committed to the empowerment and education of Latina lesbian, bisexual, and questioning women in the Chicago area. In 1999 Noriega was founding cochair and senior bid consultant responsible for bringing the 2006 Gay Games to Chicago. In 2011 Mayor Rahm Emmanuel appointed Noriega as chair and commissioner of the Chicago Commission on Human Relations. She continues to serve in that position and as a member of the LGBTQ Immigrant Rights Coalition and the Chicago Task Force on LGBT Aging. In this oral history–based essay Noriega addresses the importance of providing a safe space to talk about issues; in particular, she discusses the pláticas, *gatherings where members of Amigas Latinas could socialize and attend discussions on different topics. She also honors the influence and wisdom of her Mexican* abuela *and addresses the challenges of being a Latina lesbian and a mother of two in a society where sexual differences are perceived as either a failure or a betrayal of one's own culture.*

I WAS RAISED NOT TOO FAR FROM WHERE I CURrently live, Logan Square, in the city of Chicago—I don't know when we moved from Twenty-Sixth Street, which is a predominantly Mexican neighborhood, to what is now Wrigleyville, on the North Side, but I do know that we were one of the first Latina/o families to move there in the early 1960s. My parents purchased a two-flat, which was probably a big move for them. It was a very working-class neighborhood and had a lot of diversity. In that context I didn't perceive myself as being biracial—Mexican and Irish—or different, because everybody had family members who didn't speak English, or they had strong ethnic identities themselves.

I thought it was normal that all the children struggled with or knew some other language. I had friends whose parents were Mexican, Irish, Greek, German, or from the Appalachians, and now I realize I even had friends whose parents had escaped communist countries. When I was growing up in what is now Wrigleyville there were communities of Native Americans and Gypsies, all of whom I don't see much of anymore, but all of it made me think that my mixed-race family was not that different.

It's hard for me to talk about my childhood, because I didn't really have much of one. I went to three different grammar schools and dropped out of three different high schools. My father was an alcoholic, and my parents were divorced, and so there was a lot of trauma and drama. I started running away when I was twelve, and I got pregnant when I was fifteen. Then I hired a lawyer and petitioned the state to let me become emancipated at age fifteen so I could get married. I was divorced by the time I was twenty, and by then I had two children; so like I said, I've never felt like I had a childhood to speak of.

I did not like being a high-school dropout, and I really wanted to go to school, so I got my GED, and after I divorced I went to Northeastern Illinois University in Chicago. It was at Northeastern that I began to get an idea of what feminism was. It was the late 1970s, and I am so sure I attended the last consciousness-raising group that existed and through that came to recognize the durability of the women in my life. And rather than thinking of life as something to respond to or suffer through, I realized that life was something I could direct and that I even had affirmative examples of how to do that, like my *abuelita*. I lived with her from when I was six months old to when I had to start going to school. My time in her household was a stable and loving part of my life, but it also caused conflict, because I only knew Spanish, and when I went home to my parents' house on the weekends I couldn't communicate. On top of the drama in my parents' home, their response to the issue of language was to forbid me to speak Spanish. Compared to today, where bilingualism is valued, speaking Spanish at the time when my father was growing up here in Chicago could be met with violence. And so although there was such a sense of pride in being Mexican, some immigrants felt that their children would be better served if they didn't speak Spanish. But aside from all the trauma, I look back now and realize I was fortunate enough to have been loved and raised by an incredible woman. My *abuelita* had no formal education, didn't know how to read or write, but was very giving, directed, forceful, and nurturing; and she was a survivor—surviving in this country as a widow, without knowing the language, and yet she owned a home, could put food on the table, and could provide moral guidance. She was my first experience of women living together and being able to provide and be happy.

When I came to feminism, it was in an academic environment, at a time when there were even fewer—when compared to now—Latinas/os in higher education. I wanted to be educated, but being in an academic environment was so different from my experience of being Latina, a teenage mom, and on welfare. I felt my experiences were so different, but I really loved the ideals of what feminism stood for. From that I gravitated to friendships with some of my professors and women at the women's center on campus who were lesbians. In some ways I was naïve, as many of us were in our twenties. Because I didn't have a chance to go to high school, and I was so focused on providing a better life for my children while at the same time working and trying to figure out this thing called college, I wasn't even thinking about what gay was. I had seen poverty and hardship in my life and was determined that was not going to be our story. I didn't have money or preparation to be in college, and I was a single mom, but my perseverance compensated. It took me six years to get my undergraduate degree at Northeastern. I waitressed, delivered pizzas at night, and unloaded trucks on the third shift, and then at some point I realized that my little income was being deducted from my school grants, and so I was being penalized because I was working, so I just went straight on welfare to finish up the degree.

I was different from the women on campus but very much the same in terms of how we were trying to take control of our own lives. I was fortunate to take Sarah Hoagland's first feminism and philosophy class at Northeastern. She was an out lesbian, and her analysis just blew my mind. School, and her class in particular, opened me up to new ideas and a deeper understanding of what the world was about in terms of race, class, and gender. It was almost overwhelming to think of who I could be in this newly defined world. Balancing being a mother, going to school, and exploring all these new ideas was challenging. Grand ideas of changing the world are fun. However, making sure you have food on the table and the kids have done their homework, as you think of changing the world, certainly grounds you.

Most other students and certainly most of the lesbians I knew did not have children, but when I started to meet other women who were Latina and lesbian, having young children was not viewed as an anomaly. I didn't have to defend or explain what was different about me. And it was refreshing, because I wasn't faced with resolving that conflict of what at the time felt like contradictory identities: how could I be a feminist, a lesbian, and Latina?

Now all of that has changed, and I can't tell you how much pleasure it gives me to see young people exploring their queer identities at such young ages, and in a cultural context, but at the time it was such a struggle for me. Without any firm answers here in Chicago, I decided to go to Mexico. The first time, I went to Mexico with my son; the second time, I took my daughter and stayed for about a month, and my goal was to find lesbians, to see if there really were Mexican lesbians. Oh, my god! Yes, there were definitely lesbians in Mexico. I had a wonderful time, but more importantly it gave me some balance and perspective so I could come back to where I was born, here in Chicago in the United States. For those of us who were born here, the way we form our Latina/o identities is based on our parents and grandparents and what their ideas are from their countries of origin and the time frame of when they left. So although right now in other Latin American countries they are adopting gay ideals, that's not a topic that my *abuelita* would have discussed, because that was not within their realm when they left, nor was it acceptable here in the United States. (Some would argue that it is still not acceptable, but I would say it is so much better now.) And then layer on top of that all that they wanted for their children: to succeed, to be accepted, or at least to not be singled out in a negative way. It is strange that many people come to this country for freedom, whether economic, religious, or political, but being gay, rather than viewed as a freedom to be exercised, is somehow perceived as some familial failing or an indication that you have become too American. But the opportunity to be an American is the reason many of our parents came here, so that their children could have the opportunity to have the comforts they didn't have or, at a minimum, to not have to experience hunger. The idea was that you can have a job, you can support your family, and you can have a bed. Basic stuff such as a bed provides what we consider a basic comfort.

My *abuelita* would always say to me, "You are an American, you are an American, you are an American . . ." and compared to her, I definitely was an American. She described coming here as a slave child, taking care of other people's children, sleeping on the floor while the other children slept in beds. She came here not knowing anything, yet in her home I slept in a bed. I know that being able to provide a bed might seem small, but I so understand the power of being able to provide for your children something you never had. It's a mixed bag, so going to Mexico was for me a way to understand her, to understand that being a lesbian wasn't because I was biracial, it was because it is a normal part of the everyday world, and it is not limited to just white people.

So after I graduated in 1981 with a double major in criminal justice and human services, a friend of mine let me know of someone who was hiring for a production project. The woman interviewed me in her home on Easter Sunday. I told her my degree was in crisis management. She said, "OK, great, we need you." It was the era of typesetting, and I was coordinating the production of film catalogs in a secondary market. My job was to get all the copyrights and permissions from the film companies, coordinate the work of the artists and writers, and handle all the million and one details of production and deadlines—I loved it. Once the project was over, they permanently hired me, so I was a project manager in the advertising department, headed by a lesbian, working with other bi and gay people in an artistic environment. From that experience I started doing chapbooks for female poets of color, because I now had access to and knowledge of the production process and knew how to solicit volunteers, my coworkers and vendors, to donate their design, layout, typesetting, and print services. A chapbook was nothing more than the work of a writer, printed and distributed to friends and family—it was a medium of independent expression in the 1980s. But to be self-published required typesetting, layout, printing, and distribution, a production process that was expensive and posed major obstacles. A chapbook might not sound so important in today's age of immediate information and communication, but at the time it was a struggle to get a woman's voice heard, and getting your work published was even more difficult, and even more so for women of color.

From this experience I learned the significance and importance of my own actions, and I also began to have a little more confidence and to understand that my response to inequity in the world, although it might be different from someone else's, was my way to respond and that it was good for me. I was better able to integrate who I was and how I responded to what I saw around me. And at that time I was definitely affected by witnessing situations where lesbian women either had their kids taken away or were struggling with the concept of motherhood. I knew a few women who had suffered the trauma of having their own parents argue on behalf of a homophobic father to take their children away because they didn't want their grandchildren exposed to lesbianism, and there wasn't a way, there wasn't a mechanism, by which to address that concept—the fear that lesbianism could hurt our children. Where could you go when you couldn't even be out for fear of losing your job or fear of losing your family? So I started organizing picnics, and that evolved into celebrating on Mother's Day. It was so cool because when the children would come together at the house they could talk. They would go into a room, close the door, and with privacy start talking to each other. At a time when silence or denial was the means by which to deal with being gay, creating a space for our families to talk was powerful.

Sometimes I would fill the house full of lesbians and lesbian couples, and the purpose for me was to create a family environment. When you go to family gatherings, if you have a family, you have lots of different people, lots of different age groups, and you get to bond across age or generational differences, and who you are within the family context is reaffirmed—but many of us didn't have that, so we had to create our own. It gave us moms the opportunity to talk to each other, and you could talk about the difficulties of having vindictive fathers doing hateful things or process the difficulty your children were having because you were a lesbian. It also gave women who were partnered with mothers the opportunity to talk, as they had their own issues that we might now recognize as typical issues of blended families, such as how do you discipline children who are not your own? How do you demand respect or create a loving household when your family or the school belittles you? How do you create an affirming environment? You love this woman, but you have conflict with her kids, or you really are invested, and you want to be a good parent to these kids. This struggle seems so outdated now, as this was before the time when we could even dream of having our own families or even of legally adopting.

In the 1970s and 1980s there was no community center as we see it today. Our community center was our home and the bars, but I wanted more, and so I became involved with Latina Lesbians en Nuestro Ambiente (LLENA), although I was pretty much on the periphery of it. Being in a space full of Latina lesbians was both a breath of fresh air and exhilarating. I didn't have to negotiate difference, and who I was was okay. My humor was not off-key. I felt more appreciated, more recognized, so maybe more full; I was more whole. At our parties and our meetings we would have great discussions. They were often fiery and chaotic and then would spill over into after-meeting drinks in a bar.

There was such an urgency to be heard and to be understood, but the problem with talking without ground rules is you begin to bump up against different realities, and so language, immigration status, classism, sleeping together, different things would come up. But I so enjoyed that time because prior to that I hadn't known any Latina academics, or even community leaders, and then on top of it, that they were lesbians only served to further enhance the value of the conversations and the whole experience to me. It was like we were trying to create an ideology that was feminist and Latina, infused with academics, with women from different parts of Latin America, and with women who would have never considered themselves academics or feminists. You had all these different perspectives coming together at once, and that's what made it so beautiful.

It was also in LLENA that we organized cultural activities, poetry readings, and performance art. And toward the end we became adept at organizing the party and raising the money, but I began to have a problem with it when we were raising money without any program goals, so I began to fall away from it. LLENA lasted just a couple of years, but did a lot of work in those couple of years, maybe 1989 to 1992. In that short period of time it created a lot of conversation.

It was such a positive experience for me as it really expanded who I could be in the world as a Latina lesbian. When you come from a working class background, and your immediate struggles are to be a good mom and get your GED, that is overwhelming enough that you don't even know that you can be so much more. LLENA modeled for me a bunch of different ways to be Latina and lesbian. LLENA also provided a means for me to grow professionally, so that I could then apply my newly recognized skills to the job market. On behalf of LLENA I was part of the International Women's Day Dance Collaborative, and from that I recognized that if I could organize the details of the event and solicit so much in terms of donations and support that I could perhaps do sales. Once my daughter went to college, I quit my stable job and I tried a sales job. My second day on the job, I was going out with the boss and the other sales guys. I got in the owner's car—they were taking me out for lunch—and bam, reality hit! They started telling jokes, "Hey what did you do this weekend? I shot cans. What kinda cans? Black-CANS, Mexi-CANS, Puerto Ri-CANS."

Second day on my job, and I was thinking, "So this is normal?" I was thinking I was perceived to be white, but right now I was so scared! And then I was thinking of my daughter—my daughter was in college now, and she was flipping out because I had just quit my stable job, so I was going to have to make this job work. It all flashed in my head that I had to make it work. So even though that job didn't work, I decided to try my hand at selling in the gay community and began selling ad space for one of Chicago's LGBT newspapers, *Outlines*, now known as *Windy City Times*.

I loved talking to people, and I felt like I had professional training and a model of the sales cycle, and that was going to be my contribution to supporting a needed institution in the LGBT community. The challenge was to sell the LGBT community on the importance of community and to sell business on the market viability of the community. Back then in the 1990s advertising to the gay community was not the known entity it is now, and before I could close a sale I would often have to have a discussion, a basic Gay 101, to address whatever issues the buyer might be having about what being gay was all about.

I was at *Outlines* for a few years before an advertisement came in for help to open a regional office for the national organization of Lambda Legal in Chicago. In 1993 I applied and got the job. My first task was to organize a contingent to march in the Gay Pride Parade that very weekend. That was a pretty immediate challenge in which I recruited my family, but thereafter it was about setting up systems and establishing relationships in the midwestern states. Lambda was always very well received in Chicago and in the Midwest at large for being cognizant of the many different communities that make up the LGBT community, and because the people at Lambda honestly worked to serve the diversity of the community. Recognizing the community to be many communities in one when first opening the midwestern office, and not as an afterthought, meant we could focus on doing the work. It was while I was at Lambda that I began to recognize that I had become a professional lesbian.

I was able to do some Lambda programming in Spanish because I was a part of Amigas Latinas. My partner, Evette, was one of the organizers of Womyn of All Colors and Cultures Together (WACT), and out of that she was able to get a group of Latinas together in 1995. I became part of Amigas Latinas and was able to integrate Amigas outreach with Lambda outreach.

Amigas was pretty organized as a group, especially in comparison to my experience with LLENA. We had regularly scheduled *pláticas* that were based on the WACT model of coming together in private homes and sharing food—Evette's pitch line was, "A girl's gotta eat." But the difference was that with WACT there was no organized discussion part, while with Amigas there was a preselected topic. We had mailing lists, palm cards, and flyers, and outreach was about calling people, going to the bars and personally inviting people—there was no Internet and no texting. In fact Evette carried a pager that rotated with the leadership to take crisis calls. And although it is true that there is a huge Mexican and Puerto Rican population in Chicago, we would get women from all over Latin America. I can't even tell you how many different countries would be represented at every single meeting, every event. We discussed it all in our *pláticas*: what it's like to be Latina and lesbian, bisexuality, dating, abuse, how do you come out to your family, how do you come out at work, how out is out, drugs and drinking issues, religious conflicts, safe sex, S&M. The topics would come out of what people needed to talk about, and the women really wanted to talk. First, women would eat, and if you didn't get to announcing when it was time to sit and talk, the women would ask, "Is it time yet? Are we going to sit down to talk?" You would be surprised, or maybe we were surprised, by how well attended our *pláticas* were—twenty, thirty, forty women, everybody came, and everyone had a good time. I attribute the success of the *pláticas* to the ground rules that Evette set. She was really good about that.

One of the reasons why I think I was attracted to her was because she worked with teenage moms, and so she was always facilitating their crises and chaos, but she had a total respect for teenage moms, which is of course what I had been. She had no judgment or the fifty million questions that I grew tired of answering. Best of all she was Latina and, like me, was born in Chicago, and so she knew what it was like to have a Latina/o identity without the language. In terms of Amigas, she could facilitate in a really affirmative way so as to allow everyone a voice and to create safety when sharing intimate or emotional moments. She was able to create this safe space to discuss these very difficult topics. I describe them as difficult topics, but women wanted to have challenging and intelligent conversations in this safe environment. You walked away feeling like you better understood who you were and who your sisters were, so different and so much the same. In those ways I felt like we were creating community, and that's why Amigas Latinas still exists, because we built a base. We were offered opportunities to know and love each other across our differences, and that created the bonds that to this day exist. I loved it, as I was in an environment that was larger than me, and every Latina was different and yet she was me.

When I was part of the leadership, it was all about our kids, and of course I got together with the moms. We had holiday celebrations with piñatas, clowns to entertain, crafts, and food. This gave other women who may or may not have had their children with them—or they would bring their nieces and nephews, grandchildren, or whomever—an opportunity to come and have a great time without having to organize it. It was also an opportunity for women who were struggling with their identities—because they had internalized all the negative messages of what it meant to be a lesbian—to witness and participate in an environment where it was all about the kids, and we were all lesbians, we were all mothers and grandmas and aunts, we were everything.

We did different kinds of activities and addressed a variety of issues, all of it in affirmative ways. That's why Amigas played such an important role in the community, plus it was fun. Initially, we would pass the hat for copying the flyers and postage, but then we started to get more serious about how to address the issues the membership was dealing with, and so we decided to begin focusing on structure and on fund-raising. One opportunity that came along, which was a challenge too, was when the National Latino/a Lesbian and Gay Organization (LLEGÓ) conference came to Chicago in 1998. At that time Amigas was only three years old, and we really didn't have a structure or the knowledge of how to put on a conference or help coordinate it. But we worked with the Association of Latino Men for Action (ALMA) and LLEGÓ staff and board and other volunteers from around the country. It was really hard trying to be this host committee and coordinate workshops and events and raise money and get people to agree on things. But we did it, and despite the challenges one of the good things that came out of the conference was that Amigas' name was out there in an official way—we even did a workshop about LLENA and Amigas and the potential of Latina lesbian organizing in the future—and other women got involved with Amigas. As a result we decided to form our first steering committee.

We were on the path to take this new and exciting next step, and then one of our founding members who was helping lead the charge suddenly died. It was a very emotional time for those of us on the steering committee, and we could have just stopped right there, the loss was so heavy, but we took our grief and created a scholarship fund in her name as a way of honoring her love of teaching. For about seven years, from 1999 to 2006, we did the Aixa Diaz Latina Youth Scholarship Fund. We raised thousands of dollars, and every year we would give away two to four scholarships to youth who had advocated for change, promoted tolerance and acceptance in their high schools, and were on their way to college.

So the evolution of Amigas went from passing the hat to hosting a LLEGÓ-sponsored conference and forming a steering committee. When Aixa died it was very traumatic, but her death marked a real turning point for Amigas, and in the next couple of years we decided to become an official 501(c)(3) organization, to raise money and develop programs to address the growing needs of our people, and to celebrate who we were as a community.

After twelve years of operating Amigas out of our house, and after serving on the first board, I rotated off the board in 2007. The relationship I had with Evette was one of constant and never-ending work. The Amigas work was really good work, and Lambda was good work as well, and being able to do both at the same time helped one to inform the other, for me. But every single weekend was Amigas and Lambda— we would never have a day off. We were always negotiating our obligations, and sometimes we would be just bone tired, and so rotating off the leadership was one way for me to open up the space for new people and allow me to rejuvenate. Evette next stepped down from the board about three years later. We continue to support Amigas' mission and work—without having to do all the heavy lifting. In 2011 Evette and I were civil unioned, and in 2012 we celebrated sixteen years of being together. It has been great to be able to pass the torch to new leaders who could bring new energy and ideas.

Looking back now, I feel those years were transformative for me and for the community. It shaped how I walked through the world, how I raised my children, and prepared me for the challenges I take on today. I hope that my legacy is that of helping to create the infrastructure upon which new organizations can be built, identifying Latina/o issues within the context of our civil rights issues, and promoting the value of having room to include new ideas. It is necessary to recognize the importance of an individual's growth and healthy work/life balance so that the organizing work does not fall on just one person or is not guided by a single or unchanging perspective—founder's syndrome. You want organizations to be fluid, responsive to new issues, infused with new ideas, and you want to create opportunities for succession, for youth to build their leadership skills and experience. As we pass the torch we need to provide support for the youth who are doing their own organizing work on their own terms. My philosophy is to let them define the problem and the solutions, and not only will they learn from their successes and failures, but I and others who are older will have something to learn as well. One of the biggest compliments is to see something that you had a hand in creating continue to exist and do good work beyond your departure. I feel that way toward both Latinas Amigas and the Midwest office of Lambda Legal.

ORAL HISTORY INTERVIEW CONDUCTED BY LETITIA GOMEZ IN CHICAGO, ILLINOIS, ON JUNE 19, 2012. CHAPTER WRITTEN BY LETITIA GOMEZ.

GLORIA A. RAMIREZ

The Queer Roots of the Esperanza Peace and Justice Center in San Antonio, Texas

Gloria Ramirez has been a force behind San Antonio's Esperanza Peace and Justice Center since it first opened its doors in 1987. Born and raised in the Austin area, Ramirez attended the University of Texas at Austin, where she got degrees in history and education. Since her early childhood Ramirez suffered racism and discrimination, and these experiences would be fundamental to her later career as an activist. For Ramirez, activism is a comprehensive effort of justice and commitment. As the title of her essay states, the roots of her activism are queer, in a broad sense of the word; queer activism means being part of the world, where injustices and abuse take several forms. Gloria Ramirez's account of the Esperanza Center's history is as much a telling of her relationship with Esperanza leader Graciela Sánchez as it is a powerful portrait of over two decades of the social and political life of southwest Texas.

GROWING UP IN A CHICANA/O BARRIO IN AUSTIN, Texas, in the 1950s, I sailed through elementary school, doing well in school and gaining respect from the girl gangs that threatened everyone else. Even then I had an acute awareness of the racial dynamics that infused the schools. When I began first grade I did not speak English, but I immediately caught on with a facility for language and writing that was to be my hallmark. I remember some of the handful of white kids who went to the predominantly Chicana/o schools I attended on the East Side of Austin—their impact on me was such that I wanted to be white too. I felt ashamed of my dark skin and indigenous looks.

I was the second child of six and the oldest girl in my family. I bore the responsibility of caring for younger siblings, but I was not required to take on any other traditional female roles as long as I was engrossed in reading or playing outside in the trees or creeks behind our home.

Both of my parents, native to Central Texas, had dropped out of school in the third grade to help their parents, who were either illiterate or did not speak English. My father had attended the segregated Navarro Mexican School in Lockhart, and my mother had attended Zavala Elementary in Austin. My mother's father suffered an accident while driving a wagon and died when she was ten years old. My father, the oldest of nine children, bore the task of helping his father in the fields. Throughout their lives my parents honored their deep roots in Central Texas, frequently returning to Lockhart to reminisce about their youth and eat barbecue. They never forgot their ties to Mexico, even though our family history there was tenuous at best. They had both come from campesino stock, working the fields in their youth. Their English was minimal, which required me to translate for them from a young age as they dealt with doctors, nurses, postal workers, and a variety of other people coming by our modest two-bedroom home on Castro Street. I never felt quite up to task of making adult decisions, but I managed to fool everyone into believing I was very mature.

In 1962 we moved to south Austin, where most of the kids in the junior high I attended were white, middle-class kids. It was a complete cultural shock. There, I experienced severe racism and discrimination by both teachers and students. My seventh-grade English teacher made me stand in front of the class saying words that began with "ch" while the class raucously laughed at my inability to pronounce the words correctly. On my way home from school, kids often chased me or threw rocks at me, calling me "nigger." I also suffered for my indigenous looks, with kids yelling out war whoops when they saw me or making fun of me in other ways. My early teen years were miserable, but I suffered these indignations quietly, because I did not want my parents to suffer also. My youngest sister was born during this time, and things became harder for my parents as well. My older brother was not allowed on the football team, and my quiet, shy father had to go and speak to the coach to allow him in. I can't imagine how he felt speaking up to a white man in his broken English, but he did it. My parents had always taught us to respect authority and do as the "mayordomo" asked. My brother made the football team and was eventually cited as an all-city defensive guard.

I made it through junior high vowing (in anger) to show everyone that I, indeed, was as good as everyone else. I took speech classes for three years and made my way in high-school band from last chair to third chair out of thirty-six clarinets. My band director confided that if I had had a better-quality clarinet I could have challenged the first chair. Having a vague recollection of the radio mentioning the University of Texas when I was growing up, I had decided that was where I would go after graduating from high school, and so I did. My brother joined the marines and went to Vietnam. My younger siblings all had a difficult time getting through school, with some graduating and others not. I was the only one to go to college.

At the University of Texas at Austin, I tried out for the marching band but was not accepted. Had I been accepted to the Longhorn Band, my life would have turned out quite differently. Instead I joined MAYO, the Mexican American Youth Organization on campus, becoming part of the Chicana/o movement of the late 1960s and 1970s. With my brother being in Vietnam, I became active in the antiwar movement. And with my parents having worked in the fields, it was natural for me to support the United Farm Workers movement as well. My passion became one of reclaiming my language and culture, so I minored in Mexican American studies. After I declared I was going into bilingual education, most of my high school friends abandoned me, save for one of my best male friends, who supported my decision to become an educator. Another best friend from high school, a white woman who had lauded JFK's assassination in 1963 while we were in junior high, confided in me that she felt blacks were inferior and should not be given equal status as whites. I parted company with her, telling her that she was racist, and quietly walked out on her at the student union lunchroom. I became devoid of white friends, but did not quite fit in with the Chicanas/os either. The *fronterizos* from border towns made fun of my perfect English and lack of cultural knowledge, but they quickly stopped when they had to write papers for their classes and needed help.

I found my footing in the role of secretary of MAYO, documenting meetings and activities. My future husband was actively organizing the National Chicano Health Organization and was part of MAYO. I decided to graduate with a bachelor of arts in history after becoming disillusioned with the College of Education at UT, which did not offer minors in multicultural education or bilingual education. I applied to Teacher Corps, a federal program offering a master's degree in education that included a teaching internship in the public schools, academic courses at UT, and community work over a two-year period in the Edgewood Independent School District in San Antonio. My motivation in going to San Antonio was consistent with my desire to reclaim my language and culture and to help children in the barrios. However, my interest in teaching was at the secondary level, and I had always imagined myself teaching philosophy, history, or civics. I wound up falling in love with early childhood theory instead.

When I completed my master's in education in 1974, with certifications in early childhood and bilingual education, I found my way to Boston, joining my fiancé, who was in medical school at Harvard. There, I struggled through the desegregation phase of the Boston public schools and was hired as the first bilingual teacher in kindergarten, a sacred cow in Boston. A court order issued before I was hired had declared that Boston kindergartens must provide the same bilingual education provided at the elementary-school grades. I was the only qualified kindergarten teacher in Boston who could help in the implementation phase. I quickly made a name as an early childhood and bilingual educator there. In 1977 my fiancé and I returned to San Antonio, where he accepted a residency with the University of Texas Health Science Center, and I returned to Edgewood ISD. As I turned thirty, I declared to him that the teacher I was mentoring had become such a close friend that I almost felt as if I were in love with her. Indeed I was, and a whole new chapter of my life began.

My marriage ended in irony one day when my husband got home early after dismissing his class on sexuality. Being a man who believed himself to be pro-feminist, he struggled to be open and wanted to accept my lesbianism, but we both knew it was not possible. I moved into a dingy garage apartment to live alone.

After three years of living alone, the woman who had stolen my heart and caused such a dramatic shift in my life finally agreed to build a home with me in the suburbs. We traveled to Europe, taught together, and remained closeted, denying that we were lesbians. I lost all of my college friends, living in a self-contained little world. When she confessed an attraction to another woman, our relationship ended, and her circle of friends expanded. In the spring of 1986 I found myself in a crisis of identity, living with my ex and dependent on her and her lesbian friends for a sense of community.

I began to explore the lesbian bars of San Antonio on my own, especially the Jezebel, where I danced incognito—always going home alone. In this state of vulnerability, I met a young *lesbiana* who had returned to San Antonio after finishing her studies at Yale. She had invited a group of closeted teachers to a private screening of John Sayles's film *Lianna*. Graciela Sánchez was an out-and-out radical lesbian feminist. She quickly educated us on section 21.06 of the Texas Penal Code, which criminalized homosexual behavior and certain sexual acts between consenting adults. As the film ended, she asked, "Does anyone here give hugs?" I quickly jumped up. She sold us tickets to a screening of *Desert Hearts*, a fundraiser for the Texas Human Rights Foundation, and indicated she'd meet me there.

When Graciela arrived at the screening, she tossed her bulging red backpack next to my seat and set about distributing flyers in the theater packed with lesbians. Afterward, we all met at the Jezebel. As I watched Graciela on the dance floor, I became aware of my growing attraction to her. She would wear all sorts of pins highlighting her queer activism, her progressive politics, and her solidarity work for Central American issues. After we started seeing each other, I would wear a small round pin stating, "I'm not a lesbian, my lover is." My sense of humor survived my conflicted state of being. I had been involved with only one female lover at this point. The reluctance to identify as a lesbian was not unusual for the time. The owner of the Jezebel, who was retired from the military, refused to use the word—even though she supported the lesbian community by publishing the *Women's Community Journal* and later *WomanSpace*, from 1988 to 2007. She also featured lesbian performers at the Jezebel, like Kate Clinton, who joked that lesbians preferred to use the word *Lebanese* to identify themselves.

Graciela, on a quest to open a center for multi-issue organizing, liked my activist past. She constantly talked about the interconnection of issues and how oppressions came from the same root, which meant we all had to work together simultaneously on the same issues, but I wasn't sure I got it. I had been involved with the anti–Vietnam War and Chicana/o movements at UT Austin and had been part of MAYO there and the La Raza Unida Party while in San Antonio, but rarely did we come together unless it was around a single issue. Graciela had been involved with MEChA (Movimiento Estudiantil Chicano de Aztlán) at Yale a decade later. She too supported the United Farm Workers (UFW), and she had minored in Chicana/o studies. We had both grown up in barrios, attended public schools, and were bilingual. She was a salsa dancer and was raised by a father who grew up in Mexico and was constantly nurturing his kids with cultural offerings. I was a *polkera* who had learned to dance on my own at twenty-one and had reclaimed Mexican music. We both came from working-class backgrounds. The main difference in our activism was that Graciela had organized around Central American solidarity issues, even going to Nicaragua to make a film. Even though the age difference of ten years worried me, it did not bother Graciela.

By the summer of 1986, she and I were attending lesbian and gay events together, including the International Lesbian and Gay Association (ILGA) conference in Los Angeles—held at the same time as the annual Gay and Lesbian Latinos Unidos (GLLU) dance. We stayed with Laura Esquivel, now known as *la madre* of the Latina/o LGBT movement. By summer's end, Graciela had introduced me to Michael Stevens, editor of the *Calendar*, a semipolitical gay publication in San Antonio. It included statewide and national news articles relevant to the lesbian and gay community. Michael had lost his teaching position as an English professor after coming out while married to a woman. That had propelled him into gay activism and the formation of a gay and lesbian business alliance, the San Antonio Gay Alliance (SAGA). Both Graciela and I became part of the *Calendar* staff, writing and distributing the paper throughout San Antonio and Texas—skills we would later use. Michael died of AIDS in 1988.

Graciela and her friend, Susan Guerra, who had returned from Norway, had dreamed of finding a site where activists could work together and share resources. They had organized the first International Women's Day March in San Antonio in 1985 with other women, including author Sandra Cisneros. The keynote speaker had been Emma Tenayuca, who in the 1930s had organized a historic strike, with thousands of women marching and protesting the pennies paid for shelling pecans. Tenayuca, a Communist Party member, was eventually run out of town. When she died in 1999, the obscurity she had lived in was lifted by multiple tributes, many of which took place at the Esperanza Center.

Graciela and Susan were part of the Interchange Network, formed in 1982, which included progressive, antiwar, environmentalist, solidarity, and socially responsible groups. The network, which met once a year, had 501(c)(3) status and published a monthly news calendar. Cindy Duda, the network coordinator, agreed to sponsor the proposed site as a project. By the fall of 1986, Graciela, Susan, and Jean Durel, a former nun looking for space for the Refugee Aid Project (RAP), found a building owned by the Oblate Fathers, who agreed to rent it out for one dollar per year. RAP, the Central America Information Center, Latin American Assistance, and the American Civil Liberties Union were the first offices at the Esperanza Center, along with Habitat for Humanity, which used space there to store building materials.

Susan, who was volunteer coordinator the first year, named the center "Esperanza" to signify the empowerment of women, especially Latinas. She recalled that for the first time a collective voice of San Antonians who worked for social justice at a grassroots level was forming itself, and that our intentions were not motivated by a desire to gain power—but came from a place in the heart nurtured by memory. Our motivation in seeking social justice was rooted in family histories, neighborhood histories, school histories, and justice, or the lack of it—a concept that we had learned through personal experience. I understood at the core of my existence what this pursuit of justice meant for me. In the ensuing years, we were to actualize this thinking at the Esperanza Peace and Justice Center, which opened its doors on January 31, 1987. Graciela was not present at the opening, having left to attend film school in Cuba—accepted as the only U.S. student for the eighteen-month course. I had committed to a relationship with her and with the Esperanza until her return. As I listened to the speakers at the Esperanza opening, council member María Antonietta Berriozábal and Dr. Amy Freeman Lee, I wondered how I would fit into this crowd that included old hippies and Vietnam vets with their beat-up Volkswagens in the parking lot next to late-model cars driven by progressive academics and politicians.

Before Graciela left for Cuba, she had met with me and Letitia Gomez, a politically active *lesbiana* whom I had met at the Jezebel. Graciela convinced us to organize a statewide Latina lesbian retreat. The idea had been proposed at the Gay and Lesbian Tejano (GLT) network conference in August of 1986 in Houston, where only five of the forty-nine participants had been women. The GLT included the Gay and Lesbian Hispanics of Dallas, (GLHD), Houston's Gay and Lesbian Hispanics Unidos, (GLHU), San Antonio's Ambiente, and the Austin Latina/o Lesbian and Gay Organization, (ALLGO). They had agreed to send Graciela to a *lesbiana* retreat in Los Angeles that fall if she would organize a committee to plan a Texas retreat for 1987. After Graciela left for Cuba, Leti and I convened the first Lesbiana Latina Retreat Committee (LLRC) on January 17, 1987, at the Esperanza Center, meeting with four of the *lesbianas* who had been at the screening of *Lianna*. I was elected coordinator. Our plan was to expand the LLRC into a statewide network of *lesbianas* that would include San Antonio, Austin, Houston, and Dallas.

I moved into Graciela's one-room casita located in the shadow of the HemisFair Tower. It was attached to an old garage full of critters that made themselves known in the dark of night. It was a lonely, frightening existence, but I managed. I would arrive home from a full day of teaching to write or type letters to lesbian and gay publications all over Texas: San Antonio's *WomanSpace*, *The Left Hand* in Austin, *Impulse* in El Paso, *This Week in Texas* in Houston, *Dimensions* in Lubbock, and others. I also became adept at getting calls through to Cuba, talking to Graciela on a regular basis. There were no laptops, no Internet, no cell phones—but by sheer determination and belief in organizing *lesbianas tejanas*, we were able to forge ahead.

By February, Austin Lesbianas—a part of the Austin Latina/o Lesbian and Gay Organization (ALLGO)—and the Indigenous Women's Network agreed to host a statewide LLRC meeting at Stonehaven Ranch in San Marcos, which was provided by a progressive white woman, Genevieve Vaughan. Leti brought in the *lesbianas* from Houston's AMIGA (All Mujeres Interested in Getting Active), founded by Linda Morales and *lesbianas* who needed to find a space separate from the male-dominated groups of that city. The retreat was set for June 12–14, 1987. Fund-raising dances took place in each of the network cities, with the Jezebel holding *tardeadas* on Sunday afternoons. Grants for the retreat were garnered throughout Texas from organizations, businesses, and individuals. A statement of purpose was finalized that read, "We come together to validate and affirm our lives as Latina lesbians. In doing so, we recognize and accept the responsibility to raise our consciousness as *lesbianas latinas* and to transform ourselves into loving, strong, intuitive, and daring beings—always rigorously pursuing the best in ourselves and each other. We know that as we change ourselves, we change the world." A logo for the LLRC, designed by artist Marsha Gómez of Austin (now deceased), featured the profile of a brown woman, with her *trenzas* (braids) superimposed on the state of Texas and extending downward into Mexico like roots.

The first issue that arose in planning the retreat involved a suggestion from Houston *lesbianas* to change the title of the retreat to the Lesbiana Latina Feminist Retreat. Eventually they understood that we risked alienating the very *mujeres* we wanted at the retreat if we added "feminist" to the title. Instead, we offered workshops on feminism by Latina lesbians. Allowing non-Latinas to participate in the retreats was another issue. We agreed to allow non-Latinas with Latina partners at the retreat, but the agenda would not be altered to accommodate them. This decision indirectly led to the start of the Texas Lesbian Conference in 1988, which a group of white lesbians in Dallas began organizing. Similarly, Latino gay men began to plan their own retreat for 1988. Both the white lesbians and the Latino gay men held planning sessions at Stonehaven. A final issue dealt with accepting indigenous forms of spiritual practice at the retreats. Tonántzin, la Virgen de Guadalupe, and indigenous ceremonies became central to every retreat. In 1989 a workshop was also offered on *curanderismo* with Elena Ávila from New Mexico (now deceased).

The Gay and Lesbian Tejanos conference followed the first statewide Lesbiana Latina Retreat in September of 1987, with over thirty *lesbianas* attending. It was decided there that the LLRC would become a statewide organization of the GLT called ELLAS, with a home base in San Antonio and chapters in Austin, Houston, and Dallas. The increased visibility of *lesbianas* in the GLT had been successfully secured.

After the retreat in 1987, ELLAS "came out" on a national and international level. *¡Ellas andaban por dondequiera!* We were everywhere! Graciela and I drove to the East Coast in June to the Sisterfire Women's Music Festival, where we met *mujeres* who would later perform at the Esperanza. There we met Tatiana de la Tierra, a poet, writer, and musicologist, who introduced us to a number of Latin American singers with her cassette compilations of music—Mujeres en Fuerza, Mujeres en Rhumba, and Las Enamoradas—which she dedicated to me and Graciela. On October 11, ELLAS attended the Second National March on Washington for Lesbian and Gay Rights, marching with the LLRC banner alongside New York's Las Buenas Amigas. There, the first national Latina/o lesbian and gay organization, eventually named LLEGÓ, was conceptualized by Latinas/os including Letitia Gomez and Linda Morales, the latter of whom would become the lead plaintiff in *Morales et al. v. State of Texas* challenging the Texas sodomy laws in 1992. Linda and Leti, both original members of the LLRC and the GLT, exemplified the strong *lesbianas* coming out of the Tejana retreats.

ELLAS was also represented at El Primer Encuentro de Lesbianas Feministas Latinoamericanas y Caribeñas on October 14–17, 1987, in Cuernavaca, Mexico, where Graciela joined us from Cuba. Issues of race, class, language, and internalized colonialism created multiple challenges, but the gathering resulted in the formation of an international network of Latina *lesbianas*, including the women of ELLAS. The group of closeted *lesbianas* who had innocently come together in 1986 to view films in a small apartment in San Antonio were now part of a national and global movement.

By 1988, ELLAS was part of the Interchange Network, with an office at the Esperanza Center. Author Neil Miller, in his book *In Search of Gay America*, wrote a chapter on San Antonio Latina lesbians, observing that the *lesbianas* organizing the retreats were a group of women struggling with basic issues of identity in the earliest stages of creating a community. He noted that issues of gender, social class, and culture were so complex and intertwined that it was hard to figure out the part sexuality played. I intimately understood what he observed, but also knew the impact the retreats had had statewide.

ELLAS Dicen, a statewide news journal, began publishing in 1988. In May, Esperanza cosponsored Sin Igual, a San Francisco–based women's salsa band, with the Guadalupe Cultural Arts Center, setting a precedent for future Esperanza events. We began to receive nationwide requests to attend the retreats, but we kept the retreats for Tejanas, allotting spaces for each city and for rural areas. *Lesbianas* outside of Texas were accepted only as presenters or vendors. Tatiana de la Tierra, now deceased, sold her music compilations at the 1989 retreat and kept contact with San Antonio ELLAS. The political artwork of Liliana Wilson, Esther Hernández, and Marsha Gómez and books like Juanita Ramos's *Compañeras: Latina Lesbians* were sold. Films like Graciela's *No porque lo diga Fidel Castro*, on Cuban lesbians and gays, and *Testimonios de Nicaragua* brought international politics to the retreats.

The retreat workshops centered on addiction, abuse, identity, culture, spirituality, AIDS, sexuality, and feminism. We were to have three Tejana retreats: the first in 1987 at Stonehaven in San Marcos and the 1988 and 1989 retreats at Alma de Mujer in Austin. Genevieve Vaughan, dedicated to the philosophy of a "gift-giving economy," provided the sites and later donated Alma de Mujer to the Indigenous Women's Network. After the third retreat, ELLAS ceased to meet statewide, but San Antonio *lesbianas* reclaimed ELLAS in 1991 as a local organization under the umbrella of the Esperanza. In 1993 ELLAS of San Antonio became its own nonprofit organization. Texas *lesbianas* continued to attend each other's events and became a presence at the annual Texas Lesbian Conference. In 1994 Tejanas from the retreats participated in the Lesbiana Latina Leadership Conference in Tucson, Arizona, funded by LLEGÓ. ELLAS San Antonio continued meeting until 1996, with an annual ELLAS Night Out dance, retreats at Alma de Mujer, and a presence at the annual International Women's Day March sponsored by the Esperanza. They also awarded annual scholarships to young *lesbianas* in the arts. The Tejana *lesbiana* retreats successfully reintegrated *lesbianas* into local organizations and stimulated their involvement in queer politics at the state, national, and international level.

The Texas Lesbian Conference (TLC) was initiated in Dallas by the organizations Among Friends and Lesbian Visionaries in 1988. The TLC modeled itself after the ELLAS network, with representatives from Dallas, Austin, Houston, and San Antonio. ELLAS women like myself and Linda Morales were part of panels centered around the topic of diversity at the first TLC, but attendance was primarily white.

Linda Morales, concerned about the lack of women of color, volunteered AMIGA to cosponsor the second TLC with Houston's Womynspace. Queer cultural theorist Gloria Anzaldúa, who was close to the Esperanza, and Emma Pérez, historian and feminist critic, were the 1989 keynote speakers. While Latinas were well represented at the second TLC, black lesbians were not.

San Antonio lesbians stepped forward to sponsor the third Texas Lesbian Conference in 1990, "Lesbians in the 1990s, Speaking Out," with Esperanza's support. This time black lesbians were well represented at all levels, assuring that lesbians of color would be visible at all TLCs. The conferences, which lasted from 1988 until 2004, were in that way unique in the history of U.S. lesbians. San Antonio again sponsored the TLC in 1994, 1998, 2001, and 2004. However, we were caught unprepared for the 1990 TLC, which suffered direct homophobic attacks that threatened the Esperanza Center's very existence.

At the first anniversary celebration in January 1988, the Esperanza Center's character was somewhat reflective of the Chicana/o activist community, with Rebecca Harrington of the United Farm Workers speaking and the salsa band Toucan playing. By the fall of 1988, Graciela had returned from Cuba to take on the directorship of Esperanza. The *Interchange News Calendar* stopped publishing, and in November 1988 *La Voz de Esperanza* began as a four-page news journal. By the Esperanza Center's second anniversary celebration in January of 1989, Chicana/o activists were as visible as progressive whites. But, while *lesbianas* were comfortably ensconced at the Esperanza, gay men were barely on the scene. All of that would change by the spring of 1988 in a series of events that would bring Latinas/os from the lesbian and gay communities together while distancing us from "mainstream" gay male politics and issues.

Graciela's return to the Esperanza was highlighted in a full-length article in the *San Antonio Light* on January 22, 1989, with the headline, "Working for Peace and Justice: The Local Progressive Movement is Pulling Together for Future." The article led to a visit by an Oblate Father, who cautioned Graciela not to mention that they were the owners of the building, especially when talking about the lesbian and gay community. He stressed that the publicity would negatively affect the Oblates. Nevertheless, we continued to work with the lesbian and gay community along with white progressives and Chicana/o activists. On November 10 the Esperanza held a *plática* with Margaret Randall, who spoke on "Taking Risks, Personal and Political." She was brought to San Antonio by Carolyn Warmbold, wife of the editor of the *San Anto-*

nio Light, working in tandem with ELLAS, feminists from the San Antonio chapter of the National Organization for Women, and Central American solidarity activists from the white and Chicana/o communities. As a lesbian, a solidarity worker, a feminist, an incest survivor, and a political exile in Cuba, Randall exemplified the interconnection of issues within her own life. This event typified Esperanza's programming—consistently bridging communities and connecting multiple issues.

On May 19, 1989, the Esperanza began a journey into the queer visual experience when Mim Scharlack, a former dancer in Hollywood who had lost many gay friends to AIDS, including Liberace, paid tribute to them in the exhibit *The AIDS Series*. David Zamora Casas, the curator, recalled in an article published in *La Voz de Esperanza* that the Esperanza Center was the only space that would house an exhibit dealing with AIDS. The exhibit brought all sorts of people together—gay and straight, white and of color, male and female—all working together with AIDS workers to get the center ready for the exhibit, which turned out a diverse crowd of three hundred folks. The proceeds from the sales of art went to the San Antonio AIDS Foundation and the Esperanza Center.

The first lesbian and gay art exhibit at the center, *Equal Rights for Whom?—Art Exhibit in Support of Human Rights for All*, followed on June 21, with five hundred people at its opening. Because the title seemed ambiguous, Graciela challenged David to come out with what he really wanted to do. David agreed that his intent was to have a queer art exhibit. Of the twelve artists exhibiting, only two were lesbians. Using his mother's maiden name, he invented another *lesbiana*, Carmen Zamora, to add to the list—but that did not escape the critical eye of Graciela, who insisted on gender and racial parity at all events. We later found out that the woman's name was used to hide the identity of one of the male artists, who in choosing to remain closeted had asked David to provide a pseudonym.

David's enthusiasm for curating was matched only by his flamboyant nature. He would draw crowds and the media when he showed up wearing the hooped skirts of a *china poblana*, freshening up his red lipstick and twirling his Dalí-esque mustache. The San Antonio chapter of the Human Rights Campaign Fund (HRCF) and the San Antonio Lesbian and Gay Assembly (SALGA) made their public debuts at this exhibit. Both of the organizations had sought help from the Esperanza but not without challenges. SALGA had been formed by a group of about a dozen lesbian and gay individuals, of whom Graciela and I were part. I had named the organization using the acronym SALGA. The organization enjoyed a short lifespan of a few years because it was undermined by white gay men who resisted the idea of bylaws that called for parity in gender and in the representation of people of color in a city that is majority Latina/o. Graciela had experienced the wrath of white gay men when they had refused to remove grapes from an HRCF function, insisting that the United Farm Workers had nothing to do with "human rights." These types of confrontations became increasingly commonplace, even though we continued our efforts to work with mainstream gay groups. By the end of June 1989, both the lesbian and gay male communities were highly visible at the Esperanza Center. Mike Greenberg of the *San Antonio Express-News* reviewed the art exhibit *Equal Rights for Whom?*, observing prophetically that an explicitly gay-lesbian show was bound to raise red flags—at least in Texas, where "homosexual conduct" between consenting adults in private was at that time a Class C misdemeanor.

The year 1990 began with a strong antiwar push as the United States invasion of Panama continued and things heated up in the Persian Gulf. The Fifth Annual Freedom March honoring Martin Luther King Jr. had more than forty groups marching behind an Esperanza Center peace banner that I had painted with the statement "Stop the War / Alto a la Guerra." Fuerza Unida, a women's sewing cooperative that was formed after Levi Strauss & Co. relocated to Costa Rica, laying off over one thousand workers, began to operate out of Esperanza. Annual Earth Day celebrations began, and *Chico Mendes: Voice of the Amazon* was screened in April at the Guadalupe Theater as our film programming expanded and environmental justice issues became more prevalent.

When the 1990 Texas Lesbian Conference (TLC) set up shop at the Menger Hotel next to the Alamo, Texas-sized homophobia surfaced. ELLAS of San Antonio had joined with the Esperanza Center, Lesbian Information San Antonio (LISA, a telephone information service), and the publication *WomanSpace* to sponsor the third annual TLC on May 18–20. Lesbians at the Alamo did not receive attention— but the screenings of internationally acclaimed lesbian films *November Moon* (W. Germany) and *Anne Trister* (Canada) at the Guadalupe Theater drew the ire of the Religious Right. City hall received two hundred calls from people outraged that lesbian films were being shown at a city-supported facility. The director of the Guadalupe Cultural Arts Center, Pedro Rodríguez, refused to shut down the films, saying that a rental agreement had been signed and that the Esperanza Center was complying with the terms. Eduardo Díaz, director of the Department of Arts and Cultural Affairs of San Antonio reacted in a *San Antonio Light* article, "Flap over Films Was Not Justified" (May 1990), declaring, "What scares me the most is the presumption that art that touches on the lesbian experience is presumed 'obscene and pornographic.'" The mayor's representatives noted that it was a first amendment issue of civil rights and that the films did not violate "performance quality standards." This would be the first major public homophobic incident the Esperanza would experience, but not the last. The incident solidified the Esperanza board's support of the lesbian community, with both straight Latinas/os and straight white board members being present at the lesbian film festival to counter protests.

The 1990 TLC made a profit of $7,000 that was apportioned for future TLCs and for scholarships for lesbians to attend other conferences, like Creating Change (sponsored by the National Gay and Lesbian Task Force) and the National Lesbian Conference of 1991. Remaining funds were divided amongst sponsors of the 1990 TLC. This distribution process was made into policy in 1993, when a statewide board of the TLC was incorporated.

The second lesbian and gay art exhibit, . . . *And Justice for All*, on June 3, 1990, followed the homophobic flurry of protests against the TLC. Esperanza's courtyard was filled with quilt panels and AIDS service tables representing the Blue Light Candle Project, the Names Project, Arts for Life, the San Antonio AIDS Foundation, HRCF, SALGA, ELLAS, and others. This time, of thirteen artists exhibiting, seven were lesbians. Keynote speaker Carolyn Warmbold, who had sponsored Margaret Randall's visit to San Antonio, made clear why the outing of AIDS and the queer community occurred so dramatically in San Antonio. She disclosed that when her husband, Ted Warmbold, editor of the *San Antonio Light*, had died of AIDS, she had had to choose whether to stay silent. However, as a progressive white woman she realized that AIDS was connected with race, class, and gender issues and did not exist in isolation. She felt that if she spoke out and acknowledged her husband as a victim of AIDS, she would be placing herself in solidarity with the many communities affected by this deadly disease. She suggested that a new motto and a new movement that connected homophobia to geopolitics be used in the fight against AIDS. In the 1990 July/August issue of *La Voz de Esperanza* she explained her decision to speak out in an article entitled "Life=Speaking Out." While the Esperanza network numbered twenty-five groups at the beginning of 1990, by the fall there were over forty, including ten AIDS or lesbian and gay organizations.

Connections to my past and my sexuality collided when I visited the Names Project's AIDS Memorial Quilt on display at the San Antonio Convention Center that summer. I ran into a panel with the name of a high school boyfriend of sorts. Tara had disappeared from my life upon entering the University of Texas at Austin. His panel had a Howdy Doody doll, a decal of the Travis High School Rebels, a UT longhorn, and other items. Unbeknownst to me, he had been a gay activist in Colorado. Another close high school friend, Dexter, had come out to me at UT. He had always had a different aesthetic—painting his trombone red with white polka dots. He even took me to a gay bar near UT and explained gay sex to me, but I never connected "it" to women. I only had a sense of "otherness" from running with other "weirdoes" in high school who were self-identified as witches, philosophers, or Rosicrucians. My friends disappeared from my life—and I missed my opportunity to come out as a lesbian earlier in my life. I never knew whether the girls I ran with eventually became lesbians too.

Organizing around the Texas sodomy laws had been part of Esperanza's work and had gradually intensified. To illustrate the severity of these laws, artist Michael Marinez set up an installation entitled *Dirty Laundry* outside the walls of the Esperanza. He painted the explicit words contained in section 21 of the Texas Penal Code on white sheets, including words like penis and anus, and hung them on a clothesline for all to see. Interspersed on the line were wired figures representing AIDS victims. The installation caused a furor, even within our own board of directors, who felt it was offensive and not necessary. I felt ill at ease with the notion of the Esperanza community being in conflict with itself, especially since our board had been so supportive of lesbian and gay programming. Eventually we came to understand that only by pushing boundaries would we have any hope of change.

A month after the installation came down, the Oblates sent Esperanza tenants a ninety-day notice saying we had to vacate so the building could be sold. After negotiating, they agreed to transfer ownership to the Refugee Aid Project (RAP). The terms of sale were never made public, but they set conditions that required tenants to follow the teachings of the Catholic Church, explicitly prohibiting pro-choice programming. Everyone remained in the building, and for a while Esperanza carried on as usual. Eventually RAP's leadership changed, making it difficult for us to remain when the new male director clashed repeatedly with Graciela, refusing to respect Esperanza's space and authority in the building. By the end of 1990 we began to dialogue with the community about finding a permanent home. The community responded, and we moved forward with a process that included searching for a building, rating sites, and acquiring financing to buy a new home by the fall of 1993, while enduring homophobic attacks inside and outside the walls of our old space at 1305 North Flores.

In 1990 the Esperanza Center had begun to submit grants to the city of San Antonio for funding of our cultural arts programming. The inequities of the city's funding process were called into question by Latina/o arts groups who had experienced serious funding cuts while mainstream groups continued to enjoy favored status. The Esperanza Center joined forces with Latina/o and progressive arts groups to form the Coalition for Cultural Diversity, moving the city toward a more equitable funding process (one that reflected the city's population of 60 percent Latinas/os). The city's peer panels and Cultural Arts Board, which I sat on for a time, began to look closely at organizations applying for funding to see if people of color (especially Latinas/os) were represented on their boards and staffs and whether their programming was diverse. The Esperanza Center's applications consistently ranked high through the 1990s, but our programming, which included art exhibits, performances, readings, and film festivals, was brought into question over a period of years by Religious Right groups and white conservative gay men, who repeatedly appeared at all Citizens to Be Heard sessions, Cultural Arts Board meetings, and city council funding sessions that reviewed final funding recommendations. As a result, our lesbian and gay programming began to be targeted at multiple levels in newspapers, radio, TV, and other media in a concerted effort to stop the city from funding Esperanza.

Amid protests and cries of "No Blood for Oil," 1991 began. On the night of January 16, Operation Desert Storm began with air strikes against Iraqi forces. That evening, as part of activities leading up to MLK Day, the Esperanza Center and the Guadalupe Cultural Arts Center copresented "The Black Experience through the Media Arts: An Evening with Marlon Riggs," premiering his documentaries *Ethnic Notions* and *Tongues Untied*. The event was publicized in the *San Antonio Express-News*, in which Riggs talked about these films. By the spring, the critically acclaimed *Tongues Untied* had ignited a national debate on public funding. The Religious Right pounced on its scheduled broadcast on the PBS series *Point of View* as a symbol of everything wrong with public funding for the arts. A nationwide airing scheduled for July 16, 1991, resulted in 195 of 320 stations refusing to air the film. By the time the furor hit the national scene, the Esperanza had already premiered *Tongues Untied*, and the documentary aired on PBS in San Antonio without censorship.

The Riggs screenings provided an opportunity to bring together the black and brown communities of San Antonio. Organizing against the Gulf War provided another opportunity. The San Antonio Coalition for Peace in the Middle East met weekly, giving rise to a thorough analysis of the war in a special issue of *La Voz de Esperanza* in March 1991. After numerous protests, marches, and teach-ins, the organizing culminated in the Funeral of Forewarning. The "funeral" began with a prayer service at Our Lady of Guadalupe Catholic Church on the West Side (the historic Mexican side of the city), where a hearse left with a procession headed to Bethel African Methodist Episcopal Church on the East Side (the historic African American side of the city). The procession ended at Fort Sam Houston National Cemetery, where everyone arrived for a silent vigil. The East and West Sides would come together again in 1996 along with the lesbian and gay leadership of the Esperanza, organizing against the Ku Klux Klan, who marched into town only to find people effectively counterattacking its presence with singing, dancing, and poetry readings that drew the media's attention away from the KKK.

With the lesbian and gay community quite visible in multi-issue organizing and on the board of directors at the Esperanza Center, it was only a matter of time before homophobic attacks would find their mark. Local media made a practice of ignoring LGBT organizing, neglecting to mention significant events. When twenty-eight thousand lesbians and gay men turned out for the Statewide March on Austin for Lesbian and Gay Rights on March 17, 1991, the *San Antonio Light*'s coverage consisted of only four lines. In response, the San Antonio Lesbian & Gay Media Project formed. The *Express-News* continued to add to the print homophobia with a series of editorial cartoons, *Nacho Huarache*, that directly attacked Graciela, director of the Esperanza, and the issue of public funding for the arts, specifically the funding of the Esperanza Center. Despite meeting with the editorial boards, the homophobic cartoons and editorial comments against us continued.

The third lesbian and gay art show, *Freedom of Choice*, in 1991, solidified the presence of annual lesbian and gay art exhibits at the Esperanza. As 1991 ended, Monica Palacios, "Latin Lezbo Comic," took center stage at the Jump Start Theater, cosponsored by the Esperanza Center. She was attacked by local media, as would be other lesbian artists, like Laura Aguilar and Ana Fernandez, who showed in later exhibits. Homophobic and misogynistic attacks continued into the 1990s even as the Esperanza upped the ante in 1995 with a national touring exhibit at the new Esperanza building sponsored by the Women's Caucus for Art Conference. The attacks became viler, with a feces-covered bra being hung on one of Esperanza's pear trees and break-ins at our new space.

The *Marquise*, an LGBT publication, began publishing in 1991. Its first editor, Randy Sherman, was an ally of the Esperanza Center who supported our programming. In 1994 the *Marquise* was taken over by conservative white gay men, new to San Antonio, who used it to target the Esperanza Center. It accomplished its mission when the Bexar County Christian Coalition joined the *Marquise* in pressuring the city council to zero out Esperanza's funding on September 11, 1997. The city council denied the Esperanza funding recommended by peer-review panels and the Cultural Arts Board, as in previous years, because of homophobia and a concerted, long-term effort to defund the center. Journalist Joe Patrick Bean (now deceased), himself a white gay man, noted later in the gay publication the *Texas Triangle* that the *Marquise* folded immediately after the Esperanza's defunding, with the publisher devoting more than four pages in its last issue (in October 1997) to gloating about it.

The Christian Coalition had not gone after the Esperanza solely because of our lesbian and gay programming. We had endured obscene calls, death threats, and break-ins at both the old space and the new space. We had received this abuse because of our queer programming, but also because of our solidarity work in Central America, because of our support of Cuba, because we were feminists and pro-choice, because we were antiwar, and so on. With the 1996 lesbian and gay film series "Out at the Movies" our detractors found their footing and convinced city council to withhold recommended funding for 1997, and they were supported by white gay males. In response we filed a lawsuit against the City of San Antonio on August 4, 1998.

On May 15, 2001, the Esperanza Peace and Justice Center won its suit against the City of San Antonio. Our arts programming had been characterized as political and obscene for years, beginning with the Oblate Fathers, who had forced us out of our original home, and with the 1990 Texas Lesbian Conference films that elicited two hundred calls to city hall. The decision on *Esperanza et al. v. the City of San Antonio* gained back funding for the 1997 defunding and for 1998, when we were denied the opportunity to apply for funds after the city declared that filing suit would be a basis for denying grant awards. The judge found that the city committed unconstitutional-viewpoint and animus-based discrimination in both 1997 and 1998. He concluded that the denial of our grant application in 1998 was not merely because the Esperanza filed suit, but also because of our social and political views, which the city discriminated against. The ruling also cited the city for violating the "open meetings" laws of Texas when they met behind closed doors to defund the Esperanza. The ruling was hailed as a victory by arts groups throughout the United States, and the Esperanza Center won newfound respect. With our victory came many accolades and honors from lesbian and gay publications and organizations locally and nation-wide. In 2001 the Human Rights Campaign Fund (HRCF) of San Antonio honored Graciela Sánchez at their annual Black Tie Dinner in November, but did not acknowledge that some of the very same white men of their organization were the ones who ultimately caused the defunding of the Esperanza. HRCF, which had allowed grapes at its functions, denying the validity of the United Farm Workers movement as a human rights issue, never got the significance of multi-issue organizing and the need for diversity in organizations. Graciela pointed that out to them as she received the award at the dinner.

When the *San Antonio Current*, the alternative weekly, celebrated its twenty-fifth anniversary in 2011, it cited the Esperanza Center's opening in 1987 as one of the big moments in its timeline of coverage. Highlighting "Human-rights cover-all" as one of its feature articles, with the subtitle "Esperanza's fight for arts funding downed specter of political favoritism," the *Current* noted that the Esperanza Peace and Justice Center was "born in the culture clash of 1987, fashioning itself as a hub for all manner of social and political causes that had human rights at their core. And its story, in many ways, has tracked the path of progressive thought in San Antonio, the state, and the nation over the past quarter-century. It is a protest-filled history, sparking derision and hate, but also respect and social change."

The queer roots of the Esperanza Center from its inception in 1987 have played an important part in the development and history of the city of San Antonio. I had left behind the racism I had encountered in my hometown of Austin, coming to San Antonio with hopes of recovering my language and culture and finding out who I really was. Never did I imagine that I would go beyond being the premier early childhood teacher that I was to discovering that there was so much more to my story—were it not for the Esperanza Center.

In the midst of the lawsuit in 1999 Graciela and I ended our relationship. Graciela and I agreed that it was important to keep our personal struggles out of the limelight and to preserve the Esperanza's good work and reputation. For me, it became important to hold on to my community at the Esperanza Center and to not walk away. Graciela continues as director and I as editor of *La Voz de Esperanza*. We continue to advocate for a wide variety of issues and continue to bring communities together while working toward peace and social justice as well as the preservation of our *cultura* and historical *conciencia* in San Antonio, Texas.

CHAPTER WRITTEN BY GLORIA A. RAMIREZ.

MOISÉS AGOSTO-ROSARIO

Latinas/os and the AIDS Treatment Advocacy Movement

Moisés Agosto-Rosario was born and raised in Puerto Rico and moved to New York City seeking medical treatment when he found out he was HIV positive in the mid-1980s. In New York he encountered the AIDS Coalition to Unleash Power (ACT UP) and immediately became involved in AIDS activism, Latina/o organizing, and Latina/o LGBT health activism. In particular, he became linked to AIDS treatment advocacy for under-served populations. Agosto-Rosario has become one of the world's best-known AIDS activists whose work focuses on advances in medical testing and dissemination of treatment. He was instrumental in the development of treatment advocacy at the National Minority AIDS Council in Washington, D.C. Dividing his time between the United States and Puerto Rico, Agosto-Rosario is currently an active writer with the Colectivo Literario Homoerótica, a literary collective of gay and lesbian writers on the Island. This personal essay illustrates his early encounters with AIDS activism and treatment advocacy, self-racialization in the United States, and sexual freedom as an HIV-positive person.

WHEN I FIRST MOVED TO NEW YORK CITY AT the age of twenty-three in 1988, I already knew I was HIV+. I was not an activist, and I moved for two reasons: to continue my graduate studies on Latin American literature and to find adequate health care for my condition. The only insurance coverage I had in Puerto Rico was the one offered by the University of Puerto Rico. I did not want to go into a health-care system that wasn't adequate, but more than that, I felt the fear of being stigmatized as an HIV+ person and a gay man and of how it could affect me and my ability to finish my studies. At the age of twenty-two I got tested in San Juan at the municipal medical center called Centro Latinoamericano de Enfermedades de Transmisión Sexual. This was 1986. I was told I was positive, that I maybe had six months to live, and to take vitamins and exercise because there was nothing they could do. I found a book at a bookstore in Old San Juan titled *Living with AIDS*, and it became my bible. I thought if there were people who could beat cancer, maybe I could survive AIDS. For a year I did not talk about it with anyone, until one day in a deep depression I shared what I was going through with Dr. Reynaldo Ortiz, a psychology professor at the university. He offered me free counseling plus the opportunity to talk to others—and maybe start the first support group in Puerto Rico for gay men with HIV. Reynaldo also invited a colleague of his, Dr. Jose Toro, who was helping another HIV+ guy. A support group was formed. Still, appropriate medical care was lacking in Puerto Rico, and the stigma and bias at the time were too rooted in the minds of people who were both gay and HIV+, which prevented them from actively seeking medical care. In preparation for my trip to New York, Reynaldo gave me a list of places to go for care and treatment, and he kept me and the rest of the group informed with articles from newsletters like John James's *AIDS Treatment News* and some medical information materials from Project Inform—both based in San Francisco. With the information we got from Reynaldo, I knew exactly where to go in New York. I quickly got connected with the then Community Health Project (now the Callen-Lorde Community Health Center), a clinic that was developed as a community response to the AIDS epidemic impacting the lesbian, gay, bisexual, and transgender communities, but mostly gay men, in New York City. It was the only free clinic where most disenfranchised gay men could go for care, including Latinos. All my Latino friends who were in the city would go to it, and I would refer all my Latino friends who left Puerto Rico after me to this clinic.

One day, coming out of the gym, I connected with a guy with whom I'd been intensively flirting. As soon as we started talking about the possibilities of having sex, I disclosed my HIV status. To my surprise he was okay with it and disclosed his status, which was HIV negative. Before we said goodbye he told me about a new group of young gay AIDS activists that had been organized for a year and that needed people to translate into Spanish their materials for civil disobedience and information about the disease to disseminate to the Latina/o community. They met Monday nights at the New York Gay Community Center on Thirteenth Street, at the same place where the HIV/gay clinic was. I did not know exactly what an AIDS LGBT activist was, but I did know that I could help with translation and maybe meet other people like me for support.

The following Monday I went to the meeting. The place was packed with dozens of young gay men in their twenties and thirties, fired up, cute, and very passionate about fighting the government's silence about the devastation of the disease, as well as ready to demand a cure. Since AIDS was stigmatized as a "gay disease," they thought the government did not want to do what it should to contain it and avoid a catastrophic epidemic. There was neither interest in investing in biomedical research to find a cure or an adequate treatment nor enough attention to what was needed to understand how to treat the bizarre set of physical symptoms and opportunistic infections taking advantage of a weak immune system. People were getting sick and dying so fast, and those that were sick and surviving had to experience the most horrible ways of discrimination, like losing their jobs or their homes. At that time there was nothing but one drug, azidothymidine (AZT), and unless you were in the loop or in some sort of health-care system, access to this drug was not easy.

At that first meeting, as I walked inside the room, an electrifying feeling took hold of me instantly. When I heard the facilitator say, "Welcome to the AIDS Coalition to Unleash Power: ACT UP," the response from the audience was powerful, with cheering and political chants: "ACT UP, fight back, fight AIDS," or "People with AIDS under attack, what do we do? ACT UP, fight back." I looked around and it was like a religious experience; I was home, I was safe, and I knew it was the place I needed to be. I wanted to join them and be a part of that group, because it was about my life, and it smelled to me, then, like this group was going to be making history.

I looked around and the majority of the activists were white gay men, some white lesbians, and few, very few, African Americans, Asians, and Latinas/os. But for me, at the moment, that racial makeup had no meaning; I was coming from Puerto Rico, where the politics of race play differently. In the national discourse, we are first Puerto Rican instead of being from one race or another. And since in Puerto Rico the politics were more shaped by class, I did not know how the politics of race were played in this new setting.

At the end of the room was the information table. There were newspaper articles and tons of documents with information about clinical trials and the different working committees. The ones that got my immediate attention were the Treatment and Data Committee (T&D) and the Majority Action Committee (MA). Personally, I wanted to see and learn about all the possible clinical trials and treatments that were being developed. The MA got my attention because in their fact sheet I saw that both the members and issues were related to what they called people of color and that Latinas/os were among those listed—and in the United States a Puerto Rican was a Latina/o, therefore a person of color. I realized that if I wanted to navigate this new world of political race identities in ACT UP and New York, I had to embrace a new identity and be a person of color. So I did, and I looked for when the next meeting for each committee was and made plans.

The first meeting I went to was the MA meeting, and I just observed what went on. I had some learning to do in terms of how politics played in the United States with respect to each of the groups considered minority communities, especially the Latina/o community of which I was part. People are more comfortable with the things that are familiar to them. For people of color, the concept of minorities joining forces wasn't that difficult to understand, as well as being Latina/o—there was a language affinity and we were just a few. The political discourse of those who were already members of the committee made me feel I was expected to represent or look out for their interests. But it didn't sync that quickly until I had my own experiences of discrimination. I quickly learned about the disparities between people of color and white people regarding health care, and that stayed with me. Then I went to the T&D meeting, and the landscape of skin color and gender was uniform and homogeneous—with mostly white men. I was the only Latino in the group, and in the first row I was able to see a woman. I took all the information on the table and listened carefully. It was not only a political interest that motivated me but also a personal one, and I was sure that was the case for most of those in the room. They started discussing a protocol for a clinical trial, and they were dissecting it, looking at the methodology, questioning the randomized procedures, the double-blind process, the number of patients recruited. But what really impressed me the most was the discussion about science itself: whether the right questions were asked, or what the mechanism of the drugs was, and so on. It was amazing to witness civil society engaged in treating science politically and in self-educating themselves on the subjects of immunology, biomedical research, virology, and pharmacology, among many other science and medical topics.

The majority of the members were well educated, and as I got to know them better I realized most of them had good health care and the means and influence to advocate for themselves and to have access to most of the high-level scientists and medical individuals researching AIDS. The lack of diversity and representation, however, made me decide that treatment was the work I wanted to do. It was clear to me that without treatment or a cure, the epidemic wasn't going to end, and as far as representation, I just had to make sure more people of color got involved on issues related to treatment.

I realized I had a lot of catching up to do and started doing my homework: I taught myself about the science of AIDS, and as of today I continue to do so. It was a very difficult process. All my life until then I had spoken Spanish—my English was not the most perfect, and on top of that my college degree was in Spanish literature—therefore I was not acquainted with medical or research terminology. I not only had to buy and read science books, I also had to get medical dictionaries to understand the science and to be able to translate it—all this while in graduate school. By the time I was better prepared, I was able to integrate myself into the group, but for some reason I still couldn't be part of the sort of elite few that led the group's work. Then I also understood why I was the only person of color in the group and why no one really paid much attention to my effort to fit in: there was no need for mentoring—people were dying, and the need for action overshadowed the need for mentoring.

But I also understood it was my prerogative to push myself in learning and continuing to do AIDS treatment work, which at that point was clear to me as the work I wanted to do. One way for me to make myself visible was to volunteer not only to translate social and political statements from the activist group, but also to translate into Spanish the information that was generated from the T&D committee. Other Spanish-speaking people came to the group, like Luis Santiago ("Popo") and Carlos Maldonado, who were, like me, interested in treatment issues and were part of the organization but not of the elite of the T&D committee. We came together and formed the Spanish Communication Committee within ACT UP. A couple of months later, the Latinos who were at the MA decided to form their own group. At the first meeting the majority of those who showed up were born and raised in the States; then, as the group grew, others from different diasporas—Chile, Peru, Mexico, Argentina, Colombia, etc.—joined. They called for a meeting to address their concerns about how the unique issues facing our communities were falling through the cracks, not only within the institutional responses but also within the same coalition of people of color. Gay Latinos were a minority within a minority that spoke another language and had a whole set of other issues—like immigration—that were difficult to address in a group where the majority were African American activists. ACT UP was about empowerment, so the Latinos began to claim their own space. The call for the Latino caucus was political. That was how the Latino caucus of ACT UP was born in 1990. Members I recall being at our first meeting were Robert Vázquez-Pacheco, Aldo Hernández, Joe Franco, Robert García, Juan Méndez, Luis López-Detrés, Luis Santiago, Carlos Maldonado, and Andrew Vélez. From this group, those still alive are Robert Vázquez-Pacheco, Aldo Hernández, Luis López-Detrés, Luis Santiago, Carlos Maldonado, and Andrew Vélez.

Ken Fornataro was a member of the T&D committee and was creating a community-based organization whose mission was to disseminate easy-to-understand medical and treatment information throughout the LGBT community. It was my first experience in which, coming from a direct action group, I was slowly moving to a more institutionalized setting, working more in providing a service needed. But for me, providing information about treatment was about empowering patients to make informed decisions and to be in the know about the cutting-edge science that could save their lives, and it also had a political component. If we wanted treatment activism at large, we had to know at least the basics of the science so we were not only informed patients but also informed advocates. As a Latino man I felt I had to prove my intelligence and capability of handling these issues to be able to break through the circle of established treatment activists. The reason for this was that I could feel, and see through, how the stereotype of the uneducated or unintelligent (to the standard of the white man) minority leading the treatment movement was still some sort of obstacle to overcome. Fornataro acknowledged that the information obtained, analyzed, and generated by the group was life-saving information. He also understood that not all members of the community were going to understand the medical jargon, and he knew there was a need to simplify the information so people could benefit from it. For example, not only was knowledge about antiretroviral drugs under research important, but so was knowledge of trials that were proving that some of the most common opportunistic infections could be prevented with medication, helping patients extend their lives if using these medications as prophylaxes. So he developed a one-page fact sheet with information about HIV-related diseases, symptoms and treatments, and nutrition and exercise, emphasizing how having muscle mass was good to fight infections. Fornataro asked me to work with him on a volunteer basis to produce these fact sheets in English and Spanish. It was the first time I had made the connection of the importance for people living with HIV to be literate about the medical aspects of their disease. Before the AIDS Treatment Data Network fact sheet and newsletters, there were publications for people with AIDS, some of them covering a broad range of issues and some specializing in HIV medical, research, and treatment information. For example, San Francisco's Project Inform newsletter was solely about treatment and was the forum for the iconic AIDS treatment activist Martin Delaney to report back about the activism going on at the time, activism focused on the Food and Drug Administration and their process for approving HIV medications, the National Institutes of Health (NIH) and the lack of research infrastructure specific for AIDS science and biomedical research, and the Centers for Disease Control and Prevention and the poor handling of epidemiological data to better trace the development of the epidemic. The scope of this very specialized activism went beyond focusing only on government agencies and infiltrated the pharmaceutical industry as well. Something very revolutionary was happening, and civil society was becoming part of the design of a clinical protocol, proposing, advocating, and translating the results into public-health policies and the development of programs. Normally, the time it would take to develop and approve a drug was fifteen to twenty years. We advocated for shortening that process to a more efficient one that would give faster approval to the drugs at the completion of Phase 3, which tests safety and efficacy on a smaller scale, and continue with Phase 4, which measures efficacy on a larger scale after approval. That is one of the many examples of the work we did. A first generation of activists started to increase pressure by knocking on the doors of any institution within the fields of science and medicine that had something to do or could do something to make science and its institutions respond, with urgency and adequacy, to a disease that was showing itself to be such a powerful and overwhelming killer.

The U.S. government, in response to the demands of these individuals to have a place at the table, gathered together a group of activists from different communities in early 1991. Among those whom I remember attended were Debra Fraser-Howe from the National Black Leadership Commission on AIDS, Reggie Williams from the National Task Force on AIDS Prevention, Martin Delaney from Project Inform in San Francisco, Carol DiPaolo, Mark Harrington from ACT UP New York's T&D committee, David Barr from Gay Men's Health Crisis, and Joe Pérez, María Limón, Martin Ornelas, and Mario Solís Marich from the National Latino/a Lesbian and Gay Organization (LLEGÓ).

The NIH had created a national network for clinical research called the AIDS Clinical Trials Group. This was a network only for researchers. The treatment activist community demanded that a group of community patients' representatives (individuals who could bring to science the point of view of the patients and their environment, as well as their social, financial, and political circumstances) exist within this network. The design of research protocols for AIDS and related diseases had to factor in the feedback of the patients in order to be successful in the search for the right answers, and also had to be accessible and sensitive to those who would become the subjects of research. Having access to clinical trials also meant hope as more drugs were tested. The first group was composed, basically, of the individuals I mentioned above, and they became the Community Constituency Group (CCG) of the AIDS Clinical Trials Group of the National Institute of Allergies and Infectious Diseases. Members of the CCG were assigned to scientific committees within the network to participate in the scientific discussion but also to bring back to the CCG information on issues that were of great importance for community involvement, in terms of taking advantage of circumstances or influencing policies or practices that could be detrimental to the community of patients.

The members of this first CCG quickly realized that they needed to train other activists from their networks who could cover the turnover of this first CCG after two or three years, and they also began to develop how they could start educating their communities on scientific and medical issues; it was clear that those patients knowledgeable about their medical care did better and stayed healthier longer. Funds came from the NIH to help these networks to facilitate skill building and training among young activists in their communities. LLEGÓ was one of those networks. At that time I was already the editor-in-chief of *SIDAAhora*, the Spanish-only and first AIDS-related magazine in the country, a publication of the People with AIDS coalition in New York. Because of my connection to the T&D committee of ACT UP, the work I had started to do with the AIDS Treatment Data Network, and my commitment to making AIDS treatment information available to the Latina/o Spanish-speaking communities in New York and beyond, people started to identify me as a treatment activist. Through the magazine, Mario Solís Marich and Joe Pérez from LLEGÓ contacted me and invited me to Washington, D.C., to be a participant at the AIDS clinical trials training. From that group of trainees, people like Laura Gutierrez, Victor Rivera, and I became part of the CCG, working with Joe and Mario, who were already members but whose turnover time was close. My insertion into this world allowed me, through *SIDAAhora* and through doing workshops at community-based organizations in New York and around the country, to bring up-to-date information to the Latina/o Spanish-speaking community about the first generation of antiretrovirals, called nucleoside analog reverse-transcriptase inhibitors (NRTIs), which included AZT, zalcitabine (DDC), didanosine (DDI), stavudine (D4T), and lamivudine (3TC). At that time there was no treatment information in Spanish. It was new and important, because part of surviving AIDS at that time was keeping up with the science. As the science progressed, new treatment paradigms were reached, like medications that proved to be effective in preventing killer opportunistic infections (OIs) such as PCP (*pneumocystis* pneumonia), fungal infections, and MAC (*Mycobacterium avium* complex). There was science that proved that people did not need to die from these OIs. But in marginalized communities, because of lack of education, people with AIDS were still dying unnecessarily from these illnesses.

We also shared information on clinical trials to prevent OIs, as it was in our agenda. For example, patients were able to live longer by preventing PCP with Bactrim, Septra, or dapsone, MAC with clarithromycin, and fungal infections with Diflucan—and in communities with no access to health care, sometimes clinical trials were the only way of care for them. Prevention activism was more popular among advocates, and there was not much involvement from people of color and Latinas/os in activism related to science. After being more and more involved in treatment activism, I found that more critical issues were surfacing that sooner or later were going to impact disadvantaged communities, which were those with less access to care (not surprisingly, those were communities of color: African Americans, Native Americans, Asians, and Latinas/os).

It was not only the government that started to integrate community groups as advisors; the industry did as well. Around 1991 Burroughs Wellcome, the pharmaceutical company that created AZT, hired a consultant to create a first-of-its-kind national community advisory board to provide direct feedback to the pharmaceutical industry in their drug development. The name of the consultant was Daniel Dallabrida, and the first advisory board for the industry was born. Susie Rodriguez and I were the only Latinas/os among activists like Phil Wilson, Reggie Williams, and Robert Remian. What made this group relevant was its diversity and the caliber of its leadership, which included men and women of color.

Besides my personal interest as a person living with HIV, the disproportion of community involvement at the decision-making tables of the

NIH, the Federal Drug Administration, and the pharmaceutical industry made me understand that my commitment was also political: it was an issue of diversity, representation, and social justice. I was frustrated to see how other local and national organizations, like Project Inform, were organizing themselves around how to work with and handle treatment-specific issues. The problem I saw was that none of these organizations worked with and in communities of color. There were very few of us from these communities doing treatment work. It was very difficult to be effective without any institutional support. I started to complain about this to some of our leaders of color, and the response I got was that treatment issues were "white boys'" issues. How could they think that? I was not only a Latino man, but also a Latino man living with AIDS, and for me it was very relevant to understand the medicine of AIDS; and if it was critical for me, it had to be for many others. In 1993 I approached the executive director of the National Minority AIDS Council (NMAC), Paul Kawata. I knew our communities needed to be educated about treatments available. In fact, there was a new class of antiretrovirals under study that looked very promising; but, based on what was seen in the studies, to work effectively these drugs were going to require total adherence and compliance from the patients because the virus would quickly develop resistance if they were not taken properly. Paul Kawata was receptive to the idea of developing a Treatment Advocacy and Education Department at the National Minority AIDS Council and asked me if I would come to head it up, as he was committing himself to raising the funds. He did raise the funds, and I moved to D.C. that year. That's how the "Live long, sugar" PCP prophylaxis campaign was created and implemented. The *HIV Treatment Education Manual* was developed to support organizations for people of color in developing treatment education in their communities. Among other initiatives, the National AIDS Treatment Advocates Forum was born in 1994; this was the first national forum to train activists in all communities on issues related to treatment advocacy and education.

Bringing treatment activism to the arena of people of color—from the street-activist coalition to institutionalized organizations—raised the level of influence, diversity, and visibility of all people of color, including Latinas/os. From the Spanish Communication Committee and the Latino caucus of ACT UP, to LLEGÓ and NMAC's Latina/o activists, these advocates inserted themselves not only into government, but also within the pharmaceutical industry.

Even though treatment education became a standard component of educational services in Latina/o organizations, I still saw very little involvement of Latinas/os in the area of treatment activism and advocacy. Advocating for prophylaxis treatment at an early stage of OIs was crucial and life saving; moreover, when protease inhibitors and antiretroviral combination therapy came along, they saved and prolonged many lives, including my own.

The introduction of protease inhibitors and combination therapy was a paradigm that changed the course of the epidemic. Science has given us the hard and solid proof that by scaling up treatment and sustaining virological suppression in all those treated, we could contain the AIDS epidemic. It has been proven that if patients are in antiretroviral treatment long enough for the virus to be undetectable, they are less infectious. If the virus is undetectable in the blood, it is also undetectable in seminal fluid; with that we now know that if we scale up the use of treatment, we can stop and contain transmission in communities with the resources and capacity to provide sustainable treatment and care.

We now know that AIDS can be cured and the epidemic contained. Science has proven it, and again here I am facing a new paradigm, a new challenge: How do we translate the science into public health? How do we make it work with the National HIV/AIDS Strategy and the groundbreaking new Affordable Care Act? From 1998 to 2004, after I left NMAC, I went to work in the private sector. I was healthy again and had to get my financial life in order. Seven years were enough to do it, and in 2004 I came back to not-for-profit work, with the International Treatment Preparedness Coalition (ITPC) as a program manager working on grant-making efforts in Latin America, the Caribbean, and West, Central, and East Africa. The mission of ITPC was HIV-treatment preparedness in the developing world—in the South. I brought all my experience from the North, insisting that access to treatment was a very vital issue for those with and without HIV, that human rights and social justice were a big part of the work, and that I had something to contribute.

In 2011 a science breakthrough occurred: treatment as prevention and biomedical prevention made their entrance to the world of AIDS, and ironically treatment is now also prevention. I have come full circle in following the path of treatment advocacy, as well as coming full circle in my personal life, thanks to the health I regained after protease inhibitors and combination therapy. I wouldn't be here if I had not made the decision to learn the science of AIDS. As of the time of this writing, I am back at NMAC doing domestic work on treatment as prevention. Regarding my first love before AIDS, literature, and becoming a published writer, that, as well, has been taken care of. I enthusiastically look toward the future, and I see myself becoming old—and I see a generation free of AIDS.

CHAPTER WRITTEN BY MOISÉS AGOSTO-ROSARIO.

JOSÉ GUTIÉRREZ

We Must Preserve Our Latina/o LGBT History

José Gutiérrez, a Latino gay man born in Mexico, has been a Latino LGBT activist in Atlanta and Washington, D.C., since the late 1980s. He was a founder of organizations such as Latinos en Acción and the Latino GLBT History Project, as well as a member of SALUD, Gente Latina de Ambiente (GELAAM), and the National Latino/a Lesbian and Gay Organization (LLEGÓ). Gutiérrez has devoted many years to collecting documents, photographs, flyers, and other artifacts from Latina/o LGBT groups, bars, activists, and performers. His collection has become a unique archive on the history of LGBT Latina/os, especially in the D.C. area. In this oral history–based chapter, Gutiérrez focuses on Latina/o LGBT invisibility as a motivation for his commitment to collecting the archives. He is inspired to preserve, through material, visual, and other cultural artifacts, a history he notes others are not making a priority.

MY NAME IS JOSÉ GUTIÉRREZ. I WAS BORN IN Reynosa, Mexico, across the border from McAllen, Texas. After finishing high school I came to Austin with my first boyfriend. In the mid-1980s I moved to Monterrey to study journalism, but I was unable to complete my degree because my father and one of my sisters died. In Monterrey there were many drag queens and bars. We even had an organization for transvestites, but I can't say that there was a homosexual movement. I was aware of the homosexual movement in Latin America, and I knew of Nancy Cárdenas and the Mexican lesbian movement. I had also read works by LGBT Latin Americans, like Luis Zapata, Manuel Puig, and Sor Juana Inés de la Cruz. In 1986 I moved with the rest of my family and my boyfriend to Atlanta, where one of my sisters lived.

At that time many of my friends were dying of AIDS. This caused me intense suffering. In reality, little was known about the disease. Perhaps because of this I focused my activism on fighting AIDS. I participated as a volunteer in an agency that was called AID Atlanta. I found this agency through a Puerto Rican friend. He was HIV positive, and I would accompany him to AID Atlanta. My friend and many others died, and this motivated me to get involved. Georgia had many Latinas/os, but there wasn't much in the way of AIDS education or prevention. At that time, AID Atlanta served mostly gay white men. A friend of mine, María Rivas, worked there as a program coordinator for Hispanic outreach, and she offered me a part-time job as a health educator. My job consisted of handing out condoms, posting flyers, and distributing bilingual brochures to educate and aid the community in general. I worked on prevention in two communities: the migrant community and the LGBT community.

In 1991 a gay Latina/o bar opened in Atlanta. It was a gathering place for people from all the countries in Latin America. We were united by language, food, music, and we would share our stories. It seemed to me that we were all very isolated. Some people were living in the north, in Gwinnett, other people in Midtown or the Roosevelt area, and others in Stone Mountain. Whenever we would meet a gay or lesbian Latina/o it gave us much joy. The bar offered the opening for people to begin organizing.

Time passed and I discovered that I was also HIV positive. The fact that I lived in Atlanta and was involved in the community helped me a lot. I met good people who supported my evolution as an activist. There was a group of *compañeros* and *compañeras* who did LGBT Latina/o organizing in the state of Georgia, motivated by frustration with the lack of treatment. They were also angry about the neglect of Latinas/os living with HIV/AIDS. I believe that what motivated me to become an activist was the anger I felt at seeing my friends dying of AIDS and the feeling of impotence because little was being done to help them.

At AID Atlanta, we would meet two times a month and go to the consulates, where we would set up a table and distribute information and condoms. All our work was done on a volunteer basis. Shortly afterward, in 1991, I cofounded an organization independent of AID Atlanta with Aida Rentas, a Puerto Rican, called Latinos en Acción. The group was made up of twenty people from the greater Atlanta area. Most of us were middle class and working class. There were also older people who had never come out of the closet. Above all, it was a social group. It offered an escape for us. We would share memories of our respective countries, the fact that we were gay, lesbian, bisexual, and transgender. It was a relief. We also discussed the fear of the immigration issue. Many *compañeros* and *compañeras* were in the process of putting together their documents for immigration purposes, so there was a lot of fear, a lot of concern: "I don't want them to know. I want to be in the closet." I believe that was another barrier we had: the closet and the fear of possible deportation because one was LGBT. There was a lot of anxiety. It was better to not use your name and to not get into trouble to avoid being deported or rejected.

Latinos en Acción dedicated itself to promoting Latina/o LGBT visibility in the Atlanta Gay Pride Parade. We were an unknown community to the parade organizers; it seemed that the white LGBT leaders of Atlanta were discovering us. In that regard, it was comical. We wore costumes and made our own float—that represented a great feat given the barriers we had. The African Americans supported us a little more than the whites. I don't know if that was because of the similarities between us of being minority groups. Nonetheless, there were not many activist African American groups when I lived in Atlanta.

Over several years, Latinos en Acción also did other types of community work. We organized picnics and *bailes* and did HIV prevention work. In 1993 I came to the National March on Washington for Lesbian, Gay, and Bi Equal Rights and Liberation. It was fabulous, with a lot of activities, and I met several people. Juan Rodríguez, a gay Chicano activist, supported me to receive a scholarship that allowed me to attend a conference for gay men of color during the weekend of the march.

In 1994 I applied to work at an organization called SALUD that was located in Columbia Heights in Washington, D.C. I left my resume with Yajaira Arreaza. Shortly after, she offered me a job, and I moved to Washington. That was a beautiful time because it allowed me to work with Yajaira, Olga Rodriguez, Sylvia Evans, Ignacio Aguirre, Hugo Salinas, and Maria Paige, among others. SALUD did a lot of work in HIV prevention with little money. The Latina/o community had a lot of needs similar to what I saw in Atlanta.

About that time, I fell in love with the history of our community and started preserving memorabilia in my apartment, a little efficiency in Dupont Circle. Some of my friends gave me materials from the Washington, D.C., Metropolitan Area Coalition of Latina/o Lesbians and Gay Men (ENLACE), things such as brochures, banners, T-shirts, audiocassettes with music and interviews, and some videocassettes of drag artists. Tomás Gómez, Felisa Batista, Yajaira Arreaza, and other friends gave me posters and other ephemera from the 1980s and from our sisters and brothers who participated in the 1987 March on Washington, people like Leti Gomez and Yolanda Santiago. I collected flyers from El Faro, the first Latina/o LGBT bar in Washington, D.C., located in Adams Morgan. When Chaos (a gay bar that catered to LGBT Latinas/os) closed I recovered photos that they had thrown in the garbage. I put all of these in boxes in a closet or in the kitchen of my apartment. I had the notion then that these items were going to be important to preserving our history for future generations. We didn't have role models or mentors. I had studied Stonewall and knew who Sylvia Rivera was. I met Sylvia in 1994 during the twenty-fifth anniversary celebration of the Stonewall Riots in New York City. I often said to myself, "In school the teachers taught me the history of Mexico, but no one taught me about the LGBT community. What about our heroes? We know about Martin Luther King and Cesar Chavez, but why don't we know who Sylvia Rivera was?" So I started doing research about the Latina/o LGBT community. I realized that we had suffered sometimes double, or even triple, discrimination, sometimes by the white community or even by our own Latina/o community. That motivated me. And I would add that how our activism and our work are perceived depends on who is writing the history of the LGBT movement. I would get angry because in books they explained everything about the history of U.S. Latinas/os, but there was nothing on LGBT issues. And the white LGBT community did the same, because of its disregard for Latinas/os, and I said, "You know what? I am just tired of this." I was tired because we suffered segregation, discrimination and homophobia, sexism and other "isms." Our history is very important and is full of persons who have contributed in all sectors. There are many silent heroes, people who have fought to pave the way, and it is important to recognize them. However, if you don't preserve or give your materials to somebody interested in taking care of those materials, they end up in the trash. It applies to agencies, organizations, and even bars, but especially people. I want to be clear that I have always done historical preservation without compensation and have spent my own money toward it. The most important thing is the time one dedicates to collecting, identifying, and classifying. It is very gratifying to know that future generations will benefit. And you do these things without expecting something in return, just because somebody has to do it. For these reasons it is fundamental that we educate our community in the culture of historical preservation.

When I was working at SALUD, I also began to involve myself with the National Latino/a Lesbian and Gay Organization (LLEGÓ). I went to the office that was located on G and Seventh Streets, Southeast, near the Eastern Market Metro stop. It was a small house of two floors, and there I met Leti Gomez, the executive director. I also met Luigi Buitrago, Edgardo Guerrero, Carmen Chávez, and Robert Vázquez-Pacheco. LLEGÓ made policies, provided technical assistance, and created visibility. In that period of time, the LGBT Latina/o community was very strong. I was delighted because the community was more visible than in Atlanta, and a lot was being done. I remember that in 1996 LLEGÓ was the first organization I knew of to hire a Latina transgender person as part of the staff. Her name was Gabriela Montes. A few years after that, LLEGÓ incorporated the word transgender into its name, becoming the National Latino/a Lesbian, Gay, Bisexual, and Transgender Organization. Many people came to LLEGÓ, all very good, very active in their communities, with thousands of needs, people from many countries and eager to do something. For all of them, LLEGÓ was like a school—its work was very important. I was also a product of LLEGÓ; it was a cradle of Latina/o queer activists. We were like a big family. We did a professional job equal to any national organization, including the Encuentros.

In 1995 LLEGÓ organized its third national conference, "Creando Familia." I served as cochair. My job was to organize the local committee and to motivate the community. At the 1996 Encuentro, "Sembrando la Semilla," I received the Manuel Sandoval Award (Manuel Sandoval was a Latino activist who died of HIV/AIDS that year), which was a sculpture made by a Latina lesbian artist.

In that period many Latinas/os were infected with HIV, but government funding for local grants was very little. Then the movement began having success. For its part, the work of ENLACE, which was founded in 1987, was the most important at the local level. Thanks to ENLACE there was visibility in many areas, and in 1993 to 1995 it transitioned (ENLACE folded in 1995). LLEGÓ was established and fighting to gain visibility and political space on the national scene. At the same time, GELAAM (Gente Latina de Ambiente, founded in 1994) was working locally with people like Edgardo Guerrero, Carmen Chávez, Sofía Carrero, and Perry Miranda. In contrast to ENLACE, GELAAM received many grants for HIV prevention from the AIDS partnership of the D.C. government's HIV/AIDS Administration. Then there were two bars, El Faro—which was already open when I moved to D.C.—and Escándalo, which opened in 1994. SALUD was dedicated to fighting HIV, but soon after it would be closing its doors. Another group dedicated to HIV/AIDS was Factor Común, whose prime focus was HIV education. It was created by the HIV Community Coalition, where I had been a volunteer from 1994 to 1996. Later, I became a member of the board of directors.

During those three years we worked on the Latina/o float for the Gay Pride Parade, which was sponsored by GELAAM, the bar Escándalo, and LLEGÓ, and one year we won for best float. We also participated in other parades. I remember marching with Salvador Vidal-Ortiz and Edgardo Guerrero in the Festival Latino Parade that went down Pennsylvania Avenue. There were now other groups too, like Triángulo Rosa, which was led by Fausto Fernández. It was mostly social and focused on youth empowerment. Acuarela was a social group for gay Latino men. A third group, Platiquemos, was also organized by Fausto Fernández.

There was also a group of Latina lesbians who taught us a lot and opened doors for us. I speak of people like Leti Gomez, Yolanda Santiago, María Cecilia Zea, Nilda Aponte, Margarita Lopez, and Yajaira Arreaza. Finally, it is important to mention that during this period of time the transgender movement was very strong. I remember the Carrero "sisters," Sofía and Linda, who were female impersonators. They were from Nicaragua and were very beloved. They started a trend based on contests: Miss Mexico, Miss Puerto Rico, Miss Venezuela, and Miss International. I also need to mention community-based organizations like Whitman-Walker Clinic. They were doing some queer activism and queer programs like their Latino program, directed by Frank Yurrita.

In the end, the work was about filling various needs, from the fight against AIDS to the defense of the human rights of the Latina/o LGBT community. From my point of view, the Latina/o LGBT groups in Washington, D.C., were the most important in the country. Why? We worked at the local and national level, and it was a "golden era" for the Latina/o LGBT community. We gained a community that was healthier and stronger despite the barriers and limitations we had. The work was well done.

During this golden era, collaborations between agencies and groups began. For instance, ENLACE worked closely with SALUD on issues of HIV/AIDS. They also collaborated with the Washington, D.C., Office on Latino Affairs on issues of discrimination. The Whitman-Walker Clinic worked with Latinas/os in La Clínica del Pueblo on identity issues and also provided some services. SALUD and GELAAM created the first HIV/AIDS prevention program by and for Latinas/os. GELAAM and LLEGÓ worked together on an HIV/AIDS prevention program, sponsored by LLEGÓ, called Cultura es Vida. There was also networking with Latina/o heterosexual organizations, although it was minimal, perhaps because there were few groups of that type.

LGBT Latina/o activism was influenced, although only partially, by the projects and funding dedicated to the fight against HIV. On the one hand, many of us had previous experience with movements in our home countries. In my case, as I said earlier, I was familiar with the work of Nancy Cárdenas and the Mexican lesbian movement of the 1960s and 1970s. On the other hand, as much for me as for others, the fight against AIDS, the anger, the desperation, and the isolation motivated us to unite through activism. You get to a point when you say, "OK, I am not going to be quiet. I need to do something." Much of the money that we received at the local and national level was designated for HIV education and prevention. Remember, for example, at the local level, the main work of the Whitman-Walker Clinic and SALUD was education and prevention of HIV. Something similar happened at the national level.

In those years, a movement was created that involved many agencies and organizations and the people who worked in them. There was also the urgency to unite and say, "Aquí estamos"—in other words, to have representation and visibility as Latinas/os and LGBT people. Of course, there were disagreements between LGBT groups and some organizations, because we were groups of Latina/o activists working to defend our identity, culture, and heritage. We worked to rescue our history. For example, at times we would fight with white organizations that worked in HIV because they were not covering the needs of the Latina/o community. This activism in D.C. had a national effect, because the work that was being done gained visibility.

Each of the organizations that I was involved with during that period has left a legacy. Latinos en Acción opened doors for many people, created community and consciousness in the state of Georgia and specifically Atlanta. Before Latinos en Acción, we were 100 percent invisible and if visible, we were seen as strange. Latinos en Acción gave us visibility by educating many people. Moreover, it was a space of empowerment for *compañeras* and *compañeros*. We could say, "No estamos solos. I am feeling the same way that you feel. We suffer the same discrimination and isolation."

SALUD was different, more than anything because it was a job. But it helped people who were very sick, even though it had few resources to offer, and it helped open a front in the fight against AIDS. In SALUD, I had many good coworkers who educated thousands. We worked on issues of immigration and domestic violence that had not been dealt with. That was SALUD's legacy. In respect to GELAAM, I was only a volunteer for events like their fundraising shows at Escándalo or their participation in the float for D.C. Gay Pride Parade. Of LLEGÓ, I can say that it was a magnificent organization. I have a lot of respect for LLEGÓ and all of the people who worked there.

While I was involved in activism, I continued to preserve our history. One day I said to myself, "What's the point of keeping all these boxes? What's my purpose? Our history needs to be shared." Beginning in 1995 I began to buy large display panels. I made one about GELAAM, then another one about LLEGÓ, the HIV/AIDS movement, and lesbian leaders. Basically my job was to showcase the contributions of Latina/o LGBT activists. Around 1999 I gave a first presentation on Latina/o LGBT history at La Clínica del Pueblo, as part of Acuarela. Then I was invited to other places such as American University and George Mason University. I even did a presentation with college students from Wisconsin who were traveling throughout the Northeast.

In April 2000, during the National March on Washington, I presented the first exhibit on the history of LGBT Latinas/os at the bar Chaos, with the support of GELAAM. The same year, I invited my boyfriend and another friend to start a new organization, the Latino GLBT History Project. This organization has been active since then, dedicated to preservation and to educating the public about the culture, history, and contributions of LGBT Latinas/os. It has organized various cultural events, such as exhibitions in the Washington area, and for several years has been a nonprofit organization.

In the same year, 2000, after creating the Latino GLBT History Project, I was one of five cofounders of the Rainbow History Project, along with Mark Meinke. Finally, in 2006, I agreed to organize the first D.C. Latino Pride, as a space to celebrate our identities and culture and to honor our leaders.

At this moment I am somewhat retired, not as active as before due to health issues. But there are other *compañeros* and *compañeras* who are continuing the work of leaving a legacy to society. In terms of my life in Atlanta and Washington, D.C., I have had different roles. I have been an activist, but also a poet. I have been preserving what other people have created in the past, but at the same time I have been creating my own work. I want to reiterate the importance of historical preservation. As I said previously, we have suffered various forms of discrimination. Our Latina/o LGBT communities have been in the United States for years. Even though, in some moments in time, we were not organized, it did not mean that we did not exist. We were at Stonewall; we were in San Francisco before Stonewall. But we lack documentation of our presence as LGBT Latina/os. There have been many *compañeras* and *compañeros* who have struggled, and I am grateful to them. Even though they are anonymous heroes, I want to give them thanks from my heart for the work that they did.

ORAL HISTORY INTERVIEW CONDUCTED BY LETITIA
GOMEZ AND SALVADOR VIDAL-ORTIZ IN WASHINGTON,
D.C., ON SEPTEMBER 18, 2011. CHAPTER WRITTEN BY
URIEL QUESADA AND TRANSLATED BY LETITIA GOMEZ.

OLGA ORRACA PAREDES

All the Identities on the Table: Power, Feminism, and LGBT Activism in Puerto Rico

Olga Orraca Paredes was born in Puerto Rico, where from an early age she became engaged in intersectional community activism. Later, she joined pro-independence groups and the Puerto Rican feminist movement. After this early set of experiences, she began to work with LGBT groups, giving emphasis to lesbian communities. In the more than twenty years that Orraca Paredes has been an LGBT activist, she has approached activism from various fronts: from organizing with marginalized people, workers, and women to participating in street theater. An incisive observer of power relations, Orraca Paredes offers in this oral history–based narrative a provocative perspective on the contradictions within groups constituted to defend the rights of LGBT Latinas/os. Her constant political commitment exemplifies the relevance of lesbian activism in the last decades of the twentieth century in Puerto Rico.

M Y NAME IS OLGA ORRACA PAREDES. I WAS BORN in Puerto Rico in 1955, in a family of six—father, mother, three sisters, and me. It was a functional and dysfunctional family at the same time, as Puerto Rican families in my view tend to be. From the time I was very young, I enjoyed much freedom to recognize and explore my identities and to form my own perspectives. We were middle working class, and my parents always worked outside of the house. My parents were very liberal, and one of my sisters was part of the pro-independence movement. They offered me a framework of political and social interest that I have followed for much of my life.

I studied in Catholic private schools, where mostly middle- and middle-lower-class students attended. Working with some of the special events organized from time to time, I had the chance to volunteer at El Volcán—a poor, marginalized neighborhood—in Bayamón. I was fourteen then, and I realized at that age that community work was important to me. So I continued my involvement with the community irrespective of the school. Among other things, I worked with kids and participated in adult-literacy training.

One of the first big lessons I received happened while volunteering. We were in a community meeting with people from El Volcán. We had rescued and fixed up a house that we wanted to turn into a school to continue with adult literacy and workshops for children, youth, and adults. At some point, one of the people at the meeting got up and said, "We are the ones who live here, not you, so don't come in to tell us what our problems are. Listen to us, and then tell us how you might be able to help." What I interpreted was, "We are the main characters of this story." That statement impacted me profoundly, to the point that I still remember it vividly. That event signaled a departure point for my work with communities. I don't believe in community work done from a desk or office, without contact with the base. I am very careful with all the aspects of political work in terms of representation or spokespersons. It seems to me that the world is much more complex than that, and it also happens with social movements.

It was from that experience at El Volcán that I started my political and community work. At the political level, I joined the Puerto Rican independence movement and participated in study groups. In the 1970s you were not a part of an organization or social movement if you were not also reading, educating yourself, evaluating your position, or looking at other models. So I joined study groups, and I got involved with the Puerto Rican Socialist Party. In the process of working with the Left, I realized—as a woman and a person looking at life through a feminist lens—that something was missing from my identity.

In terms of the feminist movement, I started to participate, at an organizational level, with the Federación de Mujeres Puertorriqueñas. It was organized by chapters, and the reality within each of the chapters was different, because the work was developed through the lived experiences of the women in that particular group. So there were groups of intellectuals who promoted a more theoretical discussion, and then others, like where I was, where there was more work at the homes of the people, and we talked more of their reality than "reading X" or "feminist theory Y." I was able to be a part of the feminist movement, and within some of the groups I was a part of I participated with the woman who was my very first partner. We were known as a couple on an intimate and familiar level, and we were respected as such. However, the topic was not discussed.

I participated in a theater collective called Colectivo de Teatro Cimarrona, from which we did work of political activism. The collective was made up of a group of lesbian women. I cannot state, however, that Cimarrona was consciously or openly lesbian, but it was not closed off either. We went from house to house offering our presentation, doing workshops, and engaging in consciousness-raising work. So we always had a chance to discuss what we presented. We also had a space at the Avenida Central, a theater café, where the topics of our plays were almost always related to political awareness. Even when we did not name it as such, it was a place where many lesbians hung out and where everyone could join. Looking at that time in retrospect, I would say that my interest or needs were channeled through projects such as the Colectivo de Teatro Cimarrona, where we did much more consciousness-raising work, and where we lived our sexual orientation out of the closet within the group. We worked with kids, we had art-based summer camps, and we were recognized as lesbian women, some of us coupled within the group. I don't remember that we—as lesbian women driven by feminism and committed to the work—ever received anything but recognition and respect from parents. This was around the early 1980s.

When I started college in the 1970s, my experience continued to expand. I continued with community work. That experience has given me constant contact with reality. At that time I was realizing that, really, there was no room for a feminist perspective within the Puerto Rican Left, because independence was the first goal, and everything else went after. In the 1970s and 1980s everything seemed single-issued or compartmentalized. If you were feminist, then you were feminist. If you were pro-independence, then so you were . . . and every fight was validated, somehow, by itself. In the mid-1970s I started to more fully integrate into the feminist movement through the Federación de Mujeres Puertorriqueñas and other nonformalized community groups. However, within the feminist movement, I had a very similar feeling and experience of this compartmentalization once I self-identified as a lesbian and embraced that identity, which I did in college. Assuming my lesbian identity was not a traumatic experience. One day I simply said to a friend, "I am falling in love with that woman . . ." And from that moment on until today I have lived without questioning myself or being questioned by my family. However, I noticed that the feminist movement I was a part of did not make room for that identity by sexual orientation. At that moment I started to join the LGBT movement in Puerto Rico and to be much more alert to and involved with what was happening on an international level.

By the end of the 1980s and early 1990s, I formally joined the LGBT movement, precisely because I felt that such an important part of me was left out of other spaces, other struggles, that had been my priority in the past. Unfortunately, I quickly arrived at the conclusion that, as a woman, I did not have enough space there either: there was space to work, but no opportunity for women to talk for the organization or be as visible as men. There was a problem in validating our work, our perspectives, as to the direction of the LGBT movement, our analysis of the historical moment we were in, and the challenges our various communities faced. In that vicious cycle, it does not really matter where you are: if one does not have all the identities on the table, somehow something else is going to continue to emerge, be it a difference or an inequality in terms of power or control.

I decided to withdraw for a while from all organized work. During that time, I reflected about how the only way I could return to more formal work was by being utterly conscious about all the identities that formed who I was. That reflection coincided with the new international perspective on social movements, which affirmed that if we did not bring our identities and particular struggles to the work, nobody would advance.

The first organization I officially linked myself to in Puerto Rico was the Coalición Puertorriqueña de Lesbianas y Homosexuales (CPLH). Before that, I had worked with other groups without being a central member of them, and this type of participation has been for me the foundation of the work I've done for the last two decades. Wherever I've been, I am always Olga Orraca Paredes: feminist, lesbian, pro-independence advocate, a believer in socialism and social justice. Life has given me the experiences to be a unique human being, so I do the work from a human rights perspective.

Before Coalición Puertorriqueña de Lesbianas y Homosexuales was organized, the Colectivo de Concientización Gay existed, and it was a group for men and women. From that group the Colectivo de Lesbianas Feministas emerged in the late 1980s. I participated in some of its events. Around the same time, ten women formed Nosotras Diez, mostly as a study group with very particular projects. Later on, once it stopped being just ten women, it evolved into Aquelarre Lésbico. This was a very particular moment, because women began to group together into lesbian organizations. These groups gained strength later on. In the 1980s and early 1990s about seventeen LGBT organizations existed in Puerto Rico doing different work from various perspectives. At the Universidad de Puerto Rico were the Comunidad Universitaria Pro Igualdad Gai and the Grupo de Apoyo. Organizations from this period were as diverse as Reencuentro (a spiritual reflection group). There were open door churches in the mid-1990s as well as cogender groups like the Coalición Puertorriqueña de Lesbianas y Homosexuales and the Coalición Orgullo Arcoiris—the longest-running organization of continuous work within the LGBT movement. There were many women's groups too. Outside the San Juan metro area, for instance, was the Taller Zuania.

In addition to the diversity of LGBT activist organizations during this period, another important point is that many of the male activists in the 1980s dedicated their efforts to HIV, and emergent NGOs (nongovernmental organizations) dedicated their time, and most importantly their economic resources, to supporting efforts to fight against AIDS. This created a meeting place for LGBT activists, but it was also an opportunity for women's organizing around non-HIV/AIDS issues—in their own spaces.

Around 1989 to 1990, a group of lesbians and gay men called Coalición Puertorriqueña de Lesbianas y Homosexuales started a phone info line linked to the Fundación SIDA de Puerto Rico (now closed). People called to find out information about doctors, mechanics, technicians, and other service providers who wouldn't necessarily be LGBT but who were sensitive and friendly to our communities. Shortly after, the info line group separated from Fundación SIDA and started to strengthen its action goals, keeping in mind the needs of the constituents—the callers of Teleinfo Gay (the name of the project). In this way, what in principle was an info line became in practice a support phone line.

Through our experience with the hotline formed while at Fundación SIDA, we realized that working two hours a day, five days a week was not enough, so we created a volunteer group as an independent project of Fundación. Using our volunteers, we tried to offer services for longer hours and on more weekdays, although we faced serious limitations because we did not have sufficient resources or the infrastructure to do it. One of the things people in and out of the closet suffer in our communities is loneliness, and worse, isolation. One might participate in social and political events, but when you get home you might be separated from everyone and everything else. The same thing might happen at work, school, or with family. There are many challenges, not just in the context of being Puerto Rican but also in terms of our identities based on sexual orientation, gender, and gender expression.

Around 1994 CPLH started to develop an archive of materials and documents that *compañeras* and *compañeros* working in the gay and lesbian movements since the 1970s had held on to. We had a space called "La Casita" (the Little House) that, although it was never identified as such, was in practice an LGBT community center. There we saved the archives and documents people loaned or donated to us. Additionally, that space was made available for meetings of all types. Indeed, aside from being an archive and information center, La Casita offered a socialization space and facilitated the political work the LGBT community was engaged in at the time.

In 1991 the first LGBT Pride March took place in Puerto Rico. Since then it has been the event that brings together the largest number of LGBT people on the Island. In a sense, it has had a tremendous media impact—an impact with non-LGBT groups—and it has been a decisive way to offer a human rights perspective in terms of identity and respect for diversity. The *compañeras* and *compañeros* who created Coalición Orgullo Arcoiris (COA) wanted to give a formal, ample structure to an organization responsible for the second Puerto Rican Pride March. The work by COA expanded as well in order to provide other communities with an educational component that would contextualize our LGBT realities. For example, we held sensitivity trainings within and outside our communities.

For me and other activists, our links to international work between social movements in Puerto Rico and Latin America were, and still are, very important to us. Although in many instances we want to focus on our relationship to and links with continental U.S. movements and organizations, the truth is that Puerto Rico has been very involved in work done in Latin America and the Caribbean. It was in that spirit that in 1992 we hosted the Tercer Encuentro de Lesbianas Feministas de Latinoamérica y el Caribe. We mobilized a large group of women to help make the Encuentro take place in Puerto Rico. We worked in relative isolation and with little to no resources, looking for a safe place so that our lesbian *compañeras* could meet. Among the groups existing then, CPLH offered its limited resources to support the organizing.

The Encuentro de Lesbianas Feministas de Latinoamérica y el Caribe brought together *compañeras* from the Island who were, for the first time, making contact with lesbian groups in and outside of Puerto Rico. Some of these women were even more isolated because they were mothers. When we brought up the topic of being mother and lesbian in workshops and small groups, those women realized that there was no space for them there—similar to my own previous experience. Suddenly they realized that even in that space where they should be welcomed as lesbian mothers, from a feminist perspective, the response was "no." That motivated some of the *compañeras* to form Madres Lesbianas de Puerto Rico, a group that worked for more than ten years offering support to lesbians with kids, developing projects and concrete programs, and doing educational work.

During those years, the COA organized not only the Pride March but also Coming Out Day in October, a celebration that would later become LGBT Awareness Day. Some of us started to resent that in both activities women were invisible, not in the work but significantly on stage. Rather than just offering criticism, we realized that we needed to formulate alternatives. Then in 1993 to 1994, and because of this, an experienced, creative group organized to present a show. The group was the Taller Lésbico Creativo. As the years went by, the Taller started to do more grassroots work, more educational work, through interactive workshops and by using art as a main tool, not just in theater but in other creative forms as well. The Taller initiatives were brought to communities outside the LGBT community. That has been one of the main contributions of the Taller Lésbico Creativo: we still get requests, and we still try to keep a presence and develop workshops, although we do that sporadically. We have brought these workshops to the Latina lesbian community in the United States too.

A great many of the links established between the Taller and the Latina lesbian community in the United States were done through the National Latino/a Lesbian and Gay Organization (LLEGÓ), which had a presence in Puerto Rico in the 1990s. For various reasons, the first visits by LLEGÓ were received with mixed feelings. On the one hand, aside from our individual political ideologies, we recognize that we are a nation, whether we say it or not. On the other hand, because of the colonial status of Puerto Rico, we have resentments, fears, and hesitations, and it was in this context that we resented LLEGÓ's approach as an imposition along the lines of "We bring this work agenda for you." There had been an organized and documented movement here since 1974, when the penal code was revised and a discussion of Article 103, known as the sodomy law, started. This event gave an opening for some to integrate into a group called Comunidad Orgullo Gay. So we understood that, after so many years of work, our activism went beyond LLEGÓ's imposed agenda, and that agenda was inadequate. We felt it was disrespectful that LLEGÓ would come with a preestablished agenda.

I would say that our first encounter with LLEGÓ was not fluid. It provoked a lot of different emotions, but it still meant the beginning of a relationship with LLEGÓ. At least at the organizational level, and as time passed, the relationships started to get disentangled, in the sense that in Puerto Rico there were organized communities, there were people already doing work, and we dealt within our particular national context. Even today we find people living outside of Puerto Rico who wish to be a part of what happens here. And of course they have the right to be a part of it, and I think it is very important that they are, within their context, a part of the work done here. What we should not lose perspective of is that, when there is no daily context, you lose a sense of what is happening in the country. If you are not living that oppression or the situations that are happening at that moment, to say what should be our priority work goals from afar seems to be risky and counterproductive.

Some of us were linked to LLEGÓ from an ample, international work perspective. LLEGÓ offered us the possibility of staying in touch with Latinas/os in U.S. LGBT communities. It was also important to learn of experiences and perspectives about what was going on in the United States, where half of the Puerto Ricans live, because for us that was, and is, important. Because, as had happened in the creation of the Taller Lésbico Creativo, some of us realized that, in addition to critiquing something, we had the chance to make proposals that would allow us to participate from inside LLEGÓ. Knowing of their work with grassroots organizations, we noticed that within the organization there was a lack of awareness of socioeconomic and educational differences, areas that we continued to focus our efforts on. In many instances LLEGÓ had lost perspective on what the class struggles were or what it meant to be a second- or third-generation immigrant versus one who had just arrived six months ago. From that critical view I began working and collaborating with LLEGÓ's board of directors, around 1994 to 1995. As a result, I would later join the board.

Something that gets internalized is the lack of consciousness of what diversity really means. As a member of LLEGÓ's board of directors, I made such points and wove them to the Puerto Rican realities from the perspective of an insider. The board was made up of people with different perspectives—feminist or not feminist, with class-consciousness or not—and with various life experiences, because as board members we came from many parts of the United States and Puerto Rico. During my years on the board (1996–2002), such differences were a challenge, particularly in two instances where the differences were important. The first one was the organization as a space where employees worked, projects and programs were run, and money was managed. The second was the board's role in providing fiscal oversight of the organization while representing a microcosm of the LGBT communities in the United States and Puerto Rico that we wanted to serve.

Some of the women on the board argued that LLEGÓ was disconnected from the reality of our communities. We saw in many instances a lack of sensibility to many LGBT *compañeras* and *compañeros* and their daily struggles. At this point, there was a dichotomy not unusual in many organizations: the priorities based on the community needs you wish to serve and the priorities established through the available funds. As our movements become institutionalized—in terms of requiring infrastructure and maintaining a healthy fiscal balance—they start to decay. The decay may be in the fiscal aspects or in honoring the organizational objectives within the social movement. In terms of LLEGÓ, the board members took different positions on the board's role and the administration of the organization—from one position stressing the importance of being a good employer, to my position, which was that LLEGÓ should be a community-based organization. In some instances there were no meeting points, which widened the gap between these two positions.

It was during my last years in LLEGÓ that these differences—between sustaining a fiscally healthy organization and doing community-based work—became most evident. To a great extent, the board ceased being a body that served as a check on the executive administration. The board's responsibility was not just fiscal oversight, but oversight of carrying out the presumed objectives, mission, and vision of the organization. Suddenly I realized that there were three groups: the executive office, the staff, and the board of directors. A fourth group was the communities, which thought that LLEGÓ was very strong politically and financially and that it could support virtually any initiative. However, that was not the reality, because there were funds committed for particular programs, mostly tied to HIV. For many communities this was not LLEGÓ's only work priority, nor did they require any support in that area. One could say that LLEGÓ was like a four-point star, where each point defended its point of view as to where the organization should go. And at the center was the organization, being pulled from all four extremes. Some of us thought that we needed to meet at that middle point, or the star would blow up.

At a certain point, some of the board members decided we would leave our positions, but not before engaging in a real evaluation, not just of funds but also of the organization's transformation. The situation we faced was harder than we expected, given that the distance between the groups was worse than we thought. For instance, one of the least healthy elements of the board was that for many years its members had been selected by invitation only—many times the invitation came from the executive administration—and the board simply ratified it. That implied a loyalty not necessarily to the organization, but instead to the priorities and vision of the executive office.

In spite of that, we wanted to uncover the four different corners to see where we really were as an organization. We wished to know this, even though this required two types of actions: to continue with the programs and projects, mostly from governmental financing agencies to whom we held much responsibility, and to analyze what was happening in our communities, which in the end was the reason for the organization's existence.

When I was still presiding over the board in 2002 I had a health problem that forced me to completely retire from the work: I was to undergo cancer treatment. I had to focus on my health and quality of life. As I was going through such personal troubles, something similar was happening in LLEGÓ. The female board members who stayed were finding little to no support from the organization, and as a result it became harder and harder for them to remain on the board. As I said before, each group fought against the rest, meaning we recognized that we represented different priorities. Faced with this challenge, most of the people from the board deserted, and then the executive administration of the organization invited a new group of people to become board members in 2002 at the Encuentro in Miami. These new members and the former members were not on the same page, and we were handling much more information than the newcomers about what was happening and what needed to be done. This caused a distancing between the new board members and the old ones, and we stopped being welcomed by the organization. This is why we must see the processes in organizations as fluid—they move not just due to circumstances you have control over but also due to those you cannot control. Life creates circumstances—both in our personal lives and in collective groups—when it is important to stop, revise, and catch up on health, be it physical or organizational.

A while ago I read that to be moral is to wish for other people what you wish for yourself. Following that perspective as an activist, I began with the good I wish for me as a woman, a feminist, a lesbian, a daughter, a lover, a partner, but most of all as Olga Orraca Paredes. In some way, and in proportion to my search to reach a better quality of life for myself, with honesty and commitment, I believe I was able to impact other people. But most of all, I think that activism is a learning process. I think we share what we learn and what we believe. Similarly, I receive something from all people who come through my life, be it within the organized movements I am a part of or outside of them. I experience it as an opportunity to look at myself and to learn.

I've always questioned power—that which is control or privilege. I have been interested in understanding how we place ourselves in relation to power, control, and privilege. In particular, understanding that relationship is in large part how we form the "skin" in which we live and the way in which we manage ourselves. If we are not conscious of our limitations and our privileges, we miss an important part of making a serious life analysis, because that's what I think life is all about: to commit ourselves to it with all our being.

ORAL HISTORY INTERVIEW CONDUCTED BY SALVADOR VIDAL-ORTIZ IN SAN JUAN, PUERTO RICO, ON DECEMBER 23, 2011. CHAPTER WRITTEN BY URIEL QUESADA AND TRANSLATED BY SALVADOR VIDAL-ORTIZ.

WILFRED W. LABIOSA

Visibility, Inclusivity, and the Fight for LGBT Rights in New England

Wilfred Labiosa was born in San Juan, Puerto Rico. In the late 1980s he moved to Boston, where he finally settled. Labiosa was among the founders of La Coalición Somos Latin@s LGBT in Massachusetts in 1997. He was one of the forces behind the first Latina/o LGBT Pride celebration in the nation, a founding member of Unid@s, the National Latino/a LGBT Human Rights Organization (which was formed after the closing of LLEGÓ), and the cocreator of the newspaper column Visión Latina. *In this personal essay Labiosa reflects on his relationship with his family, his experiences in Puerto Rican society, his coming out process in Massachusetts, and his commitment to activism. In 2014 Labiosa was completing a PhD in social work at Simmons College, and he continues to focus on activism and organizing around the needs of Latina/o communities in the New England area. Although Labiosa's essay was originally written in Spanish as a testament to his political solidarity with the Island, it was translated into English for inclusion in this book.*

A LATINA/O LGBT PRIDE CELEBRATION IN THE NEW England area may seem unprecedented, but behind it is a movement that has been working toward it for many years. I recount here how I arrived in Boston, joined a group of Latina/o LGBT people, and began to organize the community in order for our movement to be recognized as united, educated, and strong.

I came to Boston in 1989 to go to college, and I found a different world from the one I knew. There I learned to live more comfortably with myself and with all the "parts" that made me unique. I was born in 1971 and raised in the San Juan metropolitan area in a middle-class family. Half of my family completed the highest high school levels; the other half did not, though they were hard-working people. My grand-parents stressed to me the importance of harvesting what you want. They also taught me to not be complacent and, at the same time, to be patient. And my parents—my father in particular—worked hard to give my sister and me an education and a good quality of life. Unfortunately, that "life" was only suitable within the very specific mold they had en-visioned. Activism was never among their plans for us. They dreamt that I would become a doctor, completing studies outside of the coun-try and coming back to the Island to serve in that role. In the end, I left Puerto Rico after graduating from high school and went home only for short visits.

In Puerto Rico I learned strict male and female gender roles from an early age, just as I grew up assuming that the man has to financially support his (heteronormative) family and to give himself "completely" even if unhappy. The individuality so embedded in the United States is not as important in Puerto Rico as the sense of family. In Puerto Rico *machismo* is respected, and *marianismo* revered; they are, in my view, es-sential parts of society. My family insisted from early on that I needed to marry (a woman, of course) and have a family, which I needed to keep "happy." I felt *machismo* in comments such as "you are a man, you need to take initiative and earn more money to support your family." *Marianismo*, on the other hand, appeared in comments that a woman needed to be a stay-at-home mother or support her "man." In my expe-rience, these concepts were central to the Puerto Rican society where I grew up. There was no space for out-of-the-norm situations like di-vorced people, gay couples, or single parents. Adoption was not an op-tion either. In part because of these reasons I decided to leave Puerto Rico. From a very young age, I knew that there was diversity not only of races, social classes, and religions but also of sexuality. I also felt different.

In my family there were topics of conversation we never discussed—for instance the fact that my aunt, who never got married, had had a "best friend" since I was a kid. Or a feminine male cousin and a mascu-line female cousin who would visit us with a "friend." Sometime later, those cousins came out of the closet with me, and my single aunt, when she aged, became the most homophobic of them all. Through such peo-ple, my family had the opportunity to directly address sexuality issues, but it was so taboo that we never talked about it. I never had a conver-sation about sex with my parents, because the expectation was that I would only have sex after getting married. At the present time my cousins and I live a double life: one type with our family and another among our gay friends and in our relationships. We only let some relatives enter that personal space, and within such space we have created a family that accepts us unconditionally.

While they did not talk about our sexuality, our family would always discuss politics—and everyone had an opinion about it. In Puerto Rico, one of the last colonies remaining, people are divided into three political groups: those who fight for independence, those who want to become the fifty-first U.S. state, and those who wish to remain a "free associated state." In my family every political position was evident, but I of course was different because of my pro-independence position. Because of this political position and my conservative family, I always wanted to fight for what I wanted and to defend my principles. It is not strange then to note that at home my family would always refer to "Wilfred's politics."

My parents and I moved to Massachusetts in 1984 with the expectation that my sister would also move with us and we would thus live as a single family within the same house. My sister never arrived, however, because she decided to marry and reside in Minnesota. During the first couple of years in the United States, I met people who became very important to me—people who strengthened my personality and helped increase my leadership potential. I remember a Spanish professor, for instance. Although I was unable to take her class, she always spoke to me and would say that I had to be proud of who I was and the person I was becoming. She changed my life forever.

We returned to Puerto Rico in 1986. There I finished high school. Even though I had only been gone for two years (and despite the fact that I went back to the same Catholic school in San Juan), I and the other students had changed, and it was difficult to recover my crew of friends. I never had a good friend who was gay; the two other gay men in my school never spoke to me about it and would instead make homophobic comments against the gay community and me. I became friends with a lesbian. She and I would go out sometimes, but it was not the same. In the end I played at being both out and in the closet; it really depended on where I was and with whom. During those years (1986–1989) in my school there were no groups focused on LGBT youth, like there are now. I only had allies and lesbian friends with whom I hung out and had a good time. When the opportunity to apply for colleges came up, I applied to places abroad. That's how I went to Boston University.

In Boston, aside from studying, I tried to make friends. I sought places where I would feel comfortable as a gay Latino, and at the beginning I did not find them. About halfway through the year (1991) a guy took me for the first time to "Latin Wednesdays" at Chaps, a gay club. There I found my people. That very same night I met everyone who worked at Chaps, from the manager to the drag queens. A Venezuelan promoter had established the Latin Wednesdays, but most of the staff and people in charge of the performances were either Puerto Rican or Cuban: La Loba, Vicky, Mari, Rene, Leo, Miguel, Coco López. It was a very special evening for me, since I had found out that the LGBT Latina/o community did exist, but only in these clubs' social circles. My LGBT peer group began to grow! Some of them had been there for just a few months, and others had been there for years. Even though there was no clear sense of unity outside of the club, at least we felt like family inside the club and saw each other as brothers and sisters on the streets.

The female cousin I mentioned previously moved to Boston with her partner to work. Some other friends followed, and everyone started to go out together. One night a Cuban gay friend told my cousin that I was gay. That was the best thing, since it was the first time a family member knew of my sexual orientation. That night I went out with all of them and started to express who I really was. However, when I would visit Puerto Rico I would go back to the closet at home, even though at the beach everyone knew, and I would only go out to places I felt comfortable. Even now, many of my family members know I have "my politics" and do not want to know anything about my gay life.

I stayed in Boston to get my master's degree. I began to assume a Latina/o leadership role on campus and a gay leadership role in the community. I attended meetings of different groups, but none were for me, because there were no Latina/o LGBT groups other than ones focused on HIV/AIDS or other health issues. None was focused on building rapport among LGBT Latinas/os.

After graduating in 1994 I was recruited to work with the Latino Health Institute in Boston as a mental health counselor and prevention facilitator. I took the job because I would be able to work directly with youth. I supervised the Hombres Latinos Gay Project, the first program of its kind that focused on HIV/AIDS prevention among men who have sex with men or who identify as gay. After applying for new projects and learning more about the needs of LGBT Latina/o communities, I started—with Cristian, Aníbal, Ernesto, Rafael, Marty, Letti, and others—Proyecto LUNA (Latina Lesbians and Latinos Unidos en Acción).

Similarly, I helped expand the Hombres Latinos Gay Project to the cities of Lowell and Brockton. In addition to focusing on health, those programs also included social events and activities. These were the first in the area with the words gay, lesbian, and Latina/o in their names.

Some Latina/o LGBT groups that frequented Chaps started to emerge. Strawberries and Chocolate, founded by Colombian and Puerto Rican youth in 1995, was a social/artistic group from the Chelsea and East Boston areas. Proyecto Arcoiris, founded in 1997 in the Merrimack area, was created for Puerto Rican, Dominican, and Colombian young people. El Sombrero, founded in 1998 by Colombians and Puerto Ricans in the Lynn area, engaged in HIV/AIDS prevention. A Guatemalan community leader formed the Gay and Lesbian Latino Association of New England in 1995 in Rhode Island, a group that engaged in fund-raising for nonprofit organizations.

Some leaders in Boston started to develop beauty pageants with the goal of promoting health issues. Orlando, Cristian, La Loba, Vicky, and others organized Miss Latina Salud (1994–1996), Miss Massachusetts Latin Time (1995–1997), and Miss Massachusetts Gay Latina (1998–present). These leaders showed me the Latina/o community's diversity, since there were transgender people and people of all social classes. These pageants were well known by the straight Latina/o and mainstream LGBT communities as shows filled with splendor, beauty, and camaraderie. They were also educational since the questions asked of pageant contestants, and some of the games involving interaction with the audience, focused on health-related topics—mostly HIV/AIDS, substance abuse, and hepatitis, but also smoking, diabetes, and other health issues. At the first pageant I attended I was introduced to Tish, an Anglo transgender woman who loved "Latin culture" and who managed a club in Lynn called Fran's Place. Tish took me under her wing and gave me the economic push to start a new social group. She also designated Sundays as "Noche Latina Gay" at Fran's Place and opened her doors to me to meet with group leaders and do pageants there.

I won't say that everything was great then; between 1990 and 1997 we gathered many times to attend funerals for friends who had died of AIDS-related complications. Some of us were victims of hate crimes as migrants and LGBT people. One night, leaving a club, I was beaten by youth who shouted words to me like *pato* (literally duck, but a derogatory Puerto Rican term referencing gayness or effeminacy) and spic. Some of my friends told me they had experienced similar or worse remarks. Ever since then, racism has been evident in the area, as every year that goes by there are many more immigrants and more people who are LGBT. On both sides there is racism, homophobia, and classism.

We felt racism not just from people but also within organizations and community groups. Many LGBT groups created by white people would not accept the increasing diversity in the region. Whoever was nonwhite—Asians, African Americans, and Latinas/os—was left out of such groups. At predominantly white events LGBT Latinas/os did not feel welcome, even though we were asked to join and participate. We did not have a group of our own that had nothing to do with health issues. We wanted a group that was not a club. I felt that it was time to create this type of group, but I did not know how—and I doubted that people would respond and participate. We already met in Lynn once a month, but it was not until two Latina lesbians, Evelyn and Emely, called me in 1997 that I knew the time had come. We met a day later and everything changed. That was the first meeting of what would later become La Coalición Somos Latin@s LGBT in Massachusetts. This group started to organize social Fridays once a month in different places in Boston and Lynn. In a few months it grew from 24 to 250 people. Two years later, and thanks to a grant from LLEGÓ, La Coalición decided to formalize as a nonprofit organization, which was finalized a few years later.

During the same year, 1997, some state legislatures and courts in the United States received same-sex civil marriage legislation. From 2001 to 2003 legalization of same-sex marriage was discussed in constitutional conventions in the state of Massachusetts; after much debate it was legalized in 2003. Since 1997 LLEGÓ had tried to find people and organizations in Boston who would work with them to educate Latinas/os about the LGBT community and these "new" unions. Because I had done some health presentations at LLEGÓ conferences, its leaders called me. This is how I started to be a spokesperson for the Latina/o LGBT community in public forums in the New England area.

With the support of Latina/o straight organizations, La Coalición participated in activities that brought it recognition in the state and the region. Among its objectives were to organize coalitions to advocate for the acceptance of Latina/o LGBT communities and to educate the communities about topics that impacted them. La Coalición also wanted its members to meet other LGBT people in different occupations with the goal of networking, so as to identify as a solid and strong community. The goal was for our Latina/o heterosexual counterparts to learn from our people. Although these were ambitious goals, they were all met; we became visible and were recognized by other groups and politicians as important individuals involved in local and state politics. These objectives were met through networking, social events, and politics, which we engaged in throughout the state, including during our monthly Noche Social event. Although La Coalición started as a predominantly social group, later on it became a political one. The unity among LGBT Latinas/os grew so much that we decided to organize a Pride celebration under the name Orgullo Latino LGBT. LLEGÓ offered significant financial help to start this celebration. LLEGÓ also introduced La Coalición members to national Latina/o LGBT leaders. From them I learned what were the important issues for the Latina/o LGBT communities in other states. I also found out that, until then, there had been no Latino LGBT Pride fest—of course there were activities where Latinas/os had significant visibility, but never a properly organized festival like the one we would organize later on in Massachusetts. Given this, our group decided to declare our weekend festival the first Latina/o LGBT Pride Week.

At this first celebration I shared my experiences with other leaders. We discussed topics such as the national and international importance of same-sex marriage legislation. All over the world same-sex marriage was being discussed, but what was not being considered was that all the community demands were not met, including immigration reform or legal recognition at the federal level. In the mainstream LGBT press, Latina/o LGBT leaders discussed the limited inclusion of Latinas/os in the state LGBT movement. From that weekend on, La Coalición leaders were called by local and national organizations to participate in focus groups and other activities and to represent the Latina/o LGBT community within their organizations' boards of directors. Thanks to that festival we were recognized as a central part of the Latina/o and LGBT movements.

We were a diverse group of Latina/o LGBT people from different socioeconomic levels and regions who were working in different fields, but we always decided together the message we wanted to share in local and national news. La Coalición prepared press releases and gave TV news interviews. We knew the importance of mass media contacts; we also wanted to communicate relevant themes within the mainstream Latina/o community. We trained group members on how to speak to the press. We collaborated with other organizations, like the Museum of Fine Arts in Boston, the Boston Latino International Film Festival, Boston Pride, Inquilinos Boricuas en Acción, The Network/La Red, La Fundación Derechos Humanos de Puerto Rico, and La Organización de Derechos Humanos. Every month we held events, including movie screenings, dances, parties, beauty pageants, and shows by comedians or drag queens. Rhode Island and Connecticut groups joined us. And we experienced exponential growth in the number of people attending our events and the number of companies that financially supported us.

During those years I noticed that we lacked a space in the print media where we could share our issues. I spoke about this with Carmen Oquendo-Villar, who was teaching Spanish at the time and finishing up her doctorate at Harvard. I had met her during my years at Boston University. We cowrote two columns, which we submitted to mainstream (white LGBT and Latina/o) local newspapers. Although several rejected our writing, finally in 2006 James Lopata, editor at *In Newsweekly*, accepted the idea. At the beginning the column was titled *Latinazo*, but it then became *Visión Latina*. With time it has changed newspapers, but it has always had the same objective of educating communities about Latina/o LGBT issues and promoting a feeling of pride in our Spanish language. The column is still published monthly and is read regionally in the *Rainbow Times* of New England and in many other parts of the United States, Colombia, Venezuela, Puerto Rico, Cuba, and Spain.

Though there is still homophobia, racism, sexism, and transphobia, at least LGBT Latinas/os have been included at the "tables" of other groups and in conversations about the overall future of the LGBT community. I see that what we achieved in Massachusetts is still to this day current and that organizations continue to involve LGBT Latinas/os. We are not solely doing HIV/AIDS work, but are participating in all aspects of public health. I feel like I represent my community in ways that were impossible before.

As a member of LGBT people of color communities, I try to balance my life in a country filled with inequality. I make an effort to survive in a classist space, one with power dynamics that are, unfortunately, the norm. Immigrants who choose to live in this nation receive opportunities otherwise limited in our countries of origin. But are we equal? Some may answer, "Yes," but the majority answer, "No." This is why I have joined other people in Massachusetts to develop organizations and movements that offer equity in our new home. At the same time, we celebrate who we are as individuals and as a community. Much has been accomplished because the Latina/o LGBT leaders have built coalitions and demanded a seat at the tables where our voices were not heard. Many feel comfortable advocating for our people, and we take a stand as proud Latina/o LGBT people. The Latina/o LGBT community is rich: we have culture, history, music, spirituality, politics, and diversity. Thanks to all the people I've met, and these experiences, I accept the diversity that describes me and the richness of my Latina/o culture.

These projects were also started with a personal motivation. When I was growing up I never had good Latina/o LGBT role models, and now I don't want anyone growing up to suffer the same adversity. We have never asked for special rights, only the same rights as others. Our work as leaders is not done to be remembered but to leave things in better shape for those who come after us. I'd like for the Latina/o LGBT movement to stay strong, even if I am no longer as involved. This has been just a glimpse at our Massachusetts history, but there are other leaders, and we have a rich history to share. The years I've just described show a sense of family and camaraderie that brought us the energy to organize and advocate for what we wanted. We met in times of happiness and sadness, we supported one another, we talked about the good and the bad, we shared news about our countries, we shared the personal and not so personal, but we shared. I am Boricua, gay, psychologist, leader, husband, brother, son, friend, nephew, cousin. I am so many things, but everything starts and ends with my roots, my name, and my actions and history.

CHAPTER WRITTEN IN SPANISH BY WILFRED LABIOSA
AND TRANSLATED BY SALVADOR VIDAL-ORTIZ.

ADELA VÁZQUEZ

Finding a Home in Transgender Activism in San Francisco

*Adela Vázquez was born in the Cuban countryside and raised in Ca-
magüey. She left Cuba at the first opportunity, at age twenty-one,
during the Mariel boatlift crisis. After living in several cities, performing at local clubs, and sustaining a relationship with a woman,
Vázquez finally settled in San Francisco, where she began her transition. She joined Proyecto Contra SIDA Por Vida in 1992 as a volunteer and became a full-time staff member in 1995. Under the umbrella
of Proyecto, Vázquez created and ran projects devoted to the transgender population, particularly Latinas/os. In her oral history–based
narrative, Vázquez tells the story of her "sexile" from communist
Cuba and how activism became the core of her civic engagement. She
presents her struggles in the United States with the capitalist system
as well as with sexism, racism, and socioeconomic inequality through a
specifically immigrant lens. Her narrative mirrors the challenges the
San Francisco transgender community has faced over the years.*

I AM FROM CUBA, FROM THE COUNTRYSIDE, NEAR A
sugar mill that used to be called Central Najasa; after Fidel Castro reached the presidency they called it Alfredo Álvarez Mola.
I was born in 1958, the day the revolutionary troops entered the sugar
mill. My mother was unable to get to the hospital because everything
was closed up and they had burned Central Najasa, so she had me
at home.

My grandfather was a Spaniard, my grandmother Cuban, and very
Catholic. My mom went to a nun's school and lived with an aunt. Mom
fell in love with a man who was a model for shop display windows—
this was big in the 1950s—and became pregnant. When my grand-

mother found out about my birth she came to get my mom, forced her to marry and get divorced on the same day, and then brought her home. Back then having a kid without a father was forbidden, so my grandparents adopted me. That's why I am sort of my mom's sister and my siblings' aunt. My mom was sent to New York so she could finish high school. She came back to Cuba when I was a year old or so. She fell in love with a rich man, and when she was getting ready for the wedding the wife of her fiancé arrived. The wife was pregnant. That was horrible. Finally mom left our house with one of the family's employees. He was a man much younger than she was, and they lived together for twenty-four years.

I was a very happy child, in spite of all that had happened. I had a wonderful childhood, and my grandma took great care of me. She gave me everything I wanted, and she would buy me dolls. I was always female, even before I realized that I could not be a girl with a penis and that I had to have a vagina. When I was eleven I left the house and never came back. First I went to school; then there was one thing after another, and I moved to the United States. Life was preparing me for exile.

I found out I was male when I entered for the first time a men's bathroom in the school I was in. I saw all those cocks, and I don't know why, but I realized that I had a sexual power that up till then I had ignored. I also started to notice that I was really a queen, but I was always very strong and feminine. In the Cuba of the late 1960s there was no mention of gay men. There were fags and *bugarrones*. All of my life I had been a woman. I did not have breasts or a female name, but I was. And everyone around me knew it: my girlfriends from school and the boys, the boyfriends with whom I'd get laid. When I was thirteen I told my family that I was a queen after they discovered a letter from a boyfriend I had in the carnivals in Santiago de Cuba. That was during a school break. Grandma had opened the letter, and when I came back to the house for a few days everyone was waiting for me. My stepdad asked whether I was a fag, and I said yes. And he said I had to leave the house. My mom started crying, even though she had known all along—because mothers know. Grandma said to my stepdad, "Wait a second, if anyone has to leave it is you, because you are not family. He is staying here." After that she said to me, looking at me seriously, "You are thirteen years old, and you know what you are, so you know what you want in life. Take a key to the house, don't bring anyone here, and live your life."

As I was starting tenth grade there was a call for training teachers.

It was an intensive thirteen-month course. Grandma was a teacher, so was my mom, and so I followed the same career to satisfy Grandma. I finished and graduated, and then I was sent to the sugar mill where I was born. By then I was in love with a soldier. He arrived at the sugar mill to work and to see me. One day a man from the Communist Party saw us. The soldier disappeared, and I never saw him again. I imagine that he went to jail. I was sent home, and soon after that I was detained, but only for a couple of days because my grandmother was a town's founder, and she and my mom both created such a scene at the police precinct that they let me go. However, I had to move in with my mom, who had bought a house in Camagüey. I was already familiar with the city—I would go visit her when I was given passes out of school. She was a ballet fanatic and loved concerts. So at eighteen, for the first time, Mom and I were living together. At that point Mom came out of the closet—she was bisexual!

I always thought of leaving Cuba. When the Mariel crisis happened in 1980 I was one of the first to show up to apply to leave. I arrived with a queen at Fort Chaffee, in Arkansas, where we were for about six weeks. My friend and I arrived at a barracks filled with men, and I said, "Oh god, how do I find a bed?" I had never been jailed, I had never been with habitual offenders, and I was an educated girl. I remember that I sat on the stairs and started to cry—and to smoke a cigarette. I had not been able to shower in eight days! Then a gorgeous man arrived, a *bugarrón* who was in charge of the barracks, and he had his room and bathroom upstairs. And he allowed me to move in and live with him there.

Lucy, a fellow teacher who had trained with me, had left Cuba a year before. My other friend and I had memorized her phone number. We called Lucy, and she got us out of the barracks and took us to her home near Los Angeles. Six days later another queer called me and said, "Go to the Gay Community Center. On Wednesdays there is a meeting at 6:00 p.m., and people come to sponsor Cubans." The following Wednesday Lucy took us from Hawthorne to West Hollywood. Two blocks away I had already noticed this big, old, strong, red-dyed-hair queen. That person, Rolando Victoria, became my sponsor. I lived with Rolando from July 1980 until March 1982. When I met him I was twenty-one.

I had arrived in the United States very anxious, since leaving the country you are born in is the most horrible thing. Exile is a deep sorrow that forces you to learn a culture. You don't know the language, don't know where to go, and don't know anybody. It is like being born again, but as an adult. The first cultural shock was the realization that I was not white; I was also no longer Cuban, but Latina. The other shock for me was learning to live in a capitalist country. I had never been taught how to budget, for instance. Thank god for Rolando Victoria, who was like a mother to me. He paid for me to take a private English course; he even slapped me once when I contracted gonorrhea. He was a Red Cross nurse. And he was the one who told me for the first time that we all needed to use condoms. That was at the beginning of 1982. Using a condom was something I did not think mattered to gay people. Other people no longer used condoms because there were other forms of pregnancy prevention. But Rolando saved my life. He put the fear of it in me, and I started to use condoms. In spite of his virtues, Rolando was a hardcore alcoholic. It was with him, too, that I was introduced to cocaine, through a friend of his, Freddy.

Between 1982 and 1989 I lived in several cities. The first one was Dallas, where I was from 1982 to 1983. I met a woman, with whom I stayed for several years. We met while I was doing a drag show at a sleazy bar, standing by the bar and fighting with the customers so that they did not pull my wig from me. In Dallas I was consuming an awful lot of drugs. In the end I left because of drugs.

I decided to move to Miami. My partner became pregnant in Dallas but had a miscarriage. That split us up; however, shortly afterward she went to get me in Miami. In October of 1983 we moved together to San Francisco. I worked at a gay porn theater to provide for my household and went to school to become a hairdresser. At some point my partner became a crack cocaine addict without me knowing. We split up in 1986 when I found out about her addiction. After that I fell deep into drugs again. Then I left for Los Angeles to clean up and to become Adela. That happened in 1988 to 1989.

At that point my issue was how to transition; becoming a woman was to lose my personality, to lose friendships I loved so much. When I returned to San Francisco from Los Angeles I was already a woman but not 24/7. I would cross-dress and would go out as female, but only at night. My challenges were my voice, my big hands, and my hairiness. And with all three I have lived wonderfully as a woman. For the hands, I've done my nails, and it has worked. To cover my five o'clock shadow I use a lot of makeup, and for the voice . . . see, I have this friend, she was born a woman, and when I call her in the mornings I hear her voice, which is so strong—so next to her I feel a girl, a soprano! I am quite empowered, as a woman, as trans, as a person. I am not afraid. I am willing to do anything. I am ready for whatever comes. And I think that this empowerment came because I knew so many strong women, because in my childhood the women in my house were the ones who were in charge. And that impacted me positively.

In May 1992 Instituto Familiar de la Raza sponsored me for a pageant named Miss Gay Latina. Víctor Gaitán, then an outreach worker for Instituto de la Raza, came to the hair salon where I worked to invite me to participate. I won the Miss Gay Latina 1992 pageant. When I won I had to do a lot of volunteer work, as that was part of the responsibilities of the crown's winner. At that point a lot of people were getting sick and dying of AIDS. There were hospices filled with people. Everywhere you would see transgender people suffering but no leaders who were trans. That started to bother me immensely. Personally, I was not interested in anything that sounded like community, because of my own associations of that word with communism. I came from a country that had oppressed me, but maybe in the end I really was communist— I am, as much as I am anti-Castro. Looking at the situation I asked myself, "Why are trans women not a part of this movement?"

The first thing I did for the community as a trans woman was to protest in 1993. In San Francisco trans people got disability just for being trans. In many cases disability meant no longer being a part of the workforce, so the government took us out of the workforce for being trans. In this way we were eliminated as people. You wanted to be a woman, but at the same time you had to work because you lived off your employment. So I went to the Human Rights Commission to protest. After that I ran into Héctor León—we called him La Condonera— and he asked me if I wanted to be part of an HIV/AIDS prevention campaign. "Of course," I answered. However, I had never liked going to places where people were looking for cock and telling them, "Hold on, I wanna talk to you about condoms." I wanted to do something that would please me, and I decided to be daring: I organized a series of shows after we formed AtreDivas. We were four queens with two dancers, and we would give the money we collected from these shows to different organizations, above all Proyecto Contra SIDA Por Vida, a program of the National Task Force on AIDS Prevention.

In 1992 I started volunteering at Proyecto Contra SIDA and did so until March of 1995. At that point I left the beauty salon and became an activist, working as part of the staff at Proyecto. An outreach-worker job came up at Proyecto, and I took it. The first thing I did was start a training program to organize trans women. I was asked to develop an event to bring together at least twenty-five trans women, so I had the idea for a safe-sex contest, like a beauty pageant. I wanted to focus specifically on those who have sex with trans women, because that was a large gap that nobody had yet addressed.

Whenever we went out to conduct outreach it was like an event. Many of the Latina girls who had undergone all the transition surgeries and were now changed would come to me when they were starting the hormone treatment. Latinas who had no idea what it meant to be trans would ask about it. I had a very well-known workshop, which I developed, called "The Transgender Psyche." I knew nothing about the transgender psyche, but my intention was to raise awareness of what it meant to be transgender and to teach people that it was not the same as being gay. Another workshop was about blacks among Latinas/os—Afro-Latinos—because we, Puerto Ricans and Cubans, always have black in us, and it's present among the rest of the Latinas/os, but nobody recognizes it. I did it to build visibility and raise consciousness, because sometimes people would arrive at Proyecto and say certain things about black people. In my workshops we talked for the first time among trans communities about hormone trafficking and the illicit selling of hormones. We knew it existed, but nobody talked about it. And I would bring all of these things up. I remember that I brought this transgender psyche workshop, in a more developed way, to San Diego, and two "normal" women who were crying by the end of the workshop came to talk with me. They had thrown their kids out of their homes for being trans. And later they found out their kids were women in jail, with HIV, and they were dying. The next day the two older women came back and urged parents to talk with their kids. This might be a regular occurrence now, but in the 1990s it was not.

When I started to work with Diane Félix, former executive director of Proyecto, there were issues in terms of how the agency dealt with trans people. Diane closed the office one day and said, "Today we are going to educate our staff members about trans issues." That has never happened to me anywhere else. I was the first trans woman hired at Proyecto. My responsibilities included overseeing a team of outreach workers who visited several locations and agencies in San Francisco. There was no funding to hire transgender folks until I started working there, and there were problems. Some people complained—and we were taken to task—because some of the funding destined for gay men was used to include trans women.

Proyecto was a wonderful place. I grew up inside Proyecto, and for me it was a home because to share work on HIV prevention through art was unique. I did so many things; I even formed a theater group that presented a very famous Spanish play, *La casa de Bernarda Alba*, where all the actors were trans. That created great consciousness within the community; it gave them courage. People would come to Proyecto, and the doors were always open. We had clothes to give them and services to render. Whenever we could not give people what they needed there was always a chance to connect them to other clients who could help them. I had about fifty clients in Proyecto. I also handled groups that started at fourteen people and ended up being groups of fifty. We held retreats and sometimes had so many people that we had to put a cap on the entry because of space limitations. I also did shows, and I had my followers. So the outreach was done in many ways. But I was also a role model for being a trans woman who worked and had a husband, something that was not so common then. We educated in a time period when AIDS was taboo. And at that time, there was a lot of funding.

As part of my job I facilitated the Transgender Summit sponsored by the National Latino/a Lesbian and Gay Organization (LLEGÓ) at Alma de Mujer in Austin in 1996. I also need to mention the program Cultura es Vida, directed at community building among LGBT Latinas/os and also organized by LLEGÓ. I facilitated Cultura es Vida events in Phoenix, Austin, San Antonio, and Puerto Rico. Proyecto was also a part of the first study of HIV and trans people implemented in San Francisco at the end of the 1990s. Proyecto's office was an interview site, and that was wonderful too, but it was a challenge to interview Latina transgender women who were totally hysterical with me because they were not interested in being part of the study. Back then, and now, there was an education problem among trans women. Everything is about looking good, and there is little known about HIV; but in order to educate others you have to educate yourself.

In April of 1998 a problem with the funds assigned to Proyecto was made public, and many of us did not get paid. We were without paychecks for two months. As a result, most of the male employees left their workplace. Only the women remained. So I moved from outreach worker to senior health educator. I started to do counseling even though I had no credentials or training. I formed groups where we would screen an erotic film, for instance, and later on we'd talk about what one could and could not do in real life. Sometimes up to ninety people came to those workshops—imagine! With all the salary issues, we fundraised for the programs. And we helped the clients to get ahead in other areas, like education. For example, Wells Fargo funded a college scholarship at Proyecto. Later on the city loaned Diane Félix $48,000. They said, "We are going to give you this money to work with sex workers who are injecting drug users." At that point I became a volunteer in the needle exchange program. Needle exchange does not have as much weight now; but back then we would bring needles and condoms to Golden Gate Park—and we would leave them in the bushes. People living as squatters would come to pick up the needles and condoms.

I adored Proyecto for being, among other things, a wonderful home to new artists. Some poets and theater leaders, such as Jaime Cortez, started at Proyecto. As a matter of fact, Jaime Cortez once asked me to go to a meeting with Jose Marquez of KQED, the public television and radio station of the San Francisco Bay Area. The project was called I-5, and it told the stories and showed pictures of the lives of five immigrants to the state of California. Each of us had contributed to our communities in positive ways. As immigrants of different racial backgrounds, none of us were rich; we were just successful in what we did, in our real lives. I was very honored to receive such a designation. It was Jaime Cortez who, later on, came up with the idea for the *Sexile/ Sexilio* book project. He noticed what my life trajectory had been and thought it would be important to document it. And that's how *Sexile/ Sexilio* came about.

It was very hard for me to let go of Proyecto. I felt a great sense of respect for what Proyecto had done for me. I learned to be an employee at Proyecto. I learned to design a flyer and to use computers. I could go to Puerto Rico, go to other countries, representing the agency. People trusted me. I am able to cheer those who are my clients now and who were kids then. When I am working, sometimes I run into someone who says, "When I was young I would go to Proyecto, and I found the inspiration to go to college." That does not happen anymore. One keeps those memories forever; it does not matter if there is a recession, lack of work. I run into people who went to Proyecto in the 1990s, and you gave them counseling, and they remember what you did. That is priceless.

Since then I've worked at various places, most recently as a clinical case manager at Instituto Familiar de la Raza. I work directly with a psychiatrist, a psychologist, and an administrative supervisor. The environment is much calmer, more professional. Everyone loves me very much. I make appointments for the clients and do an assessment to determine if the person needs therapy or psychiatric treatment. I also do case management. I can say that after eighteen years in the HIV/AIDS field I am capable of doing my job while sleeping. Even so, I am not as engaged in the lives of the clients as I used to be. I am calmer—a little older, a bit more centered. I left the streets because I was simply not interested anymore; I was done with that. But I like my job a lot because it has taken me to a certain place to achieve respect in the community. I have also been able to publish books where I talk about my life dreams. To come to this country was a dream already achieved. To be a woman, the other life dream, has also been realized. And nothing is bigger than my independence.

Ahora soy feliz.

ORAL HISTORY INTERVIEW CONDUCTED BY SALVADOR VIDAL-ORTIZ ON DECEMBER 10, 2011. CHAPTER WRITTEN BY URIEL QUESADA AND TRANSLATED BY SALVADOR VIDAL-ORTIZ.

Conclusion

URIEL QUESADA

QUEER BROWN VOICES MAY BE READ FROM DIFFER-
ent perspectives and disciplines and from within and
outside academia, as Salvador Vidal-Ortiz has pointed out in the introduction. Our purpose as editors has been to offer a book accessible to a variety of audiences, and we hope that each reader has found,
in his or her own way, several relevant topics. The fourteen narratives
included in *Queer Brown Voices* serve as personal expressions of democratic practices in the United States and Puerto Rico. Even when the
activists come from some kind of social margin—first because of their
sexual orientation but also because of poverty or their migratory status, to cite a few social markers—they all become involved through either a grassroots organization or a local, state, or federally funded program. They work for the people and with the people, opening spaces in
order to break the circle of exclusion they have personally witnessed or
experienced. We get the sense that social change is possible through institutional change, and the way to impact policies is through community involvement.

The personal stories in this book follow a pattern in which the nar-
rator, after a period of distance, reconnects with some cultural (or perhaps national or ethnoracial) aspect of the self. The richness and com-
plexity of the contributors' cultural environments are felt in many of
the narratives' opening pages. Sometimes the stories begin in a different country, such as Mexico or Cuba, or they happen in a dense urban
space in the United States—be it New York, Los Angeles, or Houston.
The cultural environment not only influences the formative years of
the future activist but also becomes, later on, a conduit for artistic and

political expression. We can find this link between cultural production and activism, for instance, in the works of Luz Guerra and Jesús Cháirez. In some cases, a cultural deficit is also present: for example, when the need to feel integrated leads an individual to reject Spanish at home or deny his or her sense of Latinidad. However, as the narratives show, at some point in life, the activist goes through an experience of (re)discovery of what it means for him or her to be a Latina/o. In that sense, this is too common of an immigrant experience or a retold story of second-generation Latinas/os in the United States.

ON BROWN ACTIVISM

A key topic in *Queer Brown Voices* is how LGBT activism intersects with other social, political, ethnic, and cultural factors. From an outsider's perspective, U.S. LGBT activism is often viewed as unified and consensual in its agenda and programming priorities. What *Queer Brown Voices* has shown is something different: There is not just one LGBT agenda, and what we know as "the agenda" usually represents the needs and interests of the white LGBT population. Secondly, LGBT Latinas/os have been a minority within a minority. In the Latina/o community at large there is limited room for sexual minorities. In the mainstream LGBT movement Brownness is almost invisible, and whoever wants to join the movement must adhere to a set of priorities that does not necessarily reflect his or her reality. As José Gutiérrez says in his chapter, Latino/a LGBTs have "suffered sometimes double, or even triple, discrimination." It is very interesting to note, though, the ways LGBT Latinas/os react to discrimination and exclusion. Medina and Cháirez, for instance, remember the time when Latinas/os were asked for more than one form of identification at gay bars; Luz Guerra recounts how Puerto Ricans were called "spics," and thus their background stigmatized and sometimes pathologized. However, nobody in *Queer Brown Voices* becomes frozen in resentment or disappointment. They look for a group or create one of their own. They start conversations on how to be visible and how to address the most pressing needs of the community. After gaining experience, the local organizations reach out to similar groups within the state for networking purposes and also with a state-level agenda in mind. Then organizations from across the country work together at the national level.

Most of the contributors to *Queer Brown Voices* have in common an early awareness of social inequality and a commitment to working with underprivileged populations. In some cases (Gomez, Medina, Veloz) family experiences with activism serve as an inspiration and an ethical model. In other cases (Esquivel, Guerra, Ramirez) a history of exclusion, discrimination, and oppression influences a future involvement in activism. In all cases the personal background informs the activists' attitudes toward social change.

Brown queer people's agenda goes beyond visibility to address discrimination, access to health care, equal rights, and cultural identity, among other issues. As we have seen in the fourteen narratives that form this book, being queer and Brown means having an ethical, active involvement with the world. All of our contributors have gone above and beyond in search of a more just, equal, and democratic world. They produced newsletters that showed solidarity with national and international issues. They created new spaces, which could be physical but also cultural, social, or identity-based. They opened up the organizations' scope to make alliances with other minorities whenever possible. Some of the activists went on to government and private industry jobs at high levels as the next step in their leadership careers.

Mainstream white organizations demanded Latinas/os play an "ethnic" role. In those instances it was okay to be Latina/o, but only if one stayed on the sideline and did not aspire to a leadership position. Latinas/os were expected to subordinate their Latinidad by supporting the white leadership agenda while at the same time overshadowing their own needs, demands, and world perspectives. When Latinas/os tried to take the lead, white gay members—mostly white men—fought back by questioning the leadership's ethical integrity or ability to conduct business. In some cases (see Veloz) the opposition caused the dissolution of the organization.

For the most part, Latina/o LGBT organizations were safe shelters. However, the organizations could not escape internal tensions, such as difficulties involved in effectively incorporating women into leadership positions (Medina, Veloz) or complaints when some funding destined for gay men was used to include trans women (Vázquez). Our contributors were aware of those tensions. In some cases they advocated for a more inclusive leadership or fought to secure equal opportunities for everyone. The results, however, were not always satisfactory, revealing how even LGBT organizations may mirror forms of discrimination found in the society at large.

Internal migration leads to networking and the creation of new organizations. Texas provides a good example of a migratory movement from small towns to big cities, where newcomers find opportunities to be involved in activism; and especially they find other Latina/o LGBT people to begin a dialogue with. Houston, for instance, is mentioned as a destination for LGBT people in the 1970s. In the context of the city's sexual openness and the racism of the time, the first Chicano/a LGBT organizations appeared. Later on, some of the founders of the Houston organization moved to Austin, where a new cultural, political, and identity environment redefined the scope of their activism.

Washington, D.C., is another major urban space where people and organizations converged. Latino/a LGBTs went to D.C. in 1987 to participate in the Second National March on Washington for Lesbian and Gay Rights and to attend workshops, but also to meet and set the foundation for what was going to be LLEGÓ, the influential national organization that was active from the late 1980s until 2004.

ORGANIZATIONS AND THE HIV/AIDS EPIDEMIC

The HIV/AIDS epidemic and the government's response to it are two major players in the narratives included in *Queer Brown Voices*. They impacted organizations at several levels, first and foremost because of the human losses. The HIV/AIDS epidemic hit groups in the most painful way when members started to get sick and die. Second, government programming support improved the organizations' visibility in the Latino/a and LGBT communities. Third, the response to the epidemic influenced a deep change in the policies and priorities of practically all of the organizations. On the one hand, most of the organizations were identified as service providers for the Latino/a community at large and for the LGBT community in particular. Money was available, even though the use of those funds was very specific. On the other hand, the organizations were forced to rapidly adapt to new rules and regulations. Perhaps they became more accountable, but at the same time they changed internally as administrative units, and also from a leadership point of view. When the funding for HIV/AIDS prevention stopped flowing, some of the groups could not evolve fast enough, while others survived with new programming priorities—or even with new nonofficial missions comparable to the organizations' missions from the pre-HIV/AIDS period. Olga Orraca Paredes's essay is particularly critical of such a change. Talking about LLEGÓ, Orraca Paredes concludes that the organization lost contact with its base when it started to respond to its funders' priorities instead of its community members' and clients' needs. She also notices the organization's progressive evolution toward a corporate-like structure that did not keep faithful to the foundational ideas of service and community participation.

Not all of the organizations were able to remain active once the federal funding stopped. The human losses due to HIV/AIDS played a critical role in the crisis and disappearance of Latina/o LGBT organized groups. The HIV/AIDS epidemic left activists drained and in mourning. Even now, it is hard for our contributors to recount those years without feeling sorrow for all the people who died; some potential contributors could not in fact write for us under such circumstances and withdrew from the project. In addition, the original purpose of several organizations changed in order to respond to the epidemic, and after HIV/AIDS funding was no longer available, they found themselves without a compass.

WHAT NEEDS TO BE DONE IN THE NEAR FUTURE?

Queer Brown Voices started as a project to break the silence that still surrounds Latina/o LGBT activism in the United States and Puerto Rico. It is a pioneering step toward a more comprehensive and inclusive history of activism, organizations, and major events. However, we the editors cannot claim that the entire job is done. There are other leaders and silent heroes who could not be included for various reasons. There are parts of the country that are not represented. If we consider that the main purpose of *Queer Brown Voices* has been to collect activists' narratives from the 1970s, 1980s, and 1990s, an immediate question may arise: "What happened next?" We are in debt to the pioneers of the previous three decades, but also to the new activists of the twenty-first century. The struggle for visibility, access to health services, and equal rights continues. As in the past, in the first years of the new century racism has been as predominant as homophobia. In general, Latinas/os face major challenges as a large minority with not enough political representation. Besides reflecting on the Latina/o LGBT activism of the movement's leaders, we need to collect the voices of the recipients of services provided by organizations led by queer Latinas/os in order to have a fuller perspective on the impact of such activism and organizing.

An important topic for future research is why most of the organizations created in the 1980s and 1990s—one of the few exceptions would be the Esperanza Peace and Justice Center—disappeared. From today's perspective those organizations may seem dated, or one might say that it all depended on the founders or on short-term agendas; however, it is necessary to explore all reasons more deeply.

When you put together the history of a social movement based on the personal narratives of several people, accuracy becomes a major challenge. *Queer Brown Voices* has shown the reader not only what the contributors remember, but also the ways they recall different moments of their personal lives and their activism. We the editors have rigorously corroborated most of the events, dates, and names mentioned in the chapters. However, it is possible that some readers will still find inconsistencies or contradictions that need to be addressed. That is not surprising if you take into account that while history depends on documents, oral histories and personal essays depend on memory.

As Leti Gomez has pointed out in the preface, this book is the collective effort of sixteen people. We consider each one of the contributors the author of his or her personal narrative, even when the narrative was originally recorded as an oral history. This decision is rooted in the very same idea of activism, where friendship, mutual respect, and support are fundamental.

Our role as editors has not been limited to collecting and critiquing other people's work. On the contrary, we have been active as key players in the organization, transcription, writing, translation, and editing of each narrative. However, each one of the contributors provides a particular narrative voice, a life experience, a political view, a perspective on what activism was twenty or thirty years ago, and a vision of what may lie ahead for new generations of activists. Those who wrote their own pieces shared with us their unique storytelling gifts. We respected the style and the social and personal concerns that guided their writing. Those who told us the story of their personal journey gave us the opportunity to compose a *testimonio*, which strived to reproduce the cadence and spontaneity of oral narration. In the end we are all part of the same project, and the final outcome represents all of us, a community of Latina/o LGBT activists.

I moved to the United States in 1997 to study Latin American Literature at New Mexico State University in Las Cruces. For the first time I saw myself as part of a minority group, be it Latina/o, immigrant, person of color, or gay. I was born and raised in Costa Rica, and these new identities changed my perceptions about many things I had taken for granted most of my life. Living at the Mexico-U.S. border also impacted me in a way I never imagined. The United States was no longer the homogenous society pictured in the media or by the entertainment industry, but a complex structure where several social, economic, and cultural layers overlapped, sometimes in an open conflict. As a member of a minority, I experienced discrimination because of my accent, the color of my skin, and my country of origin, but I also found a more welcoming atmosphere for my sexual orientation. But how could I isolate one positive aspect from the wholeness that made me a person and a citizen?

In 1999 I moved to Louisiana, where I completed my doctoral studies at Tulane and then got a job at Loyola University New Orleans. This new social space was familiar and foreign at the same time. New Orleans, with its food, vegetation, and weather, is perhaps the most Caribbean city in the United States; but it is also a Southern city, which gives New Orleans a particular flavor, from its unique hospitality to the traditional and sometimes rigid social structure.

New Orleans offered me more opportunities to explore my sexuality, but I was still perceived as "the other." I intended to join the local chapter of a national LGBT organization, but at the first meeting a group of people made a derogatory comment about my accent. After that experience I started trying to find other Latina/o LGBTs, but there were very few of us who were out and visible. Without making a conscious decision, my next move was to try to become part of the local Latino/a culture, benefited by the safety of the university environment.

I lived in Baltimore from 2006 through 2009. One day I read an ad in one of the Washington, D.C., area LGBT newspapers about the Latino GLBT History Project, and I decided to attend one of their meetings. It was the first time that I had met Latina/o LGBT activists. It was also the beginning of a learning process that continues to this day. Suddenly I realized not only that Latina/o LGBTs could get organized and fight for their rights, but also that there was a history that was relevant for people like me: immigrant, Brown, and homosexual.

At the Latino GLBT History Project I met Letitia Gomez and Salvador Vidal-Ortiz. Leti, an experienced activist, had a deep knowledge of organizations, agencies, and the subtle nuances of leadership. Salvador was a sociologist interested in oral histories. Soon we became close friends. The group's leader assigned me an archiving project as well as the design of an oral history project on the local LGBT community. Unfortunately, neither the archive nor the oral history projects took off before my return to New Orleans in 2009. However, Leti, Salvador, and I stayed in touch.

I started working with oral histories in 2010, after years of study of personal narratives, mainly Central American *testimonios*. It was clear to me that oral histories were a powerful tool to preserve the lives and experiences of underrepresented groups, people who were excluded from the official history. I traveled several times to meet Dr. Louis Kyriakoudes, director of the Center for Oral History and Cultural Heritage at the University of Southern Mississippi in Hattiesburg. Dr. Kyriakoudes and his staff generously shared their expertise with me. At the same time I did my own research about oral history projects in different parts of the country. I also read several books on recording and preservation techniques, but especially on the ethical aspects of oral history. I did my first project in Costa Rica in 2010, when I interviewed a group of young activists who opposed the free trade agreement between the United States and Central America that had been approved by the Costa Rican congress back in 2008.

I was thus ready to take on the challenge when Letitia Gomez and Salvador Vidal-Ortiz invited me to work on the *Queer Brown Voices* book project. My main limitation—perhaps also my advantage—was that I did not know the prospective contributors. I had expertise in the techniques of oral histories and personal narratives. I knew about the documentation necessary to protect our informants' rights and the best practices to properly record, transcribe, and preserve an interview. Besides that, I was the newcomer, and I would have to learn as we developed the project.

In the summer of 2011 Letitia Gomez and I conducted the first interviews in San Antonio, Texas. We met at Leti's house with Dennis Medina and Brad Veloz. The atmosphere was so relaxed that these first oral histories became celebrations of friendship and solidarity. From that point on, I built a relationship with most of the other contributors, either in person or via the Internet.

The following years were intense. I was in charge of transcribing several of the oral histories and of composing the subsequent essays. I also worked with some of the contributors who were writing their own personal narratives. Leti and Salvador did the same. In addition, they translated the chapters originally written in Spanish. These early stages of composing *Queer Brown Voices* gave me the opportunity to think about differences between LGBT movements in the United States and Costa Rica. Parallel to my work with Leti and Salvador, I started to do research about my own country. Like most of our contributors, I was very young in the 1980s. Their experiences made me revisit my own, so I read the few books available about HIV/AIDS or Costa Rican LGBT movements, talked to people whom I had never considered activists before, and discovered struggles I had not been previously aware of. Pretty soon I had to face my own homophobia as well as the homophobia of my mentors and my generation. I also acknowledged that writing is the only way to come to terms with a past that still haunts you.

We started meeting in New Orleans to put together the manuscript and prepare the introduction, preface, and conclusion. We spent many hours together writing, reading, and supporting each other. A collective book is not an easy task. It demands a strong commitment but especially the ability to listen and negotiate with coeditors and contributors. At the same time, it is a rewarding, creative process. We finalized the manuscript in May of 2014.

Even now that we have finished this book project, I feel that the learning process is far from over. *Queer Brown Voices* is an important step in preserving the experiences and points of view of a group of Latino/a LGBT pioneers, but it also represents an intense period of personal growth. I have traveled to several cities, met incredible people, dealt with different types of challenges, and also enjoyed the privilege of working with Letitia and Salvador, my supportive and hardworking coeditors. Those experiences have left in me a profound sense of friendship, commitment, and gratitude.

We hope that *Queer Brown Voices* inspires new generations of Latina/o LGBT activists. The road may look paved, but still, there is a lot to do in our struggle for a more just and open society.

Index

gay bars, Latino: Chaos (Washington, D.C.), 186, 190; Chaps (Boston), 206; El Bravo (Philadelphia), 117; El Faro (Washington, D.C.), 186, 188; Escándolo (Washington, D.C.), 188; Jezebel (San Antonio), 154; La Escuelita (New York), 117
Gay Chicano Caucus, 51, 53, 122, 123
Gay Hispanic Caucus, 52
Gay Hispanic Coalition de Dallas. See Gay and Lesbian Hispanic Coalition de Dallas
Gay Latinos Unidos. See Gay and Lesbian Latinos Unidos
Gay Men's Health Crisis, 177
Gay Pride Parade: Atlanta, 185; Chicago, 146; Houston, 71, 102; Los Angeles, 93; Puerto Rico, 197–198; Washington, D.C., 188, 190
gay-related immune deficiency, 60, 115
GELAAM. See Gente Latina de Ambiente
gender: activism, 107; antioppression theory of, 41; expression of, 18, 41, 197; HIV and, 164; as identity, 4, 5, 18, 19n2, 23n18, 197; inequality and, 13, 17; justice and, 42; normative binary in, 14; organizing related to, 5; sexuality and, 160. See also gender parity
gender parity, x, xii, 15, 24n19, 88, 89, 128, 162, 163, 196
Gente Latina de Ambiente, 135, 187
Geraldo Rivera Show, The (TV program), 86
GLHD. See Gay and Lesbian Hispanics of Dallas
GLHU. See Gay and Lesbian Hispanics Unidos
GLLU. See Gay and Lesbian Latinos Unidos
Gomez, John, 100

Gomez, Letitia (Leti), 159, 186, 187, 188, 223, 226, 227, 228
Gómez, Marsha, 158, 160
Gómez, Tomás, 186
Gonzalez, Bridget, 92
Gracia, Dolores, 21, 128, 129
GRID. See gay-related immune deficiency
Grupo Latino (Metropolitan Community Church of Greater Dallas), 74
Guerra, Luz, 15, 16, 17, 222
Guerrero, Edgardo, 187, 188
Guttiérez, José, ix, 16
Gutierrez, Laura, 178

Harrington, Mark, 177
hate crimes: targeting immigrants, 207; targeting queers, 207
Hispanic Communicators DFW, 68
HIV/AIDS: delivery of services for, to people of color, 2, 91, 184, 187, 188; impact of, ix, xiv, 2, 8, 9, 59, 73, 86, 129, 133, 172, 179, 184, 187, 216, 224, 225; Latina/o activism and, 3, 39, 40, 101, 114, 116, 119, 177, 179, 184; politics of, 166–168, 169, 224; prevention education by/for Latinos, 40, 41, 95, 114–115, 117, 124–125, 130, 131, 132, 133, 134–135, 172, 187–188, 189, 206, 207
HIV Treatment Education Manual, 180
Hombres Latinos Gay Project, 206
homophobia in Latina/o communities: Latino Civil Rights Task Force, 127; Latino Festival & Parade (Washington, D.C.), 125–127; Puerto Rican Day Parade (Philadelphia), 118
HRC. See Human Rights Campaign
Huerta, Dolores, 93, 104, 123
Human Rights Campaign, 4, 9, 162, 169
Human Rights Commission (Cuba), 216

immigrants: deportation of, 185; discrimination against, 52, 80, 141, 207–208, 210

immigration: Latino/a LGBT organizing concerning, 38, 75, 130, 138, 185, 190; "mainstream" LGBT organizations and, xiii, 209; as point of unity, 138, 145, 219, 227. *See also* immigrants

Indigenous Women's Network, 27

Informe SIDA, 60

International Treatment Preparedness Coalition, 181

International Women's Day March, San Antonio (1985), 156, 160

intersectionality, 6, 12–13, 14, 23n16, 36, 38, 43, 44, 87

ITPC. *See* International Treatment Preparedness Coalition

Jacinto, Louis, 89, 92

Jezebel (San Antonio), 154, 155, 157, 158

Kawata, Paul, 180

Ku Klux Klan, 167

Las Buenas Amigas, 1, 115, 130, 131, 159

Latina Lesbians and Latinos Unidos en Acción, 206

Latinas Lesbianas en Nuestro Ambiente, 144–145, 146, 148

Latinas y Latinos de Ambiente New York, 1

Latino/a GLBT History Project, x, xii, 190, 227

Latino Gay Men of New York, 1

Latinos en Acción, 184–185, 189

La Voz de Esperanza, 161–162, 164, 167, 170

League of United Latin American Citizens, 48–49, 57, 67, 68, 98, 121–122

Left Hand, The, 37, 157

lesbian bars. *See* Jezebel (San Antonio)

lesbian groups/organizations, Latina: Amigas Latinas, 146–149, 150; Aquelarre Lésbico, 195; Las Buenas Amigas, 115, 131, 159; Latinas Lesbianas en Nuestro Ambiente, 144–145, 146, 148; Lesbianas Unidas, 90, 91–92; Taller Lésbico Creativo, 198, 199

lesbian mothers, 35, 37, 83–84, 86, 95, 141, 143–144, 147–148, 197–198

Levins-Morales, Aurora, 33, 34

Limón, María, 21, 38, 60, 177

Lira, Jack, 3

Living with AIDS, 172

LLEGÓ (National Latino/a Lesbian and Gay Organization), xii, xiii, xiv, 1, 13, 94–95, 100, 129–137, 148, 149, 159, 160, 177–178, 180, 187–188, 189, 190, 198; AIDS clinical trials and, 178; board members, 102, 199–201; board/staff retreats, 39, 129; Cultura es Vida (CEV), 40–42, 189, 218; founding of, xiv, 20n5, 54, 58, 128–137; in Houston, 102–103; in New England, 208, 209; in Puerto Rico, 198–199; technical assistance and, 38–40; Transgender Summit, 218

LLENA. *See* Latinas Lesbianas en Nuestro Ambiente

Los Angeles Gay and Lesbian Center, 85, 86–87, 88–89

Los Angeles Pride Parade, 93

LULAC. *See* League of United Latin American Citizens

Madres Lesbianas de Puerto Rico, 198

Maldonado, Carlos, 175, 176

Marquez, Mercedes, 91

marriage: mixed-race, as illegal, 29; reproducing normative forms of, 14; same-sex, as illegal, 108; same-sex, as legal, 208, 62

Martinez, Del, 88–89

Mattachine Society, 4

MAYO. *See* Mexican American Youth Organization

Mayor's Commission on Sexual Minorities (Philadelphia), 116

MEChA. *See* Movimiento Estudiantil Chicano de Aztlán

Medina, Dennis, 93, 94, 99, 100, 122–123, 128, 129, 131

Metropolitan Community Church of Greater Dallas, Grupo Latino, 74

Mexican American Youth Organization, 153, 155

Migrant Student Program (St. Edward's University), 38

migrant workers. *See* farmworkers, migrant

Milk, Harvey, 3, 113

Minority AIDS Project, 91

Moraga, Cherríe, 33, 90

Morales, Ed, 128, 129

Morales, Linda, 61, 103, 159, 160, 161, 188

Morales v. Texas, 61, 159

Movimiento Estudiantil Chicano de Aztlán, 35, 94, 155

NACCS. *See* National Association of Chicano/Chicana Scholars

National AIDS Treatment Advocates Forum, 180

National Association of Chicano/Chicana Scholars, 62

National Black Leadership Commission on AIDS, 177

National Coalition for LGBT Health, 119

National Coalition of Black Lesbians and Gays, 128, 132

National Gay and Lesbian Task Force, 4, 164

National Institute of Allergies and Infectious Diseases. *See* AIDS Clinical Trials Group

National Institutes of Health, 177, 178, 180

National Latino/a Lesbian and Gay Organization. *See* LLEGÓ

National March on Washington for Lesbian and Gay Rights, 9, 20, 58, 93, 97, 99, 100, 124, 127, 159, 185, 186, 187, 190, 224

National Minority AIDS Council, xviii, 20n5, 130–131, 132, 133, 180, 181, 182

National Organization for Women, 162

National Task Force on AIDS Prevention, 177

National Third World Lesbian and Gay Conference, 20

New Bridges, 36, 37, 38, 40, 41

newsletters: DGA-GLHCH newsletter, 71; DGA newsletter, 68; *ELLAS Dicen*, 160; *GLHU Noticias*, 52–53, 54, 101; *La Voz de Esperanza*, 161, 162, 164, 167, 170; *The Left Hand*, 37, 157; *Noticias de ENLACE*, 57, 125; *Noticias de LLEGÓ*, 130; *SIDAAhora*, 178

NGLTF. *See* National Gay and Lesbian Task Force

NMAC. *See* National Minority AIDS Council

Noche y Día, 53, 123

No porque lo diga Fidel Castro (film), 160

Noriega, Mónica, 17

Nosotras Diez, 195

Noticias de ENLACE, 57, 125

NTFAP. *See* National Task Force on AIDS Prevention

Olivas, Arturo, 21, 56, 58, 59, 92, 124, 128, 129, 130

Toro, Jose, 172
transgenders: exclusion of, from leadership, 216; HIV/AIDS funding and, 23; inclusion of, 19n2, 41, 187, 216; movement for, 19n2, 41, 187, 216–218
Transgender Summit, 218

United Farm Workers, 93, 104, 155, 163, 169
Unity Fellowship Church Movement, 91

Vasquez, Adela, xii, 10, 13, 16, 41
Veloz, Brad, xiv, 21, 57, 228

Victoria, Rolando, 214
Vidal-Ortiz, Salvador, 188
violence: antigay, 2, 15, 125; domestic, 190; racial/ethnic, 15, 29, 45, 127, 140; sexual, 33, 42
VIVA, 90

Williams, Reggie, 177, 179
Wilson, Phil, 179

Zamora Casas, David, 162
Zapata, Luis, 183

CPSIA information can be obtained
at www.ICGtesting.com
Printed in the USA
FSOW02n1914010316
17335FS